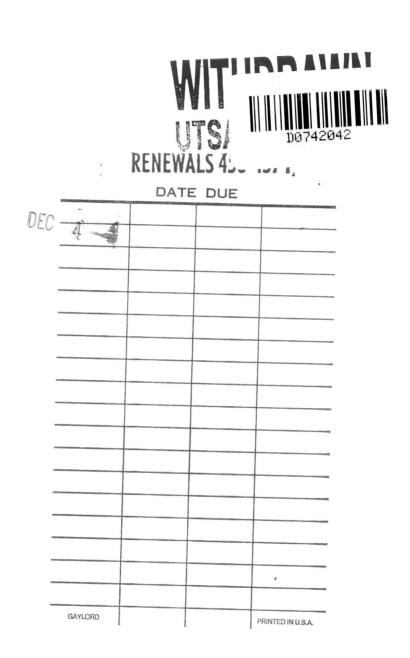

Jurek Becker

Jurek Becker

A Jew Who Became A German?

David Rock

Oxford • New York

First published in 2000 by
Berg
Editorial offices:
150 Cowley Road, Oxford OX4 1JJ, UK
838 Broadway, Third Floor, New York, NY 10003-4812, USA

Berg is the imprint of Oxford International Publishers Ltd.

Library of Congress Cataloging-in-Publication Data

A catalogue record for this book is available from the Library of Congress.

British Library Cataloguing-in-Publication Data

A catalogue record for this book is available from the British Library.

ISBN 1 85973 332 8 (Cloth)

Typeset by JS Typesetting, Wellingborough, Northants.
Printed in the United Kingdom by WBC Book Manufacturers, Bridgend,
Mid Glamorgan.

For Judy, Ben, Tom and Sam

Contents

Acknowledgements

I would like to express my thanks to the British Academy and to the Deutsche Akademische Austauschdienst for financial assistance during periods of study leave, when much of the preparatory work for this book was carried out. I should also like to thank Professor Rhys Williams for providing the photograph of Jurek Becker, taken when he visited the University of Wales, Swansea, in October 1995. I am also indebted to Jurek Becker himself for discussing many points with me both when we met in Berlin in November 1991 and in several subsequent letters.

The translations are my own, though I did consult Leila Vennewitz's translation of *Jacob the Liar* (New York, Schocken, 1990).

David Rock
University of Keele

Abbreviations used for Becker editions

A   *Amanda herzlos*
AWF *Aller Welt Freund*
B   *Der Boxer*
BK   *Bronsteins Kinder*
IB   *Irreführung der Behörden*
J   *Jakob der Lügner*
NZ   *Nach der ersten Zukunft*
ST   *Schlaflose Tage*
V   *Wir sind auch nur ein Volk*
W   *Warnung vor dem Schriftsteller*

Introduction

Sander Gilman claimed that, with his three novels *Jakob der Lügner* (Jacob the liar), *Der Boxer* (the boxer) and *Bronsteins Kinder* (Bronstein's children), Jurek Becker was the author who gave 'the most important representation of the Jew in the literature of the German Democratic Republic' (Gilman 1991: 258). Yet this prominent East German writer was born not in Germany, but in Poland, and for the first eight years of his life spoke only Polish. The question of his identity is one which has preoccupied critics from the time of the appearance of his first novel in 1969. It is one, though, which Becker himself never answered unequivocally, offering tantalisingly conflicting views at various times during his life. By his own account, he never 'felt like a German, nor have I tried to. And I've never considered myself a Pole' (*Dimension* 1978: 409). Yet when he arrived in the Soviet Sector of Germany after the Second World War, of course the eight-year-old 'outsider' did want to be a German in the sense of being just 'a normal schoolboy' like any of his peers. When he left the GDR in 1977, though, he explained that he felt more a 'GDR citizen' than a 'German', which at that time he regarded as merely a 'Begriff aus dem Geschichtsunterricht' (a concept from history lessons – *Stuttgarter Nachrichten*, 2.10.1978). And on his arrival in the Federal Republic, he was certainly made aware of the extent to which he did feel at home in the GDR, commenting: 'I will probably never feel as much at home as I once did in the GDR and never again have the sort of relationship to the world around me that I once had' (*Einmischung* 1983: 63).[1] Yet he also expressed the view that the word 'Heimat' ('homeland') had no personal meaning for him anyway (personal interview, 22.11.1991), and after living for several years in the West, he would sometimes admit to feeling settled in West Berlin and at others claim that it was all still 'fremd' (alien) to him.

The question of personal identity is, then, in Becker's case, an elusive and complex one, and emerges as a fascinating central theme in his writing. It is often discernible, too, in his typically throwaway remarks about his own biography, such as the following comment on his acquisition of the German language: 'I have long since forgotten my mother-tongue "Polish", it's the foreign language, German, that has stuck'

(*Einmischung* 1983: 59).[2] From 'the very first second', Becker felt 'like an outsider' in Germany (*Die Zeit*, 20.5.1994),[3] not only because he and his father, as 'official victims of fascism', received better food ration-cards and not only because the friendship they enjoyed appeared even to the young Becker as false, but above all because of his father's attitudes. The latter attached considerable importance to their status as 'Fremdlinge' (strangers) and was careful to underline their distinctness from those around them, speaking continually of 'the Germans' as 'the others', asking his son how 'the Germans' were treating him at school, one day finally encouraging Jurek to assert his separateness in the knowledge that 'they' will never forget anyway: 'Go ahead and let them sense that you're not one of them – they will never forget the fact anyway' (*Die Zeit*, 20.5.1994).[4] Clearly, his father's sense of identity was a complicated one: although Becker senior was not a Jew in any practising sense, he never concealed his Jewishness; on the contrary, as Becker explained in an essay written in 1994: 'I think he frequently laid his Jewishness on thicker than he really wanted to for fear of being considered conformist, out of pride, then' (*Die Zeit*, 20.5.1994).[5] His father's influence gradually diminished, though (he died in 1972), and in 1994, Becker admitted that by now he was so conscious of acting the part of a German, of pretending to belong, that he now felt that he was stuck with the part: 'Unlike him I have for many years been playing the part of being one of them, with the result that there is no longer any other one open to me' (*Die Zeit*, 20.5.1994).[6] So this Polish-Jewish victim of Nazi Germany eventually 'became a German', as he put it, yet the very title of the essay in which he made this statement, 'Mein Vater, die Deutschen und ich' (My father, the Germans and me), indicates a sense of separateness from 'the Germans', underlining his complicated relationship to his father's adopted country, Germany.

When he visited New York for the first time in 1978, he appears to have experienced specific difficulties in defining and communicating his national identity. In his prose-piece 'New Yorker Woche' (Week in New York), he describes a visit to a church in Harlem and his problem in responding to the preacher's question as to who his guests are and where they come from: 'When it's my turn, I mention a strange country of origin: *Germany*. I really don't know what this word means at all and use it nevertheless' (NZ 155).[7] His sense of cultural shock in the USA causes him to reconsider some of the labels hitherto applicable to himself and to recognise a new one: 'It strikes me that I am suddenly thinking of EUROPE, a word that had hardly ever come to mind before. Hitherto I have always given myself much more detailed names: I was a Berliner, I was a Köpenicker. Citizen of the GDR. A German – that really did seem exotic to me. And suddenly I was a European, no less' (NZ 148).[8] This minor crisis of identity on experiencing almost complete cultural aliena-tion in New York leads to the feeling of being quite 'verloren' ('lost' – NZ 147), yet it is not oases of German culture which he seeks out but the Jewish shops with their familiar names such as 'Katz, Finkelstein', and the kosher restaurants: 'I wanted very much for the first time in my life to eat the sort of food my father had told me about' (NZ 150).[9]

Was Becker, then, not really a German writer at all, but rather a 'Jewish writer', the label which critics gave to him after the appearance of his first novel *Jakob der Lügner* (1969), which they linked to the tradition of Jewish storytelling? Yet Becker was quick to reject this, too, protesting that he had only read the works of Yiddish writers such as Aleichem and Singer after already having been compared to them, and so the label 'Jewish' writer would hardly appear appropriate to someone who claimed that his first confrontation with Jewish literature came when he was almost thirty years old. Indeed, his only essay dealing directly with the problem, 'Mein Judentum' (My Jewishness – 1978), is an attempt to deny any personal sense of Jewishness through an analysis of his own tenuous relationship with his Jewish background. Yet he betrays an ambivalent attitude: whenever he was asked in the past about his origins, he would answer that his parents were Jews: 'I used this sentence like a fixed formula, one that supplies information with unsurpassable clarity. If the questioner then sometimes declared: "So you're a Jew then", I would always correct him by repeating my formula: "My parents were Jews"' (Heidelberger-Leonard 1992: 15).[10] The distinction seemed important to him, yet he admits that he was never able to explain to himself why, and with customary understatement he adds: 'At the same time, the fact that I was born into a Jewish family has been of no small consequence for my life hitherto' (Heidelberger-Leonard 1992: 15).[11] The fact that he still bore the scars of his own Jewish past is borne out in his speculation on his father's refusal to discuss the past with him: whether it was because the latter himself sought 'peace from the past years' or because he wished to protect his son, he did not 'achieve either goal' (Heidelberger-Leonard 1992: 17).

Becker's 'Wunde Judentum' (the wound of his Jewishness), as Irene Heidelberger-Leonard has called it (Heidelberger-Leonard 1992: 195), occasionally erupts quite unexpectedly, as in his virulent attack on Martin Walser's early argument for unification (1988) when Becker's fear of a resurgence of fascism and scorn for Walser provoked an outburst of anger which betrayed a sense of solidarity if not directly with the Jews then at least with others who, like him, felt alienated from Germany: 'I'm sorry, but some twenty members of my family were gassed, beaten to death or starved, and in one way or another that's a factor for me. I have not got such cosy childhood memories as Walser has. Might that be the reason why Germany belongs to people of his ilk rather than of mine?' (Heidelberger-Leonard 1992: 57)[12]

For Becker, though, shared suffering did not imply shared identity, and he argues in 'Mein Judentum' that, as he had been brought up without any sense of being part of a Jewish community, the notion of belonging to a group of people called 'the Jews' could for him be perceived only as a voluntary matter, 'einen intellektuellen Entschluß' (an intellectual decision). This is a view which Becker often felt inclined to defend vehemently, understandably so, since he saw amongst its opponents the authors of the race laws who during the Third Reich did not want to leave individuals any freedom of choice whatsoever as to whether they were Jewish or not.

This was also why he fiercely rejected presumptuous attempts by critics to pin neat labels on him and so decide for him who and what he was: 'unter anderem eben Jude' (amongst other things a Jew – Heidelberger-Leonard 1992: 19). Accepting, then, that he already counted as a Jew in the eyes of others regardless of what he said or did, he found it easier to define his 'Jewishness' in negative terms, 'Was [. . .] mein Judentum mir nicht bedeutet' (what my Jewishness does not mean to me), since this was more clear-cut: as an atheist, the Jewish religion offered him no more insights than any other religion; he did not feel any sense of pride in the great achievements of Jews, nor shame that it was Jews who set themselves up as 'Herrenmenschen' (a master race) in the Middle East, only anger that human beings treated other human beings in this way. In 'Mein Judentum', he argues that the sense of belonging to a group of people is particularly marked when the group is under attack; and since he was aware of no attacks on Jews as a group in the GDR, there were no pressures on the Jews of this part of his childhood to join together to protect themselves, no ties for him to sever, no traditions for him to accept or reject. It would, then, have taken a real effort on his part to become a Jew. Becker ends his essay, though, with a wry touch of self-irony which turns his own hitherto confident line of argument on its head, conceding the possibility that he may be wrong in this matter: though he may not have felt like a Jew, he may nevertheless be one in a variety of ways – but so what, he asks? Would it really make him any the wiser if he managed to get to the bottom of such a riddle, as he calls it? He answers his own question in the negative: 'I fear not. I fear I would just be seeking in vain to solve a mystery without which my life would be the poorer' (Heidelberger-Leonard 1992: 24).[13]

As Chaim Shoham (Röll and Bayerdörfer 1986: 225–36) has argued, many of Becker's works are attempts to cast light on the mystery of his own Jewishness. The recurrence of this central theme is hardly surprising considering his mental gaps, his lack of memories of the early years of his life and thus of precisely the seminal formative ingredients which are so critical for the shaping of human identity: the mother-tongue, memories of his family, his home in Lodz, the traditions of the world of his childhood – all these were missing in Becker's case. He was thus repeatedly drawn to the subject of the Holocaust and its repercussions, yet never saw himself as a victim. Post-war GDR society may have offered Becker a substitute identity, that of victim of fascism, but he was unable to accept this since it was 'defined negatively, in terms of the oppressor. [. . .] Those that bore the name remained objects' (Krauss 1988: 140).[14] The lifelong status of victim was for Becker the 'expression of an irreparable deformation' inflicted on the victim, and he saw evidence of such deformation in the Jewish state of Israel (*Die Zeit*, 3.10.1986). Many of Becker's Jewish Holocaust survivors also resist the label 'Opfer des Faschismus' (victim of fascism) just as their author did the 'Zwangsidentität' (enforced identity) of Holocaust victim: he regarded the attendant privileges as a form of stigmatisation, being based on emotion – sympathy – rather than the cool, intellectual stance which typified his approach: 'I should like to approach a specific subject in the coolest way possible – at any rate not in a manner whereby sympathy and bias render me incapable of thinking logically' (cited by Krauss 1988: 142).[15]

Even if his own Jewishness remained something of a riddle to him, he was certain of one thing from the time of his childhood in Berlin: the fact that he was going to be a writer. Whenever he was asked how he became a writer, he usually related the anecdote from his childhood in Berlin when his father, presented with an occasional poem by his son, read it aloud with a voice trembling with pride, arousing in the young boy the feeling that he was blessed with a rare gift (Graf and Konietzny 1991: 67). Becker also admitted the possibility that he became a writer in response to the considerable linguistic challenge which he faced in having to learn the language of his erstwhile persecutors: 'It seems strange to me too that I had to become a writer of all things, as if I had wanted to show that no task was too much for me, as if I were someone for whom a challenge is more important than a favourable starting-position' (Heidelberger-Leonard 1992: 13).[16] Becker acknowledged, too, his indebtedness to the oral tradition of storytelling which he experienced from his father's Jewish friends in Berlin after the war, which stimulated his own storytelling ambitions.

Yet the label 'Jewish' has proved an inadequate description of a writer who resisted identification with groups of any kind and who was difficult to categorise or to locate either biographically or in a literary sense: born a Polish Jew, brought up as a citizen of the GDR, which he left in protest in 1977, he was officially a 'Bundesbürger' (West German citizen) when he died, yet regarded himself as neither Pole, Jew, East German, or West German, and certainly not as a 'Jewish' writer. What he feared was, as he put it, an 'over-interpretation of his complicated self, the depths of his own identity' (*Süddeutsche Zeitung,* 6.12.1989: 39).[17] His biography points to this complexity: an early childhood spent in ghettoes and concentration camps, experiences which he repressed along with the Polish language of that infancy; then life in East and later West Germany, a life full of inner and outer conflicts, between Polish-Jewish and German-German identity; between any sense of Jewishness and a desire not to attribute any significance to this; between utopian socialism and socialism as it actually existed; between communism and capitalism. Becker acknowledged that writing for him implied an element of self-confrontation: 'The most important and probably only crucial reason for a book – is me' (in: Hage 1987: 339).[18] Hence his novels, too, reflect the aforementioned problems of identity, as Irene Heidelberger-Leonard has argued: three deal with the difficulties of being a Jew and three with the difficulties of being a socialist (Heidelberger-Leonard 1992: 193–4).

This book will give a brief account of Jurek Becker's life and will then examine his work from two main but not mutually exclusive points of view: Firstly, his treatment of his own Jewish background, his (almost forgotten) experiences of the Holocaust, and his unique contribution to German understanding of the Shoah and its repercussions – unique in the sense that it is written from the perspective of Jewish victims, but treats them as subjects not as objects. Secondly, his portrayal of his experiences in the 'three' Germanies: the GDR with its 'actually existing socialism'; the Federal Republic; and the new Germany after 1989. It will also seek to demonstrate the validity of Peter Schneider's claim that Becker was a solo-artist who restored to German literature something that had been missing for half a century (Riordan 1995: 5).

Notes

1. 'Es ist dann wahrscheinlich, daß ich mich hier niemals so heimisch fühlen werde, wie einmal in der DDR der Fall gwesesen ist. Daß ich nie wieder solche Beziehungen zu meiner Umgebung haben werde, wie ich sie einmal hatte.'
2. 'Diese Muttersprache "Polnisch" habe ich längst verloren und die Fremdsprache Deutsch ist mir geblieben.'
3. 'Ich kam mir von der ersten Sekunde wie ein Außenstehender vor.'
4. 'Laß sie ruhig spüren, daß du nicht zu ihnen gehörst – sie werden es sowieso nie vergessen.'
5. 'Ich glaube sogar, daß er sein Judentum oft dicker auftrug, als ihm selbst angenehm war: aus Furcht, für angepaßt gehalten zu werden, also aus Stolz.'
6. 'Im Unterschied zu ihm habe ich viele Jahre getan, als gehörte ich dazu, daß mir keine andere Rolle mehr möglich ist.'
7. 'Als ich an der Reihe bin, nenne ich ein seltsames Herkunftsland: *Germany*. Ich weiß ja gar nicht was dieses Wort bedeutet, und sage es trotzdem.'
8. 'Mir fällt auf, wie ich plötzlich EUROPA denke, ein Wort, das mir zuvor kaum in den Sinn gekommen ist. Bis hierher gab ich mir immer viel detailliertere Namen: ich war Berliner, ich war Köpenicker. DDR-Bürger. Ein Deutscher – das kam mir schon exotisch vor. Und auf einmal bin ich Europäer, nicht weniger.'
9. 'Ich wollte gern zum erstenmal im Leben so essen, wie mein Vater es mir erzählt hat.'
10. 'Ich benutzte diesen Satz wie eine feststehende Formel, die in nicht zu überbietender Klarheit Auskunft gibt. Wenn der Frager mitunter dann konstatierte: "Sie sind also Jude", berichtigte ich ihn jedesmal, indem ich nochmal meine Formel sagte: "Meine Eltern waren Juden."'
11. 'Dabei hat der Umstand, daß ich in eine jüdische Familie hineingeboren wurde, für meinen bisherigen Lebenslauf nicht eben kleine Folgen gehabt.'
12. 'Tut mir leid, aber von meiner Familie sind an die zwanzig Personen vergast oder erschlagen oder verhungert worden, irgendwie spielt das für mich eine Rolle. Ich habe nicht so kuschelige Kindheitserinnerungen wie Walser. Sollte das der Grund sein, warum Deutschland eher seinesgleichen gehört als meinesgleichen?'
13. 'Ich fürchte nein. Ich fürchte, ich würde nur vergeblich versuchen, ein Geheimnis aufzuklären, ohne das mein Leben ärmer wäre.'

14. 'negativ, vom Unterdrücker her definiert. [. . .] Ihre Träger blieben Objekte.'

15. 'ich möchte auf möglichst kühle Weise mich einer bestimmten Materie nähern – nicht jedenfalls in einer Art bei der Mitgefühl und Befangenheit mich denkschwach machen.'

16. 'Mich selbst mutet es seltsam an, daß ich da ausgerechnet Schriftsteller werden mußte; als hätte ich zeigen wollen, daß eine Aufgabe mir gar nicht genug sein kann, als wäre ich jemand, dem eine Herausforderung wichtiger ist als ein günstige Ausgangssituation.'

17. 'Überinterpretation seines komplizierten Selbst – Abgründe seiner Identität'.

18. 'Der wichtigste und wahrscheinlich einzig ausschlaggebende Grund für ein Buch – bin ich.'

Jurek Becker: A Brief Biography

The fact that I am Jewish in origin was something I knew from the first year of my life, but what it meant and the sort of consequences it would have, have only become clear to me with the benefit of hindsight. (Graf and Konietzny 1991: 56)[1]

Childhood in Poland

Jurek Becker was born into a large Jewish family in Lodz. Although his passport gave his date of birth as 30 September 1937, he was uncertain of the accuracy not only of the day and the month but also of the year. There were good reasons for this uncertainty.

Lodz, the second largest Polish city at that time, was an important industrial city in the west of Poland with a population of 700,000, of whom 233,000 were Jews. With its two million spindles, it had come to be known as the Manchester of Eastern Europe and had grown into a major centre of textile production. Becker's own father, along with other family members, was employed as a clerk in a textile factory owned by his uncle. Barely one week after the Second World War broke out in September 1939, Lodz fell without resistance to the Germans. When the city was incorporated into the Third Reich on 7 October, it was renamed Litzmannstadt and, under instructions issued by SS-Reichsführer Himmler applicable to all annexed territories, the Jewish population was to be 'ausgesiedelt' (resettled). On 10 December, orders were issued for the setting-up of a ghetto in the Balut slum district, which became in effect a massive prison and the largest of all the ghettoes in Poland, comprising four square kilometres of the city. The Jews were forced to vacate their homes within five days, Becker's family being moved from a house on the main street in Lodz to one on the edge of the market square in the ghetto.

The Lodz ghetto itself was completely enclosed by sixteen kilometres of barbed wire fences which were patrolled day and night by soldiers and by the local German police, with orders to shoot anyone who approached the boundaries from the Jewish side. Shootings of Jews (including children) who came too close to the fences were thus regular occurrences. Only German officials were allowed in and out. Even the Polish population was removed from the district in closest proximity to the ghetto in order to create a 'no man's land' around it. This almost hermetic isolation of the ghetto rendered communication with the outside world virtually impossible, the only scraps of news to reach the ghetto coming mostly from a few clandestine radios, ownership of which was punishable by death. Most of the information which did get through was bleak, such as the news of the mass execution of the Jews in Cracow, Lublin and Warsaw. The Lodz ghetto was thus more tightly sealed than the other ghettoes in Poland, a major factor in paralysing the will to resist and preventing Lodz from repeating the rebellions of Warsaw, Vilna and elsewhere.

The deportation of the Jews from Lodz followed a pattern different from that of most other ghettoes where the Jews were evacuated in whole families street by street. Lodz was the exception, with families being split up because the Germans, needing manufactured goods, were keen to exploit the skilled Jewish labour force, and so the ghetto was gradually turned into a work camp consisting only of those who were fit for work, hence largely adults. Meagre supplies of food were dependent on productivity at work and the inhabitants of the ghetto were deprived of anything which made life more than mere survival: even the trees in the Jewish cemetery were cut down, and it was 'probably the only city in the world without any [. . .] flowers' (Dobroszycki 1984: 344). Conditions in winter were particularly appalling, with the Jews often deprived of both food and fuel and suicides so common that grave-diggers were frequently unable to keep up with their work. During the winter of 1941–2, for instance, an average of 150 people per day died as a result of starvation, cold, exhaustion from hard labour or suicide (Herschkovitch 1989: 340–77).

The deportations began in December 1941. Families were split up and those incapable of work ('Arbeitsunfähige'), old people, the sick and most young children, were 'resettled': deportees were told that they were going to 'settlements', where they would have more to eat than in the over-crowded ghetto. At first, nothing was known for certain about the fate of such deportees: 'There was a great deal of guesswork. There were efforts to puzzle out the routes the trains took and, on that basis, to establish the transports' destinations. They clutched at straws [. . .] people did not believe or did not wish to believe that all of this [. . .] could be an unmitigated lie' (Dobroszycki 1984: xviii). In fact, they were killed in Chelmno concentration camp.

However, suspicions increased when, in September 1942, very young children, old people and the sick were deported in a barbaric way: the Germans brutally rounded them up from house to house, flinging them into the street (Huppert 1989: 326–7) – at least sixty people were murdered attempting to save their children (Loewy and Schoenberner 1990: 280). In order to save his son (who was apparently above average height), Jurek Becker's father made him out to be two years older than he really was and hence, as far as the German authorities were concerned, 'fit for work'. Jurek was thus able to live for over three years with his parents in the ghetto until they too were all eventually deported in 1943.

He now lost contact with his father, who was sent to Auschwitz, whilst Jurek and his mother were moved first to Ravensbrück and then later to Sachsenhausen concentration camp where his mother died, leaving the child to fend for himself, though Becker did once indicate that his own survival may have been at the expense of his starving mother who gave her meagre rations to her small son (Heidelberger-Leonard 1992: 96).

By the end of the war, Becker's own family, once 'a veritable tribe' (*Dimension* 1978: 417), had been reduced to three members: Jurek, his father and a distant aunt who had been able to escape to America immediately after the Germans invaded Poland. Becker was one of the few Jewish children from Lodz under ten years of age to survive this period.

Like the father and son who survive different concentration camps in Becker's novel *Der Boxer*, Jurek and his father were reunited in 1945 through the efforts of an American relief organisation. When his father entered the room in the hospital in Sachsenhausen, converted from part of the concentration camp, Jurek did not recognise him: 'a man I'd never seen before came into the room: it was my father whom I couldn't remember' (Arnold 1992: 4).[2] Yet unlike the son in the novel, Jurek Becker's identity was not in doubt, for his registration document from the Lodz ghetto had survived with him, stating the year of birth which his father had earlier given to the German authorities in Poland (Heidelberger-Leonard 1992: 32). When now asked the precise date, however, his father was unable to remember (Heidelberger-Leonard 1992: 126).

Life in the GDR

Unsure Becker's father may have been about precise details in the past, but he was quite certain about action needed for the immediate future and at once decided to take his son not back to Poland, but to the Soviet Sector of Berlin. His father had been born in Bavaria and as a child had moved with his parents to Poland. Yet according to Becker, his father's decision to go to Germany did not involve any sense of returning home, but rather the belief that the communist sector of Germany would be the safest place and anti-Semitism dead once and for all now that fascism had been eradicated in the land where discrimination against the Jews had taken on its most horrifying form. He also feared a resurgence of Polish anti-Semitism, commenting: 'After all it's not the Polish anti-Semites who've lost the war' (Heidelberger-Leonard 1992: 17).[3] His judgement of the situation proved correct in view of the pogroms against Jews which took place in Poland after the war when concentration camp returnees were driven away from their homes or even killed (Wesie 1987).

His little son, though, knew only a few words of German, and although he had spoken Polish for the first seven years of his life, even his Polish was not that of a near nine-year-old – and with good reason, as we shall see. In Berlin, Jurek now had to learn the language of his erstwhile oppressors as quickly as possible, with his father adopting a stick-and-carrot approach to his son's German schoolwork, with a deduction of five pfennigs per error but also a reward of fifty pfennigs per correct side!

Becker's conformity in the early years in the GDR was the product both of his desire 'to stop being an outsider' (Heidelberger-Leonard 1992: 109)[4] and also of his father's influence (see Chapter 5). At school, for instance, he became first a Young Pioneer and later a member of the youth organisation of the GDR, the 'Freie Deutsche Jugend', by his own account, not so much out of political conviction as of his wish to be 'a normal schoolboy' like his other friends, who were all members: 'I wasn't a normal German boy, but I wanted to be one' (Heidelberger-Leonard 1992: 109).[5] After completing his 'Abitur' in 1955, like most of the good young socialists around him, he worked for several months on an LPG ('Landwirtschaftliche Produktionsgenossenschaft', a collective farm). In contrast to his father who became something of a recluse, withdrawing from almost all social contact even with the small local Jewish community in East Berlin, the young Becker's response to the socialist society around him was a positive one for he saw the socialist 'venture' as something worthwhile (Heidelberger-Leonard 1992: 108). He was not uncritical, though, and a major reason for this was his father's enthusiasm for books and his encouragement of his son to become an avid reader: 'my father made me into an avid reader. I don't know if it is some kind of natural law, but readers turn into relatively critical people' (Heidelberger-Leonard 1992: 109).[6] The young Becker's attitudes and behaviour thus became increasingly rebellious, an early indication of the 'Unruhestifter' (trouble-maker) he was later to become in the eyes of the Party.

He hated his obligatory two years (1955–6) in the People's Army of the GDR, with all the blind obedience and discipline which it involved. And although he became a Marxist and joined the communist SED ('Sozialistische Einheitspartei Deutschlands' – the Socialist Unity Party of Germany, the official state party of the GDR) when he began studying at the Humboldt University in East Berlin in 1957, he was expelled from university by the SED in 1960 as a punishment both for being a bad student (he became more interested in writing than in studying philosophy) and for getting into trouble with the Party.[7] He had moved out of his father's apartment in 1959 to share a flat with the actor Manfred Krug on the Cantianstraße, and it was from this time onwards that the Stasi began to keep files on him (Arnold 1993: 15).

Yet for all these difficulties, Becker remained a loyal Party member during his early years in the GDR, as he acknowledged in 1983: 'All the time, I was having proceedings of one sort or another instituted by the Party against me. I was always involved in some dispute or other, in the Writer's Union too, but as far as I was concerned, a fair measure of solidarity was there' (*Einmischung* 1983: 61).[8]

Becker was twenty-three years old when the Berlin Wall was built in 1961. He was prepared at the time to accept the official argument that it was a necessary and logical consequence of the political and economic situation, sharing the hopes of a number of other GDR writers (such as Heiner Müller) that the wall would actually help matters and that many of the constraints that had existed previously would prove to be unnecessary: if the authorities no longer needed to be afraid of people running away, then they could allow life to become freer, more open and democratic. By the end of the 1970s, though, he had long since realised that not much had come of this naive hope (*Dimension* 1978: 411).

As a student Becker had written scripts for political cabarets, and for several years from 1960 onwards he earned his living by occasionally writing texts for the cabaret 'Die Distel' (the thistle) and by working as a relatively unknown scriptwriter for the East German television and film industry (see Bibliography for full list), all of which he regarded as 'handwerkliche Arbeit' (learning the skill of the trade – personal interview 1991). His first filmscript was the comedy *Mit der NATO durch die Wand* (with NATO through the wall, 1961), a short 'Stacheltier' production directed by Peter Ulbrich; his first DEFA ('Deutsche Film-Aktiengesellschaft' – the nationalised East German film company) film was another comedy, *Ohne Paß in fremden Betten* (In foreign beds without a passport); and the scripts for television which he co-authored with Klaus Poche under the pseudonym 'Georg Nicolaus' were also, as Becker admitted and the titles usually indicate, largely trivial conformist comedies: *Immer um den März herum* (Always around March – 1967), *Mit 70 hat man noch Träume* (At 70 one can still dream –1967) and *Urlaub* (Holiday – 1967/8). His experiences of scriptwriting during the 1960s, including some of the vagaries of television and film censorship in the GDR during these years, are reflected indirectly in the novel *Irreführung der Behörden* (see Chapter 5). *Meine Stunde Null* (My zero hour), which Becker co-directed with Joachim Hasler in 1969/70, is the first example of Becker's comical treatment of a serious subject: based on the 'anti-fascist' memoirs of Karl Krug and with Becker's close friend Manfred Krug playing the main part with typical dry humour, the film depicts the chaotically comical adventures of staff-corporal Karl Hartung who is captured by the Russians in 1943 and is sent back behind the German lines disguised as a lieutenant in order to abduct his commanding officer during a booze-up in the officer's mess. Despite the (in GDR terms) lavishness of the production, the appeal of the film was largely limited to the performance of its star Krug, for whom the film appears to have been tailor-made.

It was with his first novel *Jakob der Lügner* (Jacob the Liar, 1969), that Becker suddenly acquired an international reputation: it was translated into twelve languages and sold 200,000 copies in the GDR alone. In view of Becker's highly original, humorous approach to the treatment of Polish ghetto-life during the Holocaust, *Jakob der Lügner* is still regarded as a work which marks an important point in German post-war literature, both East and West, and he was awarded the Heinrich Mann Prize of the Academy of Arts in the GDR, and the Swiss Charles Veillon Prize in 1971. Originally written as a screenplay but rejected by DEFA, a very successful and award-winning film version of the novel was made in 1974. A co-production of DEFA and East German television, it was directed by Frank Beyer, already well-known and highly regarded in the GDR at the time. Adopting a conventionally realistic approach and giving an impressively sensitive portrayal of the wide array of Jewish characters, Beyer's film version keeps closely to the original plot but is unable to compensate for the absence of the gently ironic, chatty narrator always intrusive in and so crucial to Becker's novel (see Chapter 3 and Stoll in Heidelberger-Leonard 1992: 336-8). Its shortcomings are, though, minor, and it was the first DEFA film to be shown at the West Berlin *Berlinale* festival and remains the only GDR film ever to be nominated for a Hollywood Oscar.

Becker was elected to the executive committee of the Writers' Union in 1973 and won the West German Bremen Literature Prize in 1974, followed by the National Prize of the GDR in 1975. By the mid-1970s, then, Becker was a well-established writer, both at home and abroad, and hence also a specially privileged member of GDR society, with a *datscha,* a car and the freedom to travel abroad, visiting both Austria and West Germany in 1976, for instance.

Yet the seeds of Becker's disillusionment with life in the GDR had already been sown. He had been unhappy about the invasion of Czechoslovakia by Warsaw Pact troops in 1968 but had refrained from venting his feelings at this time in the international arena, as he explained later: 'But I wouldn't have dreamed of running to the *Spiegel*, for instance, to express my indignation' (*Einmischung* 1983: 61).[9] During the following eight years, though, he exploited the relatively protected and privileged position which his international reputation gave him to speak out on controversial issues, as he wryly commented in 1992, 'the more I opened my mouth, the more privileged I became!' (*Neues Deutschland*, 22.7.1992: 6).[10]

Becker's next two novels, *Irreführung der Behörden* (Misleading the authorities – 1973) and *Der Boxer* (The boxer – 1976), both critical of aspects of the 'actually existing' socialist society of the GDR, were written during the period of relaxed restrictions which followed the replacement of Walter Ulbricht as First Secretary of the SED by Erich Honecker. At the Eighth Party Congress in 1971, Honecker had declared that there would be no taboos for writers who proceeded from the 'festen Position des Sozialismus' (firm position of socialism). The November 1973 Writers' Congress was also a major event in this respect, reaffirming the relative freedom of literature within the GDR (Emmerich 1997: 251). Yet the cultural tolerance that characterised the early years of the Honecker era had begun to wane by 1976, the year when Becker's name became associated with oppositional voices. In October 1976 he had protested publicly at the expulsion of Reiner Kunze from the Writers' Union, and one month later he had signed an open letter of protest at the forced expatriation of his friend, the dissident poet and songwriter Wolf Biermann. For this Becker was ejected from the SED, and from November on, the Stasi stepped up their surveillance of him, giving him the code name 'Lügner' (liar – Arnold 1993: 24).

Nineteen-seventy-seven was another year of upheaval for Becker. In the spring he resigned from the Writers' Union in protest at the way the Party had behaved. Later that year he separated from his wife Rieke after some fifteen years of marriage, exchanging a comfortable home on the outskirts of Köpenick for a modest flat with no bathroom in the former working-class neighbourhood of Friedrichshain, where he devoted most of his time to his next novel *Schlaflose Tage* (Sleepless days). His books began to be withdrawn from the bookshops. He was not allowed to give public readings of his works – after a 'Leseabend' (reading) in an East Berlin church, he was accused of organising a 'konterrevolutionäre Veranstaltung' (counter-revolutionary event), an activity punishable by imprisonment (*Stern* 13.7.1978). Next, his new novel *Schlaflose Tage* was rejected for publication by the censor, and so, aware that he was being subjected to blatant pressures intended to intimidate him (Heidelberger-Leonard 1992: 91), Becker decided to apply to leave the GDR. With his international profile and his official status as an 'Opfer des Faschismus' (victim of fascism), he was able to obtain a unique exit visa which allowed him to live for a period of up to ten years in the West but still make regular visits to the GDR, enabling him to visit his sons Nikolaus and Leonard.

Whilst Becker was living in East Berlin he had been on the defensive *vis-à-vis* West German critics of the GDR and had generally refrained from making pronouncements about the GDR in the West German press. But when he finally left in December 1977, he took the opportunity afforded by two interviews with *Spiegel* (in 1977 and in 1980) to explain that the main reason for his break with the GDR was his frustration at not being allowed to publish his latest novel.[11] The last film which Becker had made in the GDR was also affected by the repercussions of events on the political front. Directed in 1976/7 by Frank Beyer, *Das Versteck* (The hideout), a comedy on the theme of marriage and emancipation, came out in 1978, but only five copies were released to GDR cinemas after its star, Manfred Krug, followed Becker to the West.

In 1978, Becker visited the United States where he met his second wife Hannah. He spent the spring semester as German writer-in-residence at Oberlin College, working on a collection of short prose texts which were later to be published in West Germany in 1980 under the title *Nach der ersten Zukunft* (After the initial future). Most spring from the period when he was still resident in the GDR and are largely the products of his experiences there during the early Honecker period. He submitted the original manuscript in 1979 to both Suhrkamp Verlag in West Germany and to Hinstorff Verlag in the GDR. However, having rejected his novel *Schlaflose Tage* in 1978 as too critical, GDR publishers' readers were equally wary and again turned Becker down; and so the collection was first published in the West in 1980. The Hinstorff edition of the stories (*Erzählungen* – Stories) did not appear in the GDR until 1986; and even then, four of the pieces from the original manuscript were omitted because they were still considered politically too sensitive.

It was only some fifteen years after he had left the GDR that Becker's suspicions about his surveillance by the Stasi were finally confirmed. After German unification, seven files on the author under the code name

'Lügner' were discovered in the Ministry for State Security, dating from 1959 and continuing right up to the end of the GDR. Particularly galling for Becker was the discovery that a number of 'IM' ('Inoffizielle Mitarbeiter' – unofficial collaborators) had supplemented Stasi officers' routine, tediously detailed records of his comings and goings with so-called 'Gutachten' (official reports), in which his works were crudely subjected to close scrutiny for evidence of any hostile political stance and subversive potential. *Nach der ersten Zukunft* appears to have caused the Stasi a number of headaches in this respect: the IM 'expert' with the code name 'Schönberg', for instance, in his badly written report dated 12 November 1979, noted that the manuscript contained 'such strong provocative elements [. . .] that we could not accept it with a clear conscience and sense of political responsibility' (Arnold 1993: 23).[12] Particularly disturbing for 'Schönberg' was the story 'Der Verdächtige' (the suspect), focusing directly on the taboo question of the surveillance of a loyal state functionary. As the setting is unmistakably that of the GDR, the IM reads the story as a direct expression of Becker's own experiences there, and as evidence therefore of an 'unacceptable' attitude to GDR society. The piece unwittingly illustrates very well the quandary in which Becker put the GDR authorities. Contradictions abound in the report as its writer appears intimidated by the task before him: at the start, he confidently declares himself against publication of *Nach der ersten Zukunft*, yet one page further on concludes that the manuscript cannot simply be rejected in view of Becker's achievement with *Jakob der Lügner* in establishing the GDR's place in 'die Weltliteratur der Gegenwart' (current world literature). Displaying symptoms of the selfsame persecution mania so much a characteristic both of the protagonist of the story under scrutiny and (for Becker) of the state itself, 'IM Schönberg' concludes that the author is putting pressure on the state by exploiting his international reputation: 'That's what he's counting on and that's why he's using it to put pressure on us' (Arnold 1993: 24).[13]

Life in West Berlin

Becker moved to West Berlin in 1979, and lived with only relatively brief interruptions in the inner-city area of Kreuzberg up to the time of his death in 1997. His involvement in the usually controversial debate on East–West political and literary issues in the West German media began with his arrival in the West and continued up to his death.[14] Like others who left after the Biermann affair such as Thomas Brasch, Becker, for most of the 1980s, maintained a certain amount of critical loyalty to the

GDR, particularly its ideology. He was not prepared to adopt an outright anti-GDR position, sustained his criticism of the capitalist West, and tried to keep his private options open by not permanently closing the doors to the GDR, although he did make the following admission after the demise of his former country: 'I do not think that, without unification, I would have returned to the East again, even if, for certain reasons, I attempted to give the impression that this question was still open' (personal letter, 15.12.1993).[15]

In his new-found role as commentator in numerous newspaper articles, essays, speeches, and television- and radio-interviews, though, he did not shirk from criticising hardline trends in the GDR and soon acquired a high political profile. In June 1979, he wrote personally to Hermann Kant, who was at that time President of the Writers' Union of the GDR. In his letter, not published until 1992 (Arnold 1992: 51-8), he gave vent in unmistakably sarcastic tones to the bitterness, anger and indignation which he felt at the treatment of certain GDR writers whose books had been banned and who had themselves been barred from participating in the East German Writers' Congress in Berlin. Becker did not mince his words: he accused the Party of resorting to lies and of being incapable of taking criticism, attacked the Copyright Bureau for its Mafia-like tactics, and spurned Kant's craven defence of the current cultural policy of the GDR, denouncing it as 'Unfug' (mischief): 'What you so amicably call the state's steering and planning of publishing is torment, censorship on a scale not easy to find elsewhere in Europe' (Arnold 1992: 57).[16]

He published a further three novels, two, *Aller Welt Freund* (A friend to all the world – 1982) and *Amanda herzlos* (Heartless Amanda, 1992), relating (indirectly in the case of the former) to his experiences in the GDR, and a third, *Bronsteins Kinder* (Bronstein's children – 1986, filmed in 1992) returning to the question of the Holocaust and its repercussions. He also worked on film scripts on the subject of the Holocaust: *David* (1978/9) by Peter Lilienthal, which depicts the experiences of a young German Jew who stays in Germany and, almost miraculously, manages to survive the Holocaust; and *Der Passagier* (The passenger, 1987) by Thomas Brasch, with Tony Curtis in the main role, concerning a German-American Jew and former concentration camp inmate who, through a series of flashbacks provoked by the shooting of a film in Germany, confronts his own past through his memory. In 1986, Becker began work on the first script which he had specifically written for television: *Liebling Kreuzberg* (Darling Kreuzberg), broadcast on West German television, was an immediate success, securing his financial future. It starred his old GDR friend Manfred Krug (who had also left for the West after Biermann's expatriation) and was hailed by many film critics as the best series on television (Heidelberger-Leonard 1992: 313). *Liebling Kreuzberg* was awarded the Adolf-Grimme Prize in 1987 and, with two more series transmitted, Becker became forthwith, albeit reluctantly, a national celebrity, following up his initial television success with the popular and highly regarded nine-part series *Wir sind auch nur ein Volk* (We are after all just a people) in 1994.

Throughout the 1980s his reputation was underpinned both at home and abroad by a succession of honours and awards: he was guest professor at the University of Augsburg and in 1981 was invited to participate in the first of the Peace Meetings for writers from East and West in East Berlin; he was appointed 'Stadtschreiber von Bergen-Enkheim' (City Writer-in-residence) for one year (1982-3) and elected to the Academy of Language and Literature in Darmstadt (1983); he was guest professor at Cornell University, Ithaca, New York, in 1984, the year he met his third wife Christine; from September to December 1987 he was guest professor at the University of Texas at Austin, and in 1989 he was invited to deliver the prestigious 'Frankfurter Poetik-Vorlesungen' (Frankfurt lectures on poetics) at the University of Frankfurt am Main, published the following year under the title *Warnung vor dem Schriftsteller* (Warning against the writer). In November 1989, he made a private visit to Tel Aviv. He received further prizes, the Bavarian Television Prize and the Hans Fallada Prize in 1990 (the year of the birth of Jurek and Christine Becker's son, Jonathon Samuel), and the Federal Film Prize (Gold Ribbon) in 1991. In 1993 he was Max Kade Writer in Residence at Washington University, St. Louis, and in October 1995, guest writer at the Centre for Contemporary German Literature in Swansea. In May 1996, he began writing the scripts for the latest series of *Liebling Kreuzberg*, his final work. He died of cancer on 14 March 1997 in Berlin.

Notes

1. 'Daß ich jüdischer Herkunft bin, wußte ich vom ersten Jahr meines Lebens, nur was das bedeutet und was das für Folgen hat, ist mir erst im Nachhinein klargeworden.'
2. 'ein Mann kam rein ins Zimmer, den ich nie gesehen hatte: mein Vater, an den ich mich nicht erinnern konnte.'

3. 'Schließlich sind es ja nicht die polnischen Antisemiten, die den Krieg verloren haben.'
4. 'ich wollte aufhören, ein "anderer" zu sein.'
5. 'Ich war kein normaler deutscher Junge, wollte aber gern einer sein.'
6. 'mein Vater hat mich auch zu einem Vielleser gemacht. Ich weiß nicht, ob das eine Art Naturgesetz ist, aber Leser werden relativ kritische Leute.'
7. See Chapter 5.
8. 'Ich hatte immerzu irgendwelche Parteiverfahren. Ich hatte immer irgendwelchen Streit, auch im Schriftsteller-Verband, aber es war, was mich betrifft, ein ziemliches Maß an Solidarität da.'
9. 'Es wäre mir aber im Traum nicht eingefallen, mit meiner Empörung etwa zum *Spiegel* zu laufen.'
10. 'je mehr ich den Mund aufgerissen habe, desto privilegierter wurde ich!'
11. See Chapter 5.
12. 'so starke provokante Elemente [. . .], daß man es mit gutem Gewissen und politischer Verantwortung nicht annehmen könnte.'
13. 'Darauf spekuliert er und deshalb setzt er uns auch damit unter Druck.'
14. See Chapter 6.
15. 'Ich glaube nicht, daß ich ohne die Wiedervereinigung wieder in den Osten zurückgegangen wäre, auch wenn ich, aus gewissen Gründen, den Anschein zu erwecken versuchte, als wäre diese Frage noch offen.'
16. 'Was Du so freundlich die staatliche Lenkung und Planung des Verlagswesens nennst, ist Drangsalierung, ist Zensur in einem solchen Ausmaß, wie Du es in Europa nicht so leicht nocheinmal findest.'

–2–

Souveränität' (Sovereignty): Artistic Independence as a Fundamental Aesthetic Principle

In an interview in 1991, Becker admitted that he had written 'Die beliebteste Familiengeschichte' (My favourite family story) precisely 'because for once I wanted to write something on the theme of "telling stories". [. . .] With this I believe I have a vehicle for unfolding my ideas about storytelling via a story itself' (Graf and Konietzny 1991: 63).[1] He acknowledged, too, that in many of his other novels and stories, the act or manner of speaking or writing becomes thematic: 'As long as I've been writing books, it has been my conviction that writing itself is also a theme. Not only what is represented in a book but also the way it is narrated has to become a theme as well' (Graf and Konietzny 1991: 63).[2]

Becker's narrators, therefore, frequently question the necessity and legitimacy of storytelling itself. As he once wrote of his novels: 'When I am writing a novel it becomes increasingly important for me not only to write a decent story, but also to demonstrate why I consider it worth telling' (*Die Zeit*, 3.10.1986).[3] In the story 'Die Mauer' (The wall), for instance, the narrator feels the need to justify his narration of certain events on the grounds that they must have been extraordinary, thus supplying his own aesthetic evaluative criteria: 'What happened must have been strange and unheard of, otherwise it would not be worthwhile telling you about it' (NZ 63).[4] This particular narrator also feels compelled to confess that much of his story is the product of his memory, and that certain details require verification, for his memories are not simply unreliable, but sometimes fiction rather than actual fact. The narrator of *Jakob der Lügner,* too, admitting that he has 'fragwürdige Erinnerungen' (dubious memories – J 24), feels the need prove the authenticity of his story – almost as if the author himself is all the more concerned, in view of his own lack of memories and personal sources of information, to legitimise those of his fictional narrator, who says: 'I would like, while it is still not too late, to say a few words about my sources of information before any suspicions arise' (J 43).[5]

Yet amongst Becker's narratorial and other narrative concerns we find not only examples typical of much modernist fiction, with its self-conscious preoccupation with the legitimacy of its own existence. We discover that Becker's frameworks and his stories within stories are sometimes a celebration of the event of storytelling itself, an expression of pleasure in the sovereign act of narration and the freedom that this entails. The narrator of *Jakob der Lügner*, for instance, interrupts his story about life in a Polish ghetto in order to allow himself the liberty of a casual chat with the reader and thereby, too, the opportunity to reflect on the reasons for the usually light-hearted, often cheerful narrative stance which he adopts despite his sad, tragic subject. For after all, he wants to tell a good story: 'Let's have a little chat, as befits any decent story, grant me this small pleasure, without a little chat it's all so wretchedly sad' (J 24).[6] In 'Die beliebteste Familiengeschichte', this pleasure extends to a delight in the recreation of the actual storytelling situation and ritual (see Chapter 4). The story is both a celebration of the family tradition of storytelling and a commemoration of the skills of the original master of this Jewish art, Uncle Gideon, one of several avuncular Jewish storyteller figures celebrated in Becker's works. Other noteworthy examples who testify to the power of fiction are Jakob, little Lina's 'Märchenonkel' (story-hour presenter) in *Jakob der Lügner,* and the old shopkeeper Tenzer in 'Die Mauer', of whom we read: 'he knows some stories. The most hard-boiled fellows sit in silence before him, they don't utter a word, they keep their mouths shut and stay quite still' (NZ 63).[7]

In 'Die beliebteste Familiengeschichte', then, Becker does not simply retell Uncle Gideon's story, he also chronicles the humorous family tradition of the telling of their favourite story, and succeeds in bringing alive again an important aspect of Jewish family culture, a custom which is part of his own Jewish heritage but which, he tells us, has disappeared long before his time. There were of course several different versions of this story so often retold, for with each retelling by his father 'klang sie anders' (it sounded different), yet the current narrator manages to work out his own version from the constant elements in the many variations, thereby asserting his sovereignty over his material: 'most of the precise pieces of information, which are, of course, not always avoidable when you are telling a story, represent as it were mean values. I have worked them out for myself from the deviations which my father made in almost every direction' (NZ 43).[8] Through this sovereignty which his narrator achieves, Becker succeeds in skilfully employing the techniques of the fading tradition of oral storytelling, whose exponents within his own family all perished in the Holocaust, in order to ensure its survival at least in written form.

Aesthetic problems involved in literary confrontation with the past were, then, a major concern of Becker's in his works on Jewish themes. Brought up in the GDR, he was aware of the tedious one-sidedness of the official 'Bild von Nazi-Deutschland' (image of Nazi Germany) and the tales of 'Arbeiterveteranen' (working-class veterans): 'I went to school in the GDR and was confronted with the past in a very specific way' (Hage 1987: 331–2).[9] He once admitted the possibility that he wrote his first novel *Jakob der Lügner* in reaction to the 'resistance literature' prevalent at the time in the GDR, which he regarded as distorting historical truth since examples of actual resistance on the part of the Jews such as the Warsaw ghetto uprising were 'the big exception' (*Seminar* 1983: 271): 'I once reflected on whether my first book was a reaction to my experiences in the past, or whether it was not rather a reaction to the books that were written about it, which I think are dreadful' (*Stern* 1988: 8).[10]

In an interview in 1991, Becker claims to have written a story, entitled 'Großvater' (Grandfather), in which the problem of narrating the past is the main theme: 'Above all, it is about how to relate the past, and how not to' (Graf and Konietzny 1991: 63).[11] 'Großvater', as he explained to me in 1991, was composed in the period immediately after he left the GDR in 1977. It is the opening story in the collection *Nach der ersten Zukunft*, forming an almost programmatic introduction to the volume. Narration itself becomes the subject of a dialogue between the nameless, eponymous grandfather, another oral storyteller in the Jewish tradition, and an anonymous 'wir' ('we'), presumably his grandchildren, entreating him to tell them one of his stories. The grandfather explains how his stories vary with each retelling because of the deficiencies in his own memory. Unlike the narrator of *Jakob der Lügner*, who interrupts his story in order to admit to gaps due to his own dubious memories, the grandfather prefers to carry on his story when his memory lets him down, even if this entails distorting the truth. His explanation is that he fills in any such gaps out of consideration for his listeners: 'Of course I could go and simply leave gaps in the story, too. And then you'd really thank me for that, wouldn't you?' (NZ 7).[12]

A recent critic has interpreted the work primarily as an elucidation of the aesthetic constraints placed on the storyteller, reading it as a development of 'the principles of the type of narration [. . .] which can quite correctly be read as a model of Becker's own narrative technique' (Egyptien in Heidelberger-Leonard, 1992: 279).[13] For him the grandfather's argument is a legitimate one, running as follows: since one of the principles of narration is precisely the requirement to tell a good story and so please the reader or listener aesthetically, the storyteller is bound by certain aesthetic laws which sometimes require him to modify historical truth in certain ways. Not only must he employ his imagination to close the gaps in his story left by the deficiencies of his own memory and keep his story flowing; he must also be selective, particularly in the way in which he retells the past, as the grandfather explains:

> The truth is certainly the truth. And what has happened did happen, that's just as clear too. But storytelling also has its rules. What sort of fine storyteller would go and shower his listeners with the truth, without giving them the sense and understanding of it? [. . .] Of course it makes a big difference whether you really tell a story, or whether you just throw it in your listener's face. (NZ 9)[14]

Historical truth, then, in all its details, must sometimes be avoided by the storyteller, whose real skill consists in the way in which he sidesteps this potential 'Feind' (enemy): 'The storyteller feels best, you see, when to the left and to the right of his path something is left of the truth, an enemy to be avoided, so to speak. You can take it quite literally: an enemy approaches you.'[15] The good storyteller, too, is one who recognises 'that inhibitions and reservations are not the storyteller's disgrace, but his merit' (NZ 10).[16]

Yet we must be wary here of identifying Becker with his oral storyteller. Indeed, a reading of the story which sees it exclusively in poetological terms as a debate about aesthetic issues surely misses the point. These last cited words of the grandfather are rather a case of politics masquerading as aesthetics.

To readers acquainted with the two central concerns of Becker's writing, his forgotten experiences of the Holocaust and his life in the GDR, it becomes increasingly apparent that the past in question in 'Großvater' is not the Holocaust but that of the Communist Party and its relation to Stalinism. Half-way through the story, the grandfather sighs: 'Unfortunately, over the years, quite a few things have happened which you would never, never be happy about if you heard of them' (NZ 9).[17]

The constraints which the grandfather explains relate not to aesthetic considerations but to censorship, both external and internal. This becomes clear as soon as the political context of the dialogue is hinted at, when the grandfather complains, referring to an anonymous 'sie' (they): 'I can't be careful enough. They inspect each one of my sentences. They scrutinise every single one five times to see if it can be of use to them, that is: to see if they can use it against me. That's precisely why I have to check every one of my sentences twice, before they do' (NZ 12).[18] As Becker admitted in 1991, the grandfather is, of course, a Party veteran who has lived through the Stalin era:

> The grandfather is an old comrade who is being questioned about the embarrassing past of the old comrades, which is, of course, full of unpleasant problems which he doesn't want to talk about; and the young people now want only too much to know what the history of the Communist Party of the Soviet Union was really like, and not just the way it is presented in the latest publication of the Politburo of the Communist Party of the Soviet Union. (Graf and Konietzny 1991: 63)[19]

'Großvater' can thus be seen to demonstrate the confusion which existed in GDR writing between aesthetic and political considerations and points to the dangers inherent in the modification of historical truth for political rather than aesthetic reasons. The main concern of the story is not aesthetics but censorship – here, the self-censorship of writers under political pressure.

Becker himself was no literary 'Großvater'! Whilst still resident and publishing in the GDR, he proclaimed in 1974 in the literary journal *Neue Deutsche Literatur* (New German Literature), albeit with reference to the pressures exerted on GDR writers by Western critics: 'I allow myself the right to say and to describe precisely whatever I consider right to say and describe in a book. And I allow myself the right to leave out precisely whatever seems to me to be dispensable' (*Neue Deutsche Literatur* 1974: 59).[20] He was aware, too, of the danger of linguistic straitjackets – the danger of the assimilation of, as he put it, 'things that are GDR-specific [. . .] in respect of dialect or ideology',[21] of which there was much evidence in the language of many GDR works of the time, as he commented in August 1977 in East Berlin: 'An imposed use of language can never be a sovereign use of language. Books such as these are then not solely the work of the author, and for this very reason they deserve to be criticised' (Schwarz 1990: 116).[22] Faced with the unrelenting pressure of censorship in the GDR, Becker himself strove to maintain what he called a 'souveränes Verhältnis' (sovereign relationship) to his writing.

'Souveränität' meant, for Becker, independence as a writer in the sense of being in complete artistic command of his material. It remained a key concept in his understanding of his own writing and was for him also an important element of all artistic activity. Asked, for instance, what criteria determined his choice of material, he stressed the importance of what he called 'Verfügungsgewalt' (the power over something) and the idea of narration as an expression of free will: 'I have the power over it all, absolutely' (Stöhr 1988: 10).[23] 'In my books, nobody does anything I don't want them to' (Birnbaum in Heidelberger-Leonard 1992: 101).[24]

An important aspect of this 'Verfügungsgewalt' is the adoption of the appropriate 'Erzählhaltung' (narrative stance). The reasons cited by Becker for the particular 'Erzählhaltung' in *Jakob der Lügner,* for instance, illustrate both the authorial 'Souveränität' so characteristic of his writing and also underline the distance which separates him from his various first-person narrators. The narrator of *Jakob der Lügner*, who, unlike the author, was an adult witness of events in the ghetto, interrupts his narrative at one point with the comment: 'We know what will happen. We have some modest experience of the way in which stories are sometimes apt to unfold; we have some imagination so we know what will happen' (J 34).[25] Of his narrator's disarmingly frank and naive 'Erzählhaltung', Becker commented: 'I wanted to equip a specific narrator, one I made up, [. . .] with this particular [. . .] view of things. Because it seemed to go with his character and his perspective. The man who says this is, of course, not a writer by profession but a factory-worker, and he has got a much more naive attitude to narration than I have' (Stöhr 1988: 10).[26]

Becker always denied ever having any sense of compulsion to write. Speaking of 'problems which prompt me to write about them, which I want to write about', he added: 'I don't believe in this mysterious notion of "having to write about something", which I sometimes hear about. Often, an aura is placed on literature: an author just had to do it this way or that. I never had to, I only wrote when I wanted to' (Stöhr 1988: 10).[27] Consequently, he recognised the need to achieve distance in order to maintain complete control of his material: even if an author's writing is motivated by 'Aufgeregtheit' (excitement), by 'Zorn auf bestimmte Umstände' (anger about particular circumstances), he must take care that this anger does not blind him to 'the requirements and necessities of the story he is in the process of telling' (Stöhr 1998: 10).[28] For Becker, 'the real excitement' in creative writing was one that allowed him 'to proceed with cool calculation', focused on his aesthetic goal: 'It should be economical and never lose sight of the effect of the particular piece of writing' (Stöhr 1998: 24).[29]

Becker admitted in 1989 that his reasons for leaving the GDR in 1977 were not so much political ones, but rather his private concerns about his work: he felt that he was no longer in full 'sovereign' control of his writing, producing what he deemed to be sub-standard literature, for he was in one of those situations, in which one [was] so provoked, in which one's gaze [was] so firmly fixed on the dispute that now one [could] only comment on it. [. . .] In the agitated situation at that time, I was writing in a way which was not in accordance with my own notion of writing. [. . .] In the end, I got the professions of writer and resistance fighter mixed up. (*tageszeitung,* 25.9.1989)[30]

The pressure from both the censor and also the expectations of his GDR readers, therefore, were like, as he put it,

the continuous presence of a 'huge eye': by this I mean not only the censor. By the 'eye' I mean, too, the expectations of readers who expected from literature a certain sound-level. [. . .] At that time, I would not have dared to write something which did not have recognisably political or oppositional features. Because I would have feared that, if I had done so, everyone would have said: Now he has given up, now they have crushed him, now he is avoiding the issue, now they have got him. That is a terribly non-sovereign situation. [. . .] And I think that, more than from the censor, I wanted to withdraw myself from this situation. I wanted to remain in sovereign control of my writing. (Heidelberger-Leonard 1992: 116–17)[31]

Becker did, though, also experience considerable difficulties with the censor in the GDR in the 1970s, and these were also invariably attributable to his increasingly defensive stance on the question of artistic independence. This was why he was so uncompromising in his refusal to make the necessary modifications required by the Ministerium für Kultur (Ministry for Culture) to his novel *Schlaflose Tage* (Sleepless days) and to his collection of short stories, *Nach der ersten Zukunft* (After the initial future), with the result that neither of these works were published in the GDR (see Chapter 5).

One other important aspect of Becker's notion of 'Souveränität' is his view of the author–reader relationship. In a short eulogy to Max Frisch on his seventieth birthday, Becker describes his own 'career' as a reader. His early reading was confined to books which just happened to be in his father's bookcase – works by Gorki, Rex Stout, Sienkiewicz, Karl May, Gogol, Edgar Wallace and Max Frisch. With the exception of the latter, his aesthetic enjoyment was limited to 'the suspense as to how whatever issue was being dealt with would come to a just conclusion'. With Frisch, however, he experienced 'a different kind of suspense, one focusing not so much on the outcome of the story as on which conceivable or (for me the reader) inconceivable continuation of a particular situation the author would decide upon' (*Der Tagesspiegel,* 15.5.1981).[32]

The young Becker's reading of Frisch, then, brought the realisation that aesthetic enjoyment consisted not least in stimulation of the intellect, in provocation of his own thoughts as reader about possible directions of the narrative. This experience was reinforced later by another aspect of the Swiss author's works which appears to have had a seminal impact on Becker when he was in the GDR, accustomed both to the fixed positions of an official ideology and to writers who wrote 'IM BESITZ DER WAHRHEIT', as the playwright Heiner Müller expressed it (In possession of the truth – in: Chiarloni and Pankoke 1991: 55): Becker was fascinated by the openness of the basic positions which Frisch adopts in his works: 'This marvellous uncertainty always seemed to me to be like an invitation to participate in his stories, not just to observe them. Never before had the attitude of absolute certainty, my own and that of others, seemed so suspect as it did after the impression made upon me by those stories' (*Der Tagesspiegel*, 15.5.1981).[33]

Becker's own experiences as reader underlie his attitude to readers of his own works. He always held the view (not just when he was in the GDR) that readers must become active and not play 'the role of mere recipient and purchaser of opinions'.[34] It is not the role of writers to meet readers' expectations, writers must be raising issues rather than providing solutions, as he said in 1982: 'It would be nonsensical to expect nothing but answers from books. In the East as well as in the West, writers, together, have to be searching for things' (Krüger 1982: 106).[35] Writers must therefore encourage readers 'sich für sich selbst selbständig zu fühlen' (to feel independent), to be able to stand on their own feet, helping them thereby to become aware of their own situation and of the roles which they unconsciously play in their everyday lives (Kalb 1983: 60).

This viewpoint of the author's permeates a short, almost programmatic prose-piece entitled 'Anstiftung zum Verrat' (Incitement to treason) which appears towards the end of the original edition of *Nach der ersten Zukunft*. This text is an exhortation to readers to become fully aware of the situations in which they find themselves and of the roles which they unconsciously play in their everyday lives. They can best do this by adopting different, even opposed roles:

> Interrupt whatever is a matter of course, itself almost like sleep. Get by for a few minutes without the proven arguments. Then for an hour, then for a day. Play a game: Take over the role of one's enemy. Not in a deliberately amateurish way, though, but with the utmost ambition. Until the fear of finding oneself convincing as one's own enemy gradually disappears. Do not immediately despair at the thought: Why not, then? It is the spirit of the game.
>
> Only end the game when the role has played itself out. Wait for this moment without impatience. If it does not arrive, then play on and on, if need be to the very end. (NZ 200)[36]

Are readers, then, to expect open texts from Becker which encourage them to engage actively with the text in this way? On close examination of his works, particularly those with first-person narrators, we discover almost without exception that author does not, in fact, give us entirely 'open' texts, as his above remarks might lead us to believe, but ones which are relatively closed. For instance, in many of his stories written in the period immediately before and after he left the GDR, such as 'Das Parkverbot' (No parking zone), 'Allein mit dem Anderen' (Alone with the other one), 'Der Verdächtige' (The suspect) and 'Der Fluch der Verwandschaft' (The curse of one's relatives), Becker, through the first-person narrative voice, adopts the 'role of his enemy', the roles of conformists (in most cases GDR contemporaries such as bureaucrats and other servants of the state), in order to expose their cowardly mentality from the 'inside'. It is precisely by encouraging the reader, through the narrowness of the first-person perspective, to experience events directly through the eyes of such narrators that Becker provokes the reader into standing back and subjecting the narrative voice itself to critical scrutiny. Thus, through irony, a sense of complicity between the author and the reader is established at the expense of the narrator. Becker is, of course, manipulating his readers, distancing them from the narrator and his text; but this is in turn intended to increase the reader's own critical self-awareness. This was for Becker one of the most important aspects of literature: 'Of course, one of the most important effects which literature can have, if not the most important, is to help readers to open their eyes to themselves' (W 88).[37] Readers are thus implicitly challenged to ask themselves whether they would, in fact, have reacted in the same way in a similar situation.

In 'Das Parkverbot', for instance, a fugitive seeks refuge from the police by hiding on the floor of the narrator's car which he has been forced to park in a no-parking zone while his wife goes shopping. The narrative follows the thoughts of the narrator as he grapples with the confusion in his own head caused by the 'quälende Situation' (tormenting situation – NZ 171) in which he finds himself. He does not know whether the man is a criminal or a victim of persecution. He explores the case for and against helping him, but his thoughts reveal that he is motivated not by any sympathy for this man in his desperate plight but by a desire to be rid of him and, despite his protestations to the contrary, by fear that he may become an accessory to an unknown crime. The climax of the story comes when he appears to be on the point of helping the man by driving off. However, the reader's expectations are not fulfilled – the narrator suddenly asks himself how on earth he has come to be in this situation

(NZ 173) and so decides to give the man up, the story ending with the three short sentences: 'At the moment when I saw the handcuffs closing around the man's wrists, saliva hit me in the middle of my face. The blood must have shot to my head. A policeman placed his hand soothingly on my arm' (NZ 174).[38]

The narrator's telling of the story is an attempt to rationalise and justify to the reader (and to himself, of course) his own behaviour in betraying the stranger to the police, but the more he appeals to the reader's understanding and sympathy, the more the actual text speaks out against him. By subjecting the narrative voice itself to critical scrutiny, Becker exposes the truth: that his narrator's main concern is not to help the fugitive escape but to help himself escape from the situation. Becker, then, manipulates his readers: even in the case of a story with such a first-person narrator, who, unlike the narrator of 'Die beliebteste Familien-geschichte', does not stand outside the action, enjoying 'souveräne Freiheit der Narration' (sovereign freedom to narrate), the control which the author exerts over his text is such that it is ultimately not his readers who make up their minds, but the writer who does it for them.

Notes

1. 'weil ich einmal über das Thema "Geschichten erzählen" etwas schreiben wollte. [. . .] Damit glaube ich ein Vehikel zu haben, wie ich meine Vorstellungen von Geschichtenerzählen anhand einer Geschichte ausbreiten kann.'
2. 'Seit ich schreibe, ist es für mich eine Überzeugung, daß das Erzählen selbst auch ein Thema des Buches ist. Nicht nur das darin Dargestellte, sondern die Art des Erzählens muß mit thematisiert werden.'
3. 'Beim Romanschreiben wird es mir immer wichtiger, nicht nur eine ordentliche Geschichte zu erzählen, sondern auch vorzuführen, warum ich sie für erzählenswert halte.'
4. 'Was geschehen ist, muß seltsam und unerhört gewesen sein, sonst lohnt es sich nicht, darüber zu berichten.'
5. 'Ich möchte gerne, noch ist es nicht zu spät, ein paar Worte über meine Informationen verlieren, bevor der eine oder andere Verdacht sich meldet.'
6. 'Wir wollen ein bißchen schwätzen, wie es sich für eine ordentliche

Geschichte gehört, laßt mir die kleine Freude, ohne ein Schwätzchen ist alles so elend traurig.'

7. 'er weiß Geschichten. Die abgebrühtesten Kerle sitzen stumm vor ihm und schweigen und halten den Mund und sind ganz still.'

8. 'die meisten präzisen Angaben, die beim Geschichtenerzählen doch nicht immer vermeidbar sind, stellen gewissermaßen Mittelwerte dar. Ich habe sie mir aus den Abweichungen, die meinem Vater in fast jede Richtung hin unterliefen, selbst errechnet.'

9. 'Ich bin in der DDR zur Schule gegangen und in einer Art und Weise mit dem Früher konfrontiert worden.'

10. 'Ich habe einmal darüber nachgedacht, ob mein erstes Buch eine Reaktion auf Erfahrungen meiner Vergangenheit ist, oder nicht eher eine Reaktion auf die Bücher, die darüber geschrieben wurden und die ich für entsetzlich halte.'

11. 'Vor allem handelt sie davon, wie Vergangenheit erzählt zu werden hat und wie nicht.'

12. 'Ich könnte ja auch in den Geschichten einfach Lücken lassen. Da würdet ihr euch schön bedanken.'

13. 'die Prinzipien eines Erzählens [. . .], das durchaus als Modell von Beckers eigener Erzähltechnik [. . .] gedeutet werden kann.' Egyptien's otherwise impressive interpretation misses some of the negative implications of his reading of the story.

14. 'Gewiß, die Wahrheit ist die Wahrheit. Und was passiert ist, ist passiert, das ist genauso klar. Doch hat auch das Erzählen seine Gesetze. Ein schöner Erzähler ist mir, wer seine Zuhörer ohne Sinn und Verstand mit der Wahrheit überschüttet. [. . .] Es ist doch wohl ein Unterschied, ob man eine Geschichte erzählt, oder ob man sie den Zuhörern vor die Füße wirft.'

15. 'Am allerwohlsten fühlt sich der Erzähler nämlich, wenn links und rechts von seinem Weg noch etwas Wahrheit übrigbleibt, zum Ausweichen sozusagen. Ganz wörtlich könnt ihr das nehmen: Ein Feind kommt euch entgegen.'

16. 'daß Hemmungen und Bedenken nicht des Erzählers Schande sind, sondern sein Vorzug'.

17. 'Leider hat sich im Laufe der vielen Jahre manches zugetragen, womit ihr nie und nimmer zufrieden wärt, wenn ihr es hörtet.'

18. 'Ich kann nicht vorsichtig genug sein. Sie prüfen jeden meiner Sätze. Sie drehen ihn fünfmal um, ob er ihnen etwas nützt, das heißt: ob sie ihn gegen mich verwenden können. Genau darum muß ich jeden meiner Sätze doppelt prüfen, vor ihnen.'

19. 'Der Großvater ist ein alter Genosse, der über die Peinlichkeit in der

Vergangenheit der alten Genossen ausgefragt wird, die ja voll von Unannehmlichkeiten ist, und nicht so gern darüber sprechen möchte; und die jungen Leute wollen doch nun zu gerne wissen, wie die Geschichte der KPdSU wirklich gewesen ist, und nicht nur, wie sie in der neuesten Ausgabe des Politbüros der KPdSU nachlesbar ist.' The inclusion of this story in the collection *Nach der ersten Zukunft* was one of the main reasons why the stories did not appear in the GDR until 1986 (cf. Graf and Konietzny 1991: 63).

20. 'Ich nehme mir das Recht heraus, in einem Buch genau das zu sagen und das zu beschreiben, worüber ich etwas zu sagen und das zu beschreiben ich für richtig halte. Und ich nehme mir ebenso das Recht, genau das wegzulassen, was mir entbehrlich scheint.'

21. 'DDR-Spezifisches [. . .] in mundartlicher oder ideologischer Hinsicht.'

22. 'Ein oktroierter [sic] Sprachgebrauch kann niemals ein souveräner Sprachgebrauch sein. Solche Bücher sind dann nicht allein das Werk des Autors, und schon aus diesem Grunde kritikwürdig.'

23. 'Ich habe durchaus die Verfügungsgewalt darüber.'

24. 'Niemand in meinen Büchern macht etwas, das ich nicht will.'

25. 'Wir wissen was geschehen wird. Wir haben unsere bescheidenen Erfahrungen darin, wie Geschichten mitunter abzulaufen pflegen, wir haben einige Phantasie, und darum wissen wir, was geschehen wird.'

26. 'Ich wollte einen bestimmten Erzähler, den ich erfunden habe [. . .] mit dieser [. . .] Meinung ausrüsten. Weil sie zu seinem Charakter und zu seiner Perspektive zu gehören schien. Der Mann, der das sagt, ist ja von Beruf nicht Schriftsteller, sondern Arbeiter in einer Fabrik, und er hat zum Erzählen eine viel naivere Haltung als ich.' Critics of the novel have often overlooked Becker's distance from his narrator and the latter's naive view of lies and hope.

27. 'Probleme, die mich zum Schreiben animieren, die von mir beschrieben sein wollen. [. . .] Ich glaube nicht an dieses geheimnisvolle "Schreiben müssen", von dem ich manchmal höre. Es wird oft eine Aura über Literatur gestülpt: ein Autor konnte nicht anders, als dies und jenes machen. Ich habe immer anders gekonnt, ich habe nur dann geschrieben, wenn ich auch wollte.'

28. 'die Erfordernisse und Notwendigkeiten der Geschichte, die er gerade erzählt'.

29. 'Die wahre Aufregegung ist eine, die mich kalt berechnend vorgehen läßt, auf mein Ziel konzentriert. Sie sollte ökonomisch sein und den Effekt des Schreibens nie aus den Augen verlieren.'

30. 'in denen man so herausgefordert wird, in denen man so fixiert ist auf eine Auseinandersetzung, daß man sich nur noch *dazu* äußern

kann. [. . .] In der aufgeregten Situation damals habe ich auf eine Weise geschrieben, die meiner eigenen Vorstellung von Schreiben nicht entsprach. [. . .] Zum Schluß habe ich die Berufe Schriftsteller und Widerstandskämpfer miteinander verwechselt.'

31. 'die ständige Gegenwart eines "großen Auges": Damit meine ich nicht nur den Zensor. Mit dem "Auge" meine ich auch die Erwartung einer Leserschaft, die eine bestimmte Lautstärke von Literatur erwartete. [. . .] Ich hätte damals nicht gewagt, etwas zu schreiben, das nicht erkennbar politische und widerständlerische Züge trug. Weil ich gefürchtet hätte, wenn ich es tue, werden alle sagen: Jetzt hat er aufgegeben, jetzt haben sie ihn kleingekriegt, jetzt weicht er aus, jetzt haben sie ihn. Das ist eine schrecklich unsouveräne Situation. [. . .] Und ich glaube, mehr als dem Zensor wollte ich mich dieser Situation entziehen. Ich wollte ein souveränes Verhältnis zu meinem Schreiben kriegen.'

32. 'die Spannung darauf, wie die jeweils behandelte Angelegenheit zu einem gerechten Ende kam. [. . .] eine andere Spannung; eine, die nicht so sehr auf den Ausgang der Geschichte gerichtet war wie darauf, für welche der denkbaren oder (für mich den Leser) undenkbaren Fortsetzungen einer Situation der Autor sich entscheiden würde.' Simrock, the hero of *Schlaflose Tage*, carries with him an illicit copy of Frisch's *Tagebuch* (diary), 'eine von seinem Heidelberger Vetter durch den Zoll geschmuggelte Seltenheit' (a rarity smuggled through customs by his cousin in Heidelberg – ST 104), which is later confiscated by border guards when he returns from a visit to Hungary.

33. 'Diese wunderbare Unsicherheit kam mir immer wie eine Einladung vor, an seinen Geschichten teilzunehmen, sie nicht nur zu betrachten. Nie war mir die Haltung der Zweifellosigkeit, der eigenen wie der der anderen, so verdächtig wie unter dem Eindruck jener Geschichten.'

34. 'die Rolle des bloßen Rezipienten und Abnehmers von Meinungen'.

35. 'Es wäre unsinnig, von Büchern nichts als Antworten zu erwarten. Im Osten wie im Westen haben Schriftsteller wohl gemeinsam, Suchende zu sein.'

36. 'Das Selbstverständliche, das beinahe wie Schlaf ist, kurz unterbrechen. Ein paar Minuten ohne die bewährten Argumente auskommen. Dann ein Stunde, dann einen Tag. Ein Spiel spielen: Die Rolle seines Feindes übernehmen. Doch nicht absichtlich stümperhaft, sondern mit allem Ehrgeiz. Bis die Furcht, sich als der eigene Feind überzeugend zu finden, sich nach und nach verliert. Nicht gleich verzweifeln bei dem Gedanken: Warum eigentlich nicht? Er ist die Seele des

Spiels. / Das Spiel erst dann beenden, wenn die Rolle leergespielt ist. Ohne Ungeduld auf diesen Augenblick warten. Kommt er nicht, dann immerweiterspielen, im Notfall bis ans Ende.'

37. 'Es sei doch eine der wichtigsten Wirkungen von Literatur, wenn nicht die wichtigste, daß sie Lesern den Blick auf sich selbst zu öffnen helfe.'

38. 'Im selben Augenblick, da ich Handschellen um die Gelenke des Mannes sich schließen sah, traf mich mitten ins Gesicht Speichel. Das Blut muß mir zu Kopf geschossen sein. Die Hand eines Polizisten legte sich mir begütigend auf den Arm.'

—3—

The Power of Fiction – *Jakob der Lügner*

In an essay for a symposium in Toronto in 1983, Becker explained that the idea for *Jakob der Lügner* (Jakob the Liar – 1969) had itself been an improvisation on a true story told to him by his father about a man in the Lodz ghetto who had been shot when the Gestapo discovered the clandestine radio with which he had provided his fellow-Jews with news from London and Moscow. Although his father had wanted him to write a book about this 'hero', Becker did not have 'the slightest desire' to tell stories which had already been told: 'I had often read about this man – thousands of books had already been written about him. Strictly speaking almost every book I had read about the fascist era was about this very man' (*Seminar* 1983: 273). When Becker eventually did come to compose his own unusual version of this story, he wrote a humorous film script about a Jew in a Polish ghetto who pretends to have a radio in order to give a suicidally rash friend the hope to carry on by convincing him of the Russian advance. With its unheroic hero who, except for his tale, is no different from any of his friends in the ghetto (J 9), it was rejected by the authorities in the GDR precisely because it focused not on the theme of heroic resistance, regarded as a necessary ingredient of GDR anti-fascist films at that time, but on ordinary, everyday Jews (*Süddeutsche Zeitung*, 30.7.1992). In a fit of rage at this rejection (*Stern*, 5.5.1988), Becker rewrote it as a novel, the form in which it was finally published.

His father, though, was so infuriated by the gulf between his original story and his son's humorous version that he refused to speak to him for a year on the grounds that it was not true to life. He was accused of trying to 'cheat' witnesses of the horrors of the real ghettos, and the substance of his father's criticism of the unorthodox treatment of the Holocaust was also shared by several critics when *Jakob der Lügner* first appeared. There are two other good reasons for his unconventional approach.

First, as Becker explained (Arnold 1992: 6), he was 'rebelling' against his father's emotional way of telling stories, his sentimental and melo-dramatic technique. Second, and more important for a critical consideration of the novel, he wanted to wrest humour from tragedy and vice-versa. This was one of his fundamental aesthetic principles, as he explained:

> I look for a narrative style inappropriate to my material. When I want to tell a story which, if one heard nothing but the external circumstances, one would experience as tragic, then I look for a humorous way to tell it. And if I have a story which sounds damn funny, I look for the tragedy in it. [. . .] It's been my experience as a reader that whatever came across as being somewhat irreverent, exaggeratedly irreverent, or impious, breaking the rules of good taste, or inappropriately comic, always seemed to me to be the more impressive. (Arnold 1992: 65–6)[1]

Becker thus sought to avoid sentimentality and pathos in *Jakob der Lügner* by adopting a narrative stance which would give full rein to his inventiveness and to his humorous, often wryly ironic, approach to a potentially lugubrious tale.

Predictably, his unorthodox approach aroused controversy. Though initial reactions in both East and West Germany were enthusiastic, some critical voices were raised against the dangers of trivialising the horrors of the historical situation, and occasional doubts have persisted amongst literary critics both in Germany and abroad: some, for instance, spoke of Becker's 'playful approach to a reality which has absolutely nothing playful about it' (Lüdke-Haertel and Lüdke 1988: 3),[2] and the international symposium held in Canada in 1983 criticised the work on moral grounds. For many, the Holocaust represented an order of reality which the human mind had never confronted before (Langer 1975: 3) and was considered a chapter in the history of atrocity and human suffering which was beyond words. How, then, were readers to react to a novel described on the cover of the first edition as 'a cheerfully melancholy, gentle, elaborately constructed work',[3] in which brutal events are often 'tinged with humour' (Kane 1991: 167)? Here, both the part played by the narrator and the particular effects of the humour are crucial and demonstrate that the charge of 'Verharmlosung' (playing down his subject) levelled at Becker was without foundation.

The Narrator and his Strategies

In an interview in 1977, Becker suggested that '*Jakob* is, if you like, basically not a first-person narrative at all. There is a first person, but he doesn't play a part in the action. The first person is a narrative principle' (Schwarz 1990: 122–3).[4] Becker is not entirely correct here in so far as the narrator is a real person who witnessed some of the events in his story and was told of others by Jakob himself. Yet the author points to an important distinction between his first-person narrator and many of his conventional counterparts: the narrator of *Jakob der Lügner* is a central presence, akin to the narrator of a work much admired by Becker, *Der Erwählte* (The Holy Sinner) by Thomas Mann, embodying something of the spirit of storytelling itself and occasionally even reflecting on his own role as narrator. With his private obsession with trees, he is intrusively present from the very first sentence of the novel ('I can already hear everyone saying, a tree, so what's a tree then?') to the last ('For I can still see the shadows of trees, and I can't sleep, we're going wherever we're going'),[5] framing the story which he tells within his own personal reflections. He also interrupts his story on several brief occasions for specific effects: to convey a sense of immediacy, to make his story credible and to draw his readers into the action, thereby increasing their sense of personal involvement in events and situations.

Yet unlike Thomas Mann's spirit of storytelling, Becker's narrator is 'nicht allwissend' (not omniscient – J 98): indeed, he is a specific individual, one of the few Jewish Holocaust victims to survive, and distinct from his author, he has hitherto been unable to forget his story or to retell it, no matter how hard he has tried. Like other Holocaust survivors in Becker's works such as Aron Blank and Ostwald in *Der Boxer*, he has difficulties in communication which are related to time and place (post-war Germany) and mental state: 'I've tried a thousand times to off-load this damned story, always in vain. Either I tried to tell it to the wrong people, or I made some mistake or other. I got a lot of things mixed up, I got names wrong, or, as I said, they were the wrong people. Every time I've had a few glasses of schnaps to drink, it's there. I can't help it' (J 9).[6] The time now seems right, though, to come to terms both with these persistent 'fragwürdige Erinnerungen' (dubious memories – J 24) evoked by images of trees and with his own personal sense of guilt at the fact that it is he, not Jakob, who has survived to tell the tale: 'I'm alive, there's no doubt about that. I'm alive, and nobody can force me to drink and to remember trees and Jakob and all the other things involved' (J 24).[7] Yet the narrator appears to need an anonymous reader rather than a specific listener, since previous attempts to tell his story orally have foundered on his listeners' reactions: they have either sought excuses ('But when the war ended I was just . . .' – J 25) or betrayed pity ('I can hear the pity in her voice and go crazy' – J 25),[8] and like his author, he rejects the 'Zwangsidentität' of victim as the object of pity. Above all, though, it is the presence of trees, once banned in the ghetto and now symbols of his own survival, which move him to tell his story at this point in time: 'The whole city is a mass of green, the surroundings are unique, the parks are well-tended, every tree invites my memories' (J 26).[9]

Becker's narrator, then, has his own personal problems and history, and we learn several details about him from snippets of information which he gradually divulges: that he was born, for instance, in 1921 and is forty-six years old. Becker thus locates his novel precisely in the year 1967, thereby discouraging readers' assumptions of identity between narrator and author, but also, more importantly, giving his story greater plausibility in so far as it is retold by a mature witness of the ghetto, not through the eyes of the child which Becker had been at the time. The importance of the narrator's function as witness is even reinforced, at one point, in the thoughts of his main character, Jakob, as he reflects on the need to bear witness: 'now it is as if one should memorize everything exactly as it is so as to be able to report on it afterwards. Afterwards' (J 36).[10] Credibility is therefore an important factor, and most of the narrator's personal reflections on his role as narrator, together with the details that he supplies of his own experiences, serve to authenticate his story: 'Ich bin dabeige-wesen' ('I was there' – J 40), he affirms early on.

For the sake of credibility, too, he admits that there are limits to his ability to authenticate Jakob's story and the events and characters in the ghetto, but where he can offer evidence, he does so. So he recounts several episodes from his life in post-war Germany out of a strong sense of obligation to vouch for the general accuracy of his tale: he first explains how he revisited the ghetto in Poland to verify certain tiny details (J 21), and later he announces apologetically that he will have to intrude into the ghetto time-level in order to try, if not always successfully, to give certain explanations and so avoid gaps, implying that he is a chronicler of facts which have a real historical basis: 'If possible, no gap is to be left, and so unfortunately, when it comes to explaining, I'll have to intervene clumsily and directly in the action. The explanation will plug it after a fashion, but only later on: first the gap must become visible in its entirety' (J 196).[11] The explanation referred to here concerns his visit to an ageing SA-man after the war in order to establish facts which he otherwise could not have known, namely the ultimate fate of Professor Kirschbaum, a Jewish doctor of international standing who was taken away in a limousine to treat heart-attack victim and Gestapo chief Hardtloff: 'I imagine that some people will be asking suspiciously how I managed to get into this car' (J 207).[12]

To signal his own direct involvement either as eyewitness or as participant in events both at the railway yard where they worked in the ghetto, and during their deportation to the camp, the narrator sometimes employs first-person singular and plural pronouns ('On this fine blue day, I dish out the soup' – J 37; 'Then we set off' – J 278).[13] Yet he acknowledges that he is, for the most part, reliant upon others for his information, notably Jakob whom he refers to as his most important source (J 43–4). At the same time, though, he asserts his own autonomy as narrator of the story, emphasising that it is he, not Jakob, who is telling this story: 'All the same, it's me telling the story, not him, Jakob is dead, and besides I'm not telling his story but a story' (J 44).[14] Since he was there himself, and in the absence of any other witnesses, he claims for himself the right to employ his imagination where he sees fit, allying it to his own actual experiences in order to fill in the missing details. He justifies this right by underlining the highly subjective nature of these experiences in times when the normal laws of probability did not operate,[15] whilst at the same time claiming the right to portray, too, not only what might but also what should have happened, thus preparing the way for his invention of an alternative ending to the story (J 44–5). On some occasions, then, his story is punctuated by defensive admissions that his imagination is at work (J 55), yet at others, his imagination is presented as a potent creative factor which imbues his suppositions with the force of epistemological truths: 'I can't hear what Herschel is saying [. . .] but I can imagine it, and this is not a case of vague suppositions. The longer I think about it, the clearer I know what his words were, even if he never confirmed them to me' (J 137).[16] On the other hand, the narrator can also be selective in his use of his imagination, and sometimes, invariably for deliberate effect, he refuses to fill in certain gaps, as in the instance of the unsolved mystery of Fajngold's sudden disappearance, which then becomes symbolic of the fate of so many other ghetto inmates. The narrator thus emerges as a strong character in his own right who exercises sovereign control over his material, varying his approach as he sees fit.

His presence as a distinct personality is nowhere more visible than in passages where he comments on central issues such as the question of resistance. Here he adheres to the gloomy historical facts and makes no attempt to gloss over the absence of resistance in his ghetto:

And the resistance, people will ask, where's the resistance? [. . .] Are there in this wretched town only hands that do exactly what Hardtloff and his sentries demand of them? [. . .] Condemn them, go on condemning us, those were the only hands there were. [. . .] I can tell you that since then, I have read with awe of Warsaw and Buchenwald, another world yet comparable. I have read a lot about heroism, probably too much, I have been gripped by senseless envy, but I don't ask anyone to believe me. At any rate, we kept still right up to the last second, and there's nothing I can do now about that. I am not unaware of the fact that an oppressed people can only be really liberated if it contributes to its liberation, if it goes at least a little bit of the way to meet the Messiah. We didn't do it, I didn't budge, I learnt the orders by heart, I adhered strictly to them and only asked poor Jakob from time to time what sort of news had come in. I will probably never come to terms with it, I haven't deserved any better, my whole thing with the trees no doubt has something to do with it, as well as my awful sentimentality and the generosity of my tear ducts. Where I was, there was no resistance. (J 98–9)[17]

In the manner in which he both poses and answers this question, the narrator demonstrates his honest approach, his self-critical attitude, and his awareness of his own shortcomings and limitations, thereby increasing the credibility of his story. Over and above this, his self-deprecating personal 'confession' typifies the narrative tone which prevails throughout the story: the unpretentious narration of events stands in sharp contrast to the pathos and melodrama of typical resistance novels written in the GDR at this time with their tendency to demonise the perpetrators and glorify the victims in the manner of Bruno Apitz's *Nackt unter Wölfen* (Naked amongst wolves), to which GDR readers would have recognised a veiled reference in this passage. Thus elsewhere, too, the narrator scornfully denies the existence of notions such as comradeship and solidarity amongst the Jews as they work at the railway yard: 'Don't give me all that stuff about comradeship and the like; anyone who talks like that has no idea what this place is like, absolutely no idea at all' (J 28).[18]

His honesty in broaching such sensitive questions leads the narrator to forewarn the reader at this early stage in his story of the bleak yet typical ending in store for the ghetto inmates when, regretting the lack of resistance, he declares: 'The worst that could have happened to us would have been a meaningful death' (J 99).[19] Yet at the end of the novel, the narrator once more asserts his absolute narratorial autonomy, casting aside both credibility and historical facts as he proceeds to offer the reader two endings to his story, telling a 'fictitious' one before coming to the 'real' one. Why should Becker have his would-be chronicler of the ghetto postpone the actual ending in favour of pure 'fiction'? It has been widely recognised (for instance, by Kane 1991) that GDR readers will have read parts of his preferred ending as a deliberate attempt to lay on the pathos and melodrama and thereby ironise conventional GDR Socialist Realist works with their portrayal of the Soviet army as the glorious liberators. In this ending, Jakob dies heroically trying to get out of the ghetto (the narrator can only speculate on his motives), but the salvo which kills him is answered by the vengeful thunder of the Russian artillery. The scene sketched out by the narrator reads almost as a scenario for a Soviet film version:

> I picture to myself revenge for Jakob, this being (so I have decided) the cold and starry night when the Russians arrive. The Red Army will have succeeded in surrounding the city within a very short time; the sky is being lit up by the heavy artillery fire. Straight after the salvo aimed at Jakob, a deafening roar starts up, as if inadvertently triggered off by the unfortunate marksman on the watchtower. The first ghostly tanks, direct hits on the police station, the watchtowers are burning, Germans defending themselves to the last bullet with grim determination, or Germans fleeing, unable to find any hole to crawl into – dear God, what a night that would have been. (J 270)[20]

This heroic upbeat ending is then immediately followed by the real one, with the Jews in the cattle-trucks heading for 'wherever we are going'. The narrator, though, has his own explanation for his two endings to his story:

> Jakob can reinvent things a thousand times, give reports, make up battles and circulate them, but there is one thing he cannot prevent: with complete certainty, the story is approaching its worthless ending. Or rather, it had two endings; basically only one, of course, the one experienced by Jakob and all the rest of us, but for me it also has a different one. Not wishing to boast, but I know an ending that could make you turn pale with envy, not exactly a happy one, a little at Jakob's expense, yet incomparably more successful than the real ending, one which I knocked together over the years. I said to myself: it's actually a crying shame for such a beautiful story to peter out so miserably. Make up a half-way satisfactory ending for it, one that makes sense; a decent ending allows many a weakness to be forgotten. (J 257–8)[21]

This double ending, together with the narrator's liberal use of his imagination elsewhere in the novel, was criticised for trivialising the highly sensitive subject-matter. Some critics thus found it difficult to take Becker's characters seriously because of the way the narrator 'plays' with them (Lüdke-Haertel and Lüdke 1988: 3); others viewed the work as derivative (Brecheisen 1993: 213), with all too distinct echoes of the narrator of Frisch's *Mein Name sei Gantenbein* (Let my name be Gantenbein), with his recurrent phrase 'Ich stelle mir vor' (I imagine) and his formula 'Ich probiere Geschichten an wie Kleider' (I try on stories like clothes). Even the otherwise favourably disposed Martin Kane sees signs of the narrator allying himself at times with the entirely speculative approach of an Uwe Johnson, and poses the unanswered questions: 'Does Becker's undisguised preoccupation throughout the novel with the act of creating fiction constitute a venturing into the sphere of dubious taste? Does it detract from the moral seriousness of the novel?' (Kane 1991: 169–70).

The narrator's reluctance to tell the real ending is, though, not a case of playing with 'a reality which has absolutely nothing playful about it'; rather it is testimony both to his psychological complexity and to the difficulty of his undertaking, reminding us of the potential contradiction in his ambition at the start when he explained both his need to get 'this damned story' (J 9) off his chest and also his apparently conflicting desire to entertain his readers and tell 'eine ordentliche Geschichte' (a decent story – J 24). His postponement of the real ending suggests that he has his doubts as to whether the historic details of the Holocaust are an appropriate subject for literature as he understands it, for telling tales which entertain and uplift his readers, which is precisely what he set out to do at the start. He thus resolves his dilemma by also providing us with his 'ending that might have been', legitimatising his preceding efforts.

The narrator's problems with his own tale have led several critics to observe that *Jakob der Lügner* can be read as a 'parable of the writer',[22] with Becker himself accepting the view that it could be read as a 'parable about the role of literature in modern society' (*Seminar* 1983: 290). More specifically, one might add that the ending encourages us to read the novel as a parable about the question of writing after Auschwitz, a question which Becker answers in a highly original way by emphasising the importance of narration as the creation of fictional alternatives. As the author explained in an interview: 'I consider it justifiable for an author to depart from reality – not, for instance, because he's not concerned about it, but in recognition of that reality. I have to find my own realities in order to do with them as I want: not to reproduce them' (Schwarz 1990: 124–5).[23] Stories about the Holocaust thus cannot change the terrible finality of history, but they can create an alternative reality which looks with hope towards the future: with his alternative ending, the narrator is the direct counterpart to Jakob, his unusual hero, for like Jakob, who gives hope to the entire ghetto with his fictitious news about the advance of the Russians, the narrator also brings hope with his story about Jakob and with his alternative ending which is itself another variation on the Jakob theme of creating hope through fiction. And in both cases hope is synonymous with the future.

From the start, too, the narrator, a man obsessed with trees, associates Jakob, the bringer of hope, with trees: 'At the same time, to look at, Jakob doesn't in any way remind you of a tree' (J 9),[24] and on several further occasions (J 9, 99, 291), even in the cattle-truck at the end (J 283), the narrator mentions trees and Jakob almost in the same breath, leading us to conclude that the narrator himself needs a tree, something to lean on for support: he needs to believe in his hero Jakob in order to sustain his spirits in post-war Germany where his story has met with indifference. Indeed, his telling of his tale can itself be viewed as an act of resistance against the apathy and complacency which prevails, for nobody appears interested in his story of Jakob. Thus Heinz Wetzel has argued that it 'begins with his grief and anger at this insensitivity, this renewed lack of humanity. [. . .] The persecution of the Jews does not appear in this novel as an historically unique catastrophe which is over and done with, but as the extreme nadir in the latent insensitivity and brutality of man' (Wetzel 1988: 73).[25]

In his essay with the self-explanatory title 'Deprimieren ist für mich kein Schreibmotiv' (the desire to depress people is not one of my motives for writing), Becker rejected the labels 'Holocaust-writer' and 'historian'. Indeed, the most important period in Jakob's story, the time during which his good news spreads through the ghetto, is described almost mockingly by the narrator as 'a few insignificant days [. . .] insignificant for historians' (J 83).[26] As the author explained in an interview, his intention was not documentary historical accuracy since he was writing a story, not rewriting the grim details of history, which he believed could only desensitize through their abstractness: 'A sentence by Sartre made a great impression on me: "One dead person is a catastrophe, one thousand dead is a number." [. . .] I never had the feeling that literature could have anything to do with descriptions of mountains of corpses, because it doesn't provide the key to something abstract' (Graf and Konietzny 1991: 59).[27] In creating a purely fictional ghetto in *Jakob der Lügner*, devoid of the horrific details of the real ghettoes in Poland, and where hope is still able to win a temporary victory over inhumanity and brutality, Becker was aiming not at the past but at the future, not at witnesses to these horrors but at future generations: 'books about such things are not written for the witnesses; why should I tell them stories. Books are written precisely for the others' (*Seminar* 1988: 288). Writing for others in the future meant making them aware of the dangers of history repeating itself and so contributing to the creation of social and political conditions which prevent it:

When I ask myself the question 'Why write about the past, why write about the persecution of the Jews, about fascism and National Socialism, about war?', then the answer 'So that people know what it was' is actually too minor. The more valid answer should be: 'To keep the risks of a repeat down to the minimum possible'. This means that the point of such literature should and can consist in, at best, increasing, minimally increasing, people's sensitivity; perhaps sharpening people's awareness of violence: what is violence, where does it start, what are the manifestations of violence? (Graf and Konietzny 1991: 59–60)[28]

With his aim of making his readers more sensitive, Becker has his narrator adopt a varied repertoire of narrative strategies in *Jakob der Lügner* in order to keep readers on their toes, encourage them to become actively involved and so provoke a critical reading of the novel. For instance, the sentimental first ending, whilst complementing the inner story of Jakob, also functions as a provocative illusion which the narrator dangles before his readers, and whilst he reminds us initially that it is only fiction, it is as if he is consciously playing with our expectations only to leave us with the final hopeless journey to the death camp. Just as Jakob cannot change the future and stands there at the end 'like a joker who has forgotten his text at the crucial moment' (J 275), so too the narrator cannot change the past and is compelled to tell the real ending: 'But, finally, after the ending which I've made up comes the pallid, irksome one, the real, unimaginative ending which immediately makes you want to ask the nonsensical question: What was the point of it all?' (J 272).[29] The narrator's question here is a crucial one, marking his intention actively to engage his readers by challenging them to reconsider the entire story and his own existence as narrator in the light of the real ending. We are thus left at the end with an unanswered question of central importance. Moreover, with his two problematic storytellers, the narrator and Jakob himself, and his two endings to the novel, Becker questions the whole purpose of fiction, of storytelling, in times of extreme distress: the fictional constructions of both Jakob and the narrator function as a parable of literature itself,[30] its possibilities but also its limitations, for Becker himself was aware of the danger of creating hope, of wanting 'to write a story about the value of storytelling, above all, in times of misery; whether it can help people to survive, or distract them from the worries they would have been better off taking care of' (*Seminar* 1988: 272–3). Is Jakob therefore a false prophet of liberation? For even hope itself, the central theme of the novel, is implicitly questioned at one point in terms of whether it is counter-productive, not only undermining the will to act but also actually deterring potential resistance in the belief that the liberators are on their way, when the narrator warns his fellow Jews: 'Anyone who now gets shot, so near the end, has suddenly lost a future; for heaven's sake, don't give them any reason now to send you to Maidanek or Auschwitz (if reasons can be said to have any meaning), be careful, Jews, be extremely careful and no rash steps' (J 83).[31] Asked in 1976 about the theme 'Lügen, um überleben zu können' (lying in order to be able to survive), Becker's reply was unequivocally negative, commenting that in *Jakob der Lügner*, he was consciously reflecting on 'the role played in life by the factor "hope". The story shows that it is indeed a condition for life, but not an adequate one' (*Frankfurter Rundschau* 23.11.1976).[32] His novel, though, ultimately leaves the question of the role of hope open, for a positive interpretation is also possible, as we shall see.

If the novel ends with questions unanswered, it begins quite literally with a question which the narrator can hear his presumed readers asking: 'I can hear everyone saying, a tree, so what's a tree then [. . .] ?' He then simulates an oral storytelling situation: readers become listeners, with the narrator anticipating possible objections and engaging directly in a dialogue with his audience: 'All wrong, I say then, you can stop guessing, you won't get it'.[33] This 'Gespräch über Bäume' (conversation about trees) is both a literary retort and a direct challenge to readers familiar with Bertolt Brecht's famous poem 'An die Nachgeborenen' (To those born much later), where Brecht speaks of 'times when / a conversation about trees is almost a crime / because it involves silence about so many evil deeds'. Readers are thus, from the outset, drawn into the story and the issues which emerge, with the narrator anticipating our curiosity as he begins his account of events in the ghetto: 'Don't ask about the exact time, only the Germans know that, we don't have any clocks' (J 10).[34]

To keep readers on their toes, the narrative perspective shifts constantly: sometimes the narrator uses the simple first-person form for addressing not only his readers as narrator but also his characters (usually Jakob) as fellow ghetto inmates. For instance, at a time when he is just as avid for news of the Russians as the others in his story, the narrator urges Jakob: 'laß bitte nichts aus, hörst du, bitte nichts' (listen, please don't leave anything out, please don't – J 101). Occasionally, too, he opts for a technique known in English as 'free indirect speech', but which in German is more aptly termed 'erlebte Rede' (speech experienced), since it allows both us to experience the characters' thoughts, and his characters to continue the story from their own perspective. For the most part, it is Jakob who replaces the narrator here, particularly if emotions are at play, as when Jakob experiences frustrated annoyance at Mischa's first reaction to the news of the Red Army advance:

Jakob is flabbergasted. One overcomes one's reluctance, ignores all the rules of caution and all one's reservations which are real enough, one chooses a blue-eyed young idiot to confide in and what does the snotty-nosed fellow do? He doesn't believe you. And you can't simply walk away, you can't leave him standing there in his stupidity, tell him to go to hell and simply walk away. You've got to stay with him. (J 30)[35]

Here, even the ways in which Jakob's perspective is expressed shift abruptly from the 'erlebte Rede' form, first in the simple third person ('Jakob') then in the impersonal ('man' – one), to interior monologue ('du' – you), as Jakob addresses himself. For the reader, the effect is one of increasingly sharing Jakob's experience with the narrator, whereby a triangular relationship is developed between narrator, reader and character.

The changing perspective also extends to the subsidiary characters: for instance, even the emotions of the little orphan Lina, whom Jakob has adopted, are given direct expression as she discovers what she erroneously believes to be the radio (J 145); and in the scene where Professor Kirschbaum's wife is visited by two impatient Gestapo men looking for her husband (J 197–8), the perspective shifts constantly between the three characters in the one scene, thus highlighting in a formal way the confrontation between persecutors and victim which culminates in Elise Kirschbaum's dignified yet scornful reaction to their behaviour as she puts them in their place, at which point the narrator brings his omniscience to bear, his chummy, conversational tone barely concealing his delight at just how long the impatient Germans had to wait for her husband, a minor victory of dignity and humanity over barbarity: 'She sits down in the vacant armchair, very upright, she places her hands in her lap. Now they can wait. I can safely say that Kirschbaum arrives after about half an hour' (J 199).[36]

Throughout the novel, then, we are confronted with a variety of perspectives which gives a multi-faceted representation of ghetto life, so avoiding stereotyping and over-simplification, and also draws us into the narrative, bringing us closer to the Jewish characters from whose perspective many of the events are experienced. In this way, the author breaks down the traditional psychological barriers which separate his German (and other) readers and Jewish Holocaust victims, one of the major strengths of the novel which marks it out from the main body of European Holocaust literature. These psychological barriers are also one of its themes: for instance, from the few episodes of the narrator's life in post-war Germany which we are given, we learn of the uneasiness which Germans feel towards him when they find out about his identity and his past, and of the effect which this has on him even in his most intimate moments with his lover:

We are still breathing heavily, we have never discussed it before, then suddenly she asks me: 'Tell me, is it true that you . . .'
I don't know who the hell it was who told her, I can hear the pity in her voice and go crazy. I go into the bathroom, sit down in the bath and start singing to stop myself from doing something which I know I will regret after five steps. When I come back after half an hour, she asks me in astonishment what suddenly came over me, and I say 'Nothing' and give her a kiss, turn out the light and try to fall asleep. (J 25)[37]

Such episodes in the outer frame of the novel demonstrate the inner barrier which is still in place between Holocaust victims and ourselves, 'the others' – the danger that in our reaction to the Jewish victims of the Holocaust, we automatically create a distance between them and ourselves. The shifting narrative perspective of *Jakob der Lügner* has the effect of breaking this down, for it brings the Jewish characters close to us, allowing us to experience their thoughts and emotions directly, so making it easy for us to relate to and identify with them. The figures are close to us, too, because Becker does not portray them as victims – or as saints for that matter – but as ordinary human beings with strengths and weaknesses which we can recognise as our own. This he achieves not only through his narrative strategies, but also through his brilliant use of comic elements, for which he was initially criticised on grounds of trivialisation.

Comic Elements and Plot

The comic situations in which Jakob and others become embroiled are often examples of Chaplinesque farce hovering on the brink of tragedy, set as they are against a backcloth of misery. For instance, at one point Jakob secretes himself in a German latrine in order to steal a newspaper to obtain authentic news and so bolster his flagging inventiveness. He seems to be heading for disaster when Kowalski suddenly distracts the attention of the diarrhoea-stricken German guard who takes his frustration out on him, giving him a severe beating. The scene is a peculiar mixture of comedy and genuine heroism; it is extremely funny but also moving, with the characters increasing both in moral stature and in the reader's affections; yet the narrator's self-consciousness, with his brief intrusion to justify his use of a particular epithet, prevents it from degenerating into sentimentality: '"Thank you," says Jakob in an emotional voice. Emotional is the right word, emotional for the first time in forty years, one doesn't get one's life saved every day, and then by somebody one has known for such a long time and of whom, quite honestly, one would not have expected it' (J 109).[38] In another episode, the giant Mischa's confrontation with a puny guard, which leaves Mischa with a bloody mouth, is described literally in terms of a knockabout scene from a silent movie:

> Mischa turns towards him, the one in command is a head shorter than he is and he has some trouble reaching up to hit Mischa in the face. It verges on the comical, not suitable for the German newsreel, more like a slapstick scene from the silent movie era when Charlie, the little policeman, tries to hunt down the giant with the bushy eyes, and, try as he will, the big fellow doesn't even notice him. Everyone knows that Mischa could lift him up and tear him to pieces. If he really wanted to. The fellow in command hits him a few more times, his hands must be hurting him by now, he shouts something or other of no interest to anyone and only shuts up when a thin trickle of blood runs out of the corner of Mischa's mouth. (J 33)[39]

In this passage and elsewhere, the wry humour of the Jews is in ironic contrast to the deadly earnest of their Nazi oppressors, reminding us of the humanity of the victims of a system geared methodically and systematically to dehumanise them. As Jakob slips away from the Gestapo headquarters at the start, the narrator is even able to mock the hideous logic of a system which decrees that the Jews are sub-human:

> The house has come to an end. Jakob gets ready to take off, almost twenty metres have to be covered a few minutes before eight, it's a pretty safe bet, and yet. A mouse is what one ought to be, isn't it? A mouse is so inconspicuous, so small and quiet. And you? Officially you're a louse, a bedbug, we're all bedbugs, by a whim of our Creator we've turned out absurdly large bedbugs, and when was the last time a bedbug wanted to change places with a mouse? (J 21)[40]

The inventiveness which Becker displays in his use of comedy is also in evidence in the plot of *Jakob der Lügner*, with the author demonstrating his natural talent for spinning captivating yarns. As the title indicates, Jakob's 'Radio-Lüge' (radio-lie), his fictitious radio, is the central point on which the entire novel turns, and the narrator does not let us forget that the entire sequence of lies is rooted in comedy and triggered off by the pressure of ludicrous circumstances in the shape of a young friend's irresistible yet suicidal craving for potatoes.

The way in which the sequence of incidents is set in motion demonstrates why Becker is regarded as 'one of the best storytellers to emerge from the GDR' (Kane 1991: 166). Taking a walk 'because a stroll after work seems to bring such a strange, faint whiff of normal times' (J 43),[41] Jakob is, in these perverse times, the victim of a cruel prank when a German sentry sends him into the ghetto police station to receive 'eine gerechte Bestrafung' (a just punishment) for breaking the curfew. This is itself a lie for it is not that late, as the narrator informs us, and the guard is merely playing a practical joke on his Jewish victim, but the joke is ultimately on him. Inside, Jakob overhears snippets of a radio report of a Russian attack only four or five hundred kilometres away. The good fortune of his chance eavesdropping seems to be in vain, though, for Jakob believes he is already 'a dead man' since no Jew has hitherto emerged alive from this place. But then the incredible does happen when the sleepy, friendly duty officer, who is probably new to the ghetto and does not wish to be bothered by such a trivial matter, turns out to be human, 'and therefore a weak link in the otherwise logical chain of evidence' (J 31),[42] and sends him home. Jakob is in a new quandary, though: he is fearful that his fellow-Jews will suspect him of being an informer if he tells the truth about this incident, yet also wants to communicate the good news which he is unable to authenticate. He is forced into a solution by the desperately hungry Mischa when the latter is on the point of risking his seemingly pointless life by stealing some potatoes from under the noses of the German guards at the goods' yard where they work. When the true version of events fails to convince Mischa, Jakob feels compelled literally to give his young friend a 'future' by claiming that he has heard of the Russian advance on his clandestine radio: 'He has been forced to spread irresponsible claims, that clueless idiot there has forced him through his ridiculous distrust, just because he suddenly had a craving for potatoes' (J 32).[43] The impact of Jakob's words is conveyed through a powerful metaphor: 'It's not the sentries who have fired [. . .] Jakob has fired, straight to his heart.' The transformation is immediate: for Mischa 'quite suddenly tomorrow is another day' (J 32).[44]

Spreading like a chain reaction, the ensuing sequence of events appears irreversible, with the narrator predicting: 'We know what will happen. [. . .] Mischa won't be able to keep his mouth shut' (J 34).[45] Jakob's old friend Kowalski is the first to be infected with Mischa's euphoria: its effect on him is humorously compared to an erotic experience when, 'as if in love', he whispers the words 'The Russians' (J 43). The scene then shifts to the private sphere of the Frankfurter family, as Mischa comes to ask Rosa to marry him in the belief that 'It does make sense to speak of the future.' Her father is naturally of the view that Mischa has taken leave of his senses in these 'accursed times when perfectly normal desires sound monstrous' (J 52),[46] but then Mischa, with his inside information, seizes his opportunity to tell them the news. Again a dramatic transformation takes place as Mischa's belief in the future spreads to the whole family, with Rosa making specific detailed private plans:

> The big issues will somehow or other take care of themselves, important people who'll take care of them are sure to come along; let's start with our own little personal affairs, no one's going to look after those for us. Rosa moves from pondering to whispering: first of all there would be the house in which one must feel comfortable, we could also discuss something other than the house if it occurs to you, but let's start with that. Not too small, not too big, let's say five rooms, that's not asking too much. (J 66)[47]

As the news continues to spread like wildfire, the narrator intervenes to take stock, reporting in general terms its effect on the ghetto-inmates: hope for an end to the grim situation quickly leads to a resumption of normal, everyday concerns: 'Old debts start to be important again, embarrassed creditors remind their debtors, daughters turn into brides, weddings are planned for the week before the New Year festival, people have gone stark staring mad, the suicide figures have dropped to zero' (J 83).[48]

The narrator, then, follows the spread of Jakob's news about the advancing Soviet liberators through the ghetto, observing and reporting its transforming effect on Jakob's fellow-Jews. Structurally, the novel is made up of a string of more or less separate episodes, consistent with the haphazard way in which Jakob's information is spread, giving the reader a panorama of ghetto life in the diversity of figures, some close to Jakob, others more remote, but all united in their craving for his news. However, as Werner Zimmermann has argued (Zimmermann 1988: 21), two distinct threads to the plot are discernible which run counter to one another: the one develops the story of Jakob's 'radio' and its effect on the ghetto inmates; the other records the feedback to Jakob and its influence on his relationship to his friends, which is in turn illuminated further through occasional flashbacks to the period before the German occupation when Jakob also played the part of 'something similar to a spiritual comforter' (J 250). And the more Jakob's news brings comfort to the Jews in their desperate situation, the more Jakob's personal difficulties mount up, leading to his increasing alienation from those around him which culminates in the 'Welle von Feindschaft' (wave of hostility – J 263) which threatens him at the end.

Yet Becker never fails to exploit the comic potential in the situations which unfold as Jakob becomes ever more entangled in the swiftly expanding web of his own lies, having to supply the demand he has created with snippets of entirely invented information. Thus we witness Kowalski's melodramatic gestures of horror at the news that the radio is 'broken' when Jakob's well of inventiveness temporarily dries up (J 126). At the same time, though, the reader becomes aware that reality is gradually catching up with Jakob as hope gives way to increasing scepticism and ultimately despair. On the morning when Jakob is about to disseminate a particularly encouraging piece of 'news', for instance, disastrous real events intervene as Mischa learns of the latest deportations: this time it is the street where his girlfriend Rosa lives. He manages to save Rosa, but the deportation of her parents fills her with despair; the hope which Jakob's news had given her now gives way to disbelief (J 238), and she is the first to accuse him of lying (J 247). Jakob himself now succumbs to the glaring disparity between the illusion which he has created and reality: 'According to the radio, one should soon be able to see the first artillery flashes in the distance, but day after day all you see is the same scene of repulsive desolation' (J 247);[49] and when in a moment of weakness Jakob tells Kowalski the truth about his radio, his old friend commits suicide the same night, bitter evidence now of the power of fiction as a life-sustaining force.

The strand of the plot tracing Jakob's increasing social isolation culminates in the narrator's 'fictional' alternative ending, in which Jakob's alienation is interpreted as one of the possible motives for his desperate attempt to escape from the ghetto: 'Or he is fleeing from his own people, from their persecution and hostility, from their thirst for news too, an attempt to escape from his own radio and its consequences' (J 269).[50] Yet even this bleaker strand is not without its humorous aspects. At the start of the novel, for instance, there is comic exaggeration in Jakob's elevation from mere comforter to 'messiah', 'prophet' and 'chosen one', the man 'with a direct line to our dear God' (J 69). Simultaneously, though, begin the secret condemnations by those who see the 'radio' not as a source of hope but of danger. Thus Felix Frankfurter's reaction is fear that the Gestapo will get wind of Jakob's radio, and ironically, he destroys the only real radio in the ghetto because of the threat posed by its fictional counterpart. Later on, direct reproaches are made by Professor Kirschbaum to Jakob, who is forced to defend himself by pointing out that there have been no cases of suicide since the advent of his news (J 195). Yet the reader already knows that Jakob is himself plagued by the selfsame doubts expressed by Kirschbaum. Light relief comes for Jakob in the shape of the cut in the electricity supply to the ghetto, 'eine paradiesische Atempause' (a heavenly respite – J 116): for all his satisfaction at the absence of suicides, he is relieved to be able to tell 'die lautere Wahrheit' (the pure truth) for a change. Increasingly, then, Jakob loses control of the situation, sometimes with humorous effect as his lies generate the need for further lies. It is as if his 'radio' takes on a life of its own, becoming 'Gemeingut des Ghettos' (the common property of the ghetto – White and White 1978: 211), with Jakob having to extricate himself from ensuing dilemmas through more lies. For instance, when he laments, with feigned dejection, that his radio is 'broken', the ghetto community unexpectedly comes to his rescue: Kowalski arrives with a radio repairman. The role of 'chosen one', though, rebounds completely on Jakob in the end and when the evacuation order goes up, his desperately disappointed fellow-Jews stare at him 'wie geprellte Gläubiger' (like cheated creditors – J 274–5). And at the end, as the narrator relates the journey to the camp in the cattle-truck with Jakob and the others, we are confronted with the bleak outcome: that all the hopes of salvation and plans for the future which Jakob's lies inspired were illusory.

Yet the danger of pathos is avoided through the gentle irony of the narrator's comments at the most crucial moments. As Jakob prepares to tell Kowalski the truth, for instance, the narrator informs us 'that Jakob is preparing for unconditional surrender'; then after the mask has finally fallen, we read 'it's as if a king has abdicated' (J 249–50).[51] And in his fictional ending, even Jakob's heroic death is qualified by the narrator's confession that he is unable to analyse Jakob's motives, offering us three possibilities: Jakob's desire to save his own skin in his despair in the belief that liberation is not at hand; his need to flee from the hostility of his own people; and his courageous intention to venture forth in quest of more news. It is left to readers to decide for themselves which is the most appropriate: 'So I offer them as a selection; let each reader choose the one which, according to his own experiences, he considers most convincing', and he adds challengingly: 'perhaps some readers will be able to come up with even more plausible ones' (J 269).[52]

Style and Narrative Tone

The way in which Becker spins his yarns is thus highly inventive, even if the overall form of the novel is fairly conventional, with the narrator looking back and reporting the past. What has been recognised as unique about *Jakob der Lügner*, however, is the easy-going, often gently ironic, narrative tone adopted, in view of the novel's gloomy subject-matter. For instance, in his initial review of the novel, Marcel Reich-Ranicki spoke of the 'carefree and pointedly leisurely conversational tone – as if it was all just a matter of course. [. . .] With such a gloomy theme, you can least of all do it gloomily, you do it rather with bright and cheerful, contrasting effects, with wit and humour. This is very difficult, though, and almost reckless. But Becker has managed it' (Heidelberger-Leonard 1992: 134).[53] Heinz Wetzel made a similar observation, but with more stress on the humour in terms of language and situation: 'The story comes alive in the usually quiet, restrained humour of its language and in the discreet comedy in many of its episodes' (Wetzel 1986: 112).[54] The familiar, conversational tone is achieved through the predominance of the present tense and through the use of a variety of devices such as irony, comic synecdoche and understatement to which the narrator frequently resorts when playing down the sense of menace and threat in certain situations. For instance, just before Herschel Schtamm is shot by the railway official, the latter is referred to disparagingly as simply 'die Pfeife' (the Pipe), and as he threatens to shoot anyone who approaches the cattle-truck containing Jews destined for the camps, the narrator comments mockingly on the inferior tonal quality of his voice : 'So that's what his voice sounds like, not a very successful premiere I'd say, a weak baritone I'd say; one might have wished for a more pleasant sound' (J 134).[55] Ironic understatement is also used to mock the lie which the Jews are forced to live because of the constant threat from their persecutors when the narrator sarcastically presents the latter's perverse perspective of the food distribution: 'We form a line, very disciplined and without the slightest pushing and shoving. They've taught us that, under the threat of no food. It has to look as if at the moment we're not at all hungry: What, food again already? Hardly does a fellow have time to settle down to his work properly before he is interrupted yet again by another of these many meals' (J 37).[56] Becker's tendency to soft-pedal in the direction of understatement is reflected in his efforts to wrest a comic side from almost every event and situation, particularly when tragedy threatens. Indeed, the sense of ever-present danger is nowhere more visible than in comic situations, where the existence of mortal threat creates tension which is played down through irony but then sometimes explodes into comic climax, nowhere better illustrated than in the scene where the German soldier approaches the Germans' latrine into which Jakob has just disappeared in search of snippets from a newspaper lying inside it:

> Jakob looks outside once more to see if everything is still all right, it's not, not at all, there's mine after mine all the way back, a soldier is walking towards the privy, purposefully one might say. [. . .] he's got five steps to go, all that's left for you now is the little oval hole, down into their crap. Which you can't bring yourself to do, even though you're skinny enough.

The soldier opens the door which offers no resistance; to his annoyance he sees a double sheet of newspaper opened in front of him, trembling moderately, although at such an embarrassing moment, he doesn't give it a second thought. 'Oh, excuse me!' he says, and shuts the door quickly. (J 105)[57]

The predominance of the present tense here and elsewhere in the novel serves to increase the suspense. Yet more importantly, the present tense makes the past appear to come alive, creating the illusion that we are participating in events which are actually taking place, particularly when the narrator addresses us directly or allows us to share characters' experiences directly. The contrastive effect of Jakob's flashbacks to normal times, too, brings home to the reader the abnormality of everyday life in the ghetto, nowhere more vividly than in the scene where Jakob enters the Gestapo building which used to be the local finance office and can actually smell the difference between then and now, giving us a tangible experience of the perverse veneer of civil normality concealing Nazi barbarity: 'The smell in this building has changed, somehow for the better. The stink of ammonia that used to pervade the corridor has gone, instead, inexplicably, it smells more civil' (J 13).[58] On other occasions, such contrasts enable the narrator to make ironic observations on the present: for instance, we learn that, in order to improve his prospects as a boxer, Mischa was playing with the idea 'sich ein Schwergewicht anzufressen' (eating to put on enough to make heavyweight – J 28), at which point the narrator wryly comments: 'In the region of one hundred and seventy pounds, the ghetto came between him and his plans, and since then his weight has slowly been going down' (J 28).[59]

With his gentle irony and understatement Jurek Becker is certainly no Edgar Hilsenrath, who claimed of his gruesome novel *Nacht* (Night), 'I [. . .] described it without glossing over anything, just as it really was' (*Lebenslauf*, 504).[60] Yet although the horrific details of life in the real ghettoes are, for the most part, either omitted or portrayed indirectly, the narrator of *Jakob der Lügner* does give us enough details to evoke an atmosphere of threat, degradation and misery, but they are usually presented on the level of general observation and remain firmly in the background: thus we learn that each morning Jews have to clear the streets 'von Unrat und von Verhungerten' (of garbage and of the corpses of those who had died of starvation – J 175) and 'that in winter one in five of us freezes to death, that every day half a street goes off to be transported' (J 194).[61] The narrator focuses his attention rather on Jakob, his hero, and events related to him. The real horror is not thereby denied but is only allowed to cast its shadow on this story about a storyteller and about the reasons why he tells his tale. The reader is also gradually made aware of the real horrors through the perversion of normality into its opposite whereby normal, everyday banalities become criminal transgressions, punishable by death within the Nazi scheme, as when the narrator muses: 'I try to imagine what would happen to someone found wearing a ring on his finger, walking a dog in the street after eight' (J 8).[62] This order of things – a reign of largely invisible terror – is accepted as absolute by the Jewish ghetto inmates, who seem resigned to their fate. Thus through understatement, the unspoken horrors (what Rainer Nägele has aptly termed 'the presence of absence' – Nägele 1983: 280) gradually become apparent. Becker portrays scenes of violence either fleetingly or comically, as in the above-cited scene where the giant Mischa is beaten by the midget German guard – here the effect is one of gentle mockery, by implication, of the pretensions of the Master Race. Or the author omits brutality entirely, leaving gaps for readers to fill in with their own knowledge of the past. Again a favourable contrast with Apitz's *Nackt unter Wölfen* springs to mind, where sadistic fascists are confronted by concentration camp inmates who develop heroic strength in their struggle against their oppressors.

Characterisation

Unlike Apitz's black-and-white characterisation, Becker's portrayal of both Jews and Germans is variegated: he gives us a wide spectrum of individuals within the ghetto, avoiding the stereotypical. Jakob himself has no superhuman strengths; indeed, as we have noted, he is something of an anti-hero, and at the start his feelings of helplessness, timidity and anxiety are the understandable reactions of an ordinary human being in an extraordinary situation. Only unintentionally, through the force of circumstances and his own reaction to this, does he become a saviour, but this reluctant hero remains throughout a character with whom the reader can readily identify. And above all, Becker avoids portraying the Germans just as brutal persecutors and the Jews exclusively as victims, both here and in his other works. Rather, he depicts a wide variety of types, avoiding the stereotype 'fascists' of an Apitz with their gruesome injustices: although the German persecutors play only bit parts and are small in number, some even betray humane characteristics, for which the author was criticised. They range from the cynical guard in the watchtower at the start to the humorously drawn duty officer in the 'Revier' whose playfully ironic opening line 'Was verschafft mir die Ehre?' (To what do I owe this honour?) sparks off in Jakob the astonished thought 'das ist ja ein freundlicher Mensch' (he's actually a friendly fellow – J 18), an assessment which proves correct, for shortly afterwards he proceeds let Jakob go free. On the other hand, Preuß and Meyer, the two sinister Gestapo men, are truer to type, but even here the narrator distinguishes between the tall, authoritative Preuß, whose name reflects his Prussian sense of correctness and who at least goes through the motions of politeness, and his coarse subaltern Meyer, whom Preuß continually puts in his place on account of his vulgar expressions and manners. Even the soldier who brutally punches Kowalski for knocking over some boxes betrays some evidence of a conscience as he 'drops' two cigarettes which Kowalski picks up (J 110). Consistent with the fundamental optimism of the novel (and with Becker's communist beliefs at the time), the author seems to be at pains to show that it is the system which dehumanises its subjects, in whom these traces of humanity are still discernible.

The Jewish characters are all individuals, each with some complexity of personality, yet at the same time also recognisable as ordinary human beings. Such a portrayal has the effect of breaking down our inhibitions, our tendency to see them as victims of an horrific period, remote from ourselves in time and space. Becker avoids, too, the danger of glorification of his Jewish figures, above all through his ironic narrative stance which prevents things being presented in crude black or white, leading his narrator to a realistic assessment of his characters. For instance, it may be true that Jakob ultimately does live up to the claims made for him early on by the narrator: 'He tried to explain to me how one thing followed another and that he couldn't have acted any differently, but I want to tell you that he was a hero. Not three sentences would pass his lips without some mention of his fear, but I want to tell you about his courage' (J 44).[63] Yet in our first encounter with his hero Jakob, it is the latter's fear which is stressed when his mouth is so dry that he is unable to answer the duty officer's question (J 18). Flashbacks to an early romance reveal, too, the problematic side of Jakob's personality, his tendency to be oversensitive and uncommunicative: all in all he appears to have been something of a loner. Jakob's close friend Kowalski, too, is another timid hero, a curious mixture of opposites, a would-be fox who wears his heart on his sleeve: 'Kowalski is divine. He thinks he is a fox who knows all the tricks, yet his face can conceal nothing, it tells all. You only have to be slightly acquainted with him to know exactly what's up with him before he has even opened his mouth' (J 38).[64] After Kowalski's death, the narrator comes to a balanced assessment of Jakob's old friend too, recognising that he was 'equipped with one or two questionable attributes, was suspicious, cranky, awkward, garrulous, too clever by half, but all in all, with the benefit of hindsight, suddenly endearing' (J 256).[65] Even the minor characters are rounded: the dignified Elise Kirschbaum is considered 'verschroben' (eccentric) by some, and the usually timid Herschel Schtamm, with his childishly naive faith, reveals a hidden resource of courage when he dies in the attempt to bring hope to the Jews in the cattle-truck in the railway siding.

Just as the characters are portrayed individually in terms of their weaknesses and their strengths, so too the overall spectrum of Jewish figures is wide and differentiated. Felix Frankfurter, the former actor, is the typical rationalist who tries to plan methodically for all eventualities. Herschel Schtamm is the orthodox Jew who finds solace in his Hasidic beliefs. Professor Kirschbaum, on the other hand, reflects on his tenuous relationship to his own Jewishness: like Arno Bronstein in *Bronsteins Kinder* and Aron in *Der Boxer*, his thoughts have a certain affinity with those expressed by Becker in 'Mein Judentum':

> Kirschbaum has never given a thought to being a Jew; his father before him was a surgeon, what does it mean, of Jewish origin, they force you to be a Jew while you yourself have no idea at all what that really is. Now he is surrounded only by Jews, for the first time in his life nothing but Jews, he has racked his brains about them, wanting to find out what it is that makes them all alike; in vain, they have nothing recognisably in common with one another, and he himself absolutely nothing at all with them. (J 80)[66]

As his name suggests, Leonard Schmidt, nicknamed 'Assimilinski', provides the example of the assimilated German Jew forced to live like a fish out of water in a Polish ghetto. With his Iron Cross, Schmidt was 'well on the way towards becoming a German nationalist' but has ended up in the ghetto 'because his great-grandfather went to the synagogue and his parents were stupid enough to have him circumcised' (J 128);[67] puzzled by 'the remarkable conception of legality which this odd people has',[68] he has little in common with his fellow-Jews except the shared suffering ('Leidensgefährte ist er unzweifelhaft' – 'he's undoubtedly a fellow-sufferer', J 135) and his need for Jakob's news ('plötzlich gleicht er ihnen aufs Haar' – 'he's suddenly the spitting image of them', J 132). Schmidt even exhibits something of the mentality of the Nazi fellow-traveller which has brought about his own demise: 'he probably wouldn't have the slightest objection to the entire ghetto if it hadn't been him they had stuck in there' (J 134).[69] As Claudia Brecheisen has observed, Becker demonstrates through the multiplicity of his Jewish figures and with bold and fine lines of differentiation that that there is no such thing as '**den** Juden, **die** jüdische Identität' (**the** Jew, **the** Jewish identity – Brecheisen 1993: 87).

A Jewish Novel about Hope

Jakob der Lügner is, then, a multi-faceted story about Jews and the problems of being Jewish, signalled in the very title of the novel in which Becker has taken the archetypal myth of the Jew as liar and re-evaluated it. But more than this, *Jakob der Lügner* is also a Jewish *story*: despite Becker's denial of any knowledge of writers such as Aleichem and Singer in *Mein Judentum*, his novel does embody something of the Yiddish narrative tradition,[70] as Marcel Reich-Ranicki noted in his initial review of the novel with his comment that, with his humorous treatment of a sad theme, Becker was 'vom Geschlecht der traurigen Humoristen' (from the family of sad humorists – Heidelberger-Leonard 1992: 136). It may be true, as Becker himself admitted (Schwarz 1990: 115), that the tone of *Jakob der Lügner* owes something to the literary tradition of the Jewish-style narrative established and represented by one of the foremost Christian GDR novelists, Johannes Bobrowski, with his novel *Levins Mühle* (Levin's mill), a work which Becker had read many times before writing his first novel. Yet also discernible in the storytelling situation which forms the framework of *Jakob der Lügner* is, above all, the influence of the East European Jewish oral tradition. On two occasions, Jakob himself refers enviously to the Jewish author whose work Becker claimed to have read only after writing his novel, wishing he were endowed with just half of his imagination: 'If my mother had endowed me with a brighter brain, gifted with as much imagination as Sholom Aleichem – what am I saying, half as much would be enough . . .' (J 102); and later he laments: 'but, and unfortunately this will never change, one doesn't have the inventive gifts of a Sholom Aleichem' (J 167).[71]

As Manfred Karnick has shown, the location of *Jakob der Lügner* echoes that of the Eastern European shtetl (Heidelberger-Leonard 1992: 211). Indeed. the cover picture of the first edition of the novel in Aufbau Verlag (GDR) has the title framed within the market place of a 'Schtetl'. The sense of a narrow, closed community within which everyone knows or wants to know everyone else's business is an important factor for Jakob in the role which he plays, with his knowledge that 'good news is there to be passed on' (J 26).[72] Hence the cultural shock of the alien Western Jew Schmidt, who seems to be on a different wavelength, as the narrator notes, when Schmidt makes direct reference to the deportations: 'That's the way it is; unfortunately, Schmidt is not familiar with the game of hints where certain things aren't mentioned and yet are said; he'll never be familiar with them, in his heart he is and always will be an outsider. Everything has to be spelt out to him in blunt, unequivocal terms' (J 136).[73] Yet at the same time the novel points to the destruction of these elements of the traditional world of East European Jewry which have survived in the ghetto, for as the arrival of the outspoken outsider Schmidt underlines, the ghetto itself has become a temporary residence for the Jews, the transit camp before the death camp.

The novel's ultimate message is, though, not about destruction. We noted that it begins and ends with the dominant image of the tree: its Jewish significance is suggested early on when the narrator associates Jakob, the bringer of hope, with trees (J 9). The narrator's reference to the Book of Job ('Hiobsbotschaft' – bad news) recalls, too, both the biblical story of Jewish suffering in the tale of a good man who suffers total disaster, and the close relationship of trees and hope in Job 14.7: 'For there is hope of a tree, if it be cut down, that it will sprout again, and that the tender branch thereof will not cease'; and in Job 19.10, where Job laments in despair: 'mine hope hath he removed like a tree'. In Job, then, the tree functions as a symbol of both hope and the possibility of its renewal: hope cannot be easily destroyed for even if the tree is cut down, it will survive unless the roots are torn up. Echoes of this biblical idea are further present in the surname of Herschel Schtamm ('Stamm' is the German word for 'trunk'), another bringer of hope, and in the narrator's passing observation that in the ghetto, the Germans, in their attempt to banish trees, have carefully cut them down to ground level, but have left the roots intact (J 223). The tree imagery is thus central to our understanding of the theme of hope, for just as the Germans' attempt to destroy the trees will fail because of the survival of their roots, so too by implication will the attempt to destroy hope. Jakob is proof of this failure, for his own private victory over despair brings renewal and the desire to tell his story:

> Jakob walks on and discovers, so he has told me, that he has changed. From one day to the next, his senses are suddenly much more alert; he is beginning to observe. The apathetic despair has not survived the excitement of the previous night, nothing is left of that numbness, now it is as if one should memorise everything exactly as it is so as to be able to report on it afterwards. Afterwards. (J 36)[74]

The narrator himself is also living proof of this failure: Jakob's story has helped him to survive, and he too now renews Jakob's story of the renewal of hope, passing it on to his readers. The fact that the narrator has survived, however fortuitously, is a vindication both of Jakob's lies and of fictions which generate hope under extreme circumstances. It is hope, too, which helps the Jews psychologically to resist Nazi oppression by not succumbing to its aim, their mental and physical destruction. This is why the narrator, pinpointing the moment when Jakob first tells a lie, is able to assert that even the mere attempt to generate hope justifies itself, regardless of whether it is founded on pure fiction, or even whether any of the Jews survive:

> . . . it was an important moment for him, he told me. The first lie, which maybe wasn't one at all, such a little one, and Kowalski is satisfied. It's worth it; hope must not be allowed to fade away, otherwise they won't survive. He knows for certain that the Russians are advancing, he has heard it with his own ears, and if there is a God in heaven, then they must also get as far as us, and if there is no God, then they must also get as far as us, and they must find as many survivors as possible, so it's worth it. And if we should all be dead, then he made an attempt, so it's worth it. (J 75)[75]

Notes

1. 'Ich suche den einem Stoff unangemessenen Erzählstil. Wenn ich eine Geschichte erzählen möchte, die man, wenn man nichts anderes hört als die äußeren Umstände, als Tragödie empfindet, suche ich den komischen Weg, sie zu erzählen. Wenn ich eine Geschichte habe, die saukomisch klingt, suche ich die Tragödie darin. [. . .] Ich habe selbst die Erfahrung gemacht, daß das, was mir als Leser auf gewisse Weise respektlos, übertrieben respektlos, oder pietätlos, Geschmacksregeln verletzend, unangemessen komisch daherkam, mir immer das Eindrücklichere gewesen ist.'

2. 'spielerischer Umgang mit einer Wirklichkeit, die absolut nichts Spielerisches hat.'

3. 'eine melancholisch-heitere, leise, eine kunstvoll komponierte Geschichte.'

4. 'Der *Jakob* ist, wenn man so will, im Grunde gar keine Ich-Erzählung. Es gibt da wohl ein Ich, das aber in der Handlung nicht vorkommt. Das Ich ist ein Erzählprinzip.'

5. 'Ich höre schon alle sagen, ein Baum, was ist das schon [. . .] Denn

ich sehe noch die Schatten von Bäumen, und schlafen kann ich nicht, wir fahren, wohin wir fahren.'

6. 'Ich habe schon tausendmal versucht, diese verfluchte Geschichte loszuwerden, immer vergebens. Entweder es waren nicht die richtigen Leute, denen ich sie erzählen wollte, oder ich habe irgendwelche Fehler gemacht. Ich habe vieles durcheinandergebracht, ich habe Namen verwechselt, oder es waren, wie gesagt, nicht die richtigen Leute. Jedesmal, wenn ich ein paar Schnäpse getrunken habe, ist sie da, ich kann mich nicht dagegen wehren.'

7. 'Ich lebe, das ist ganz unzweifelhaft. Ich lebe, und kein Mensch kann mich zwingen, zu trinken und mich an Bäume zu erinnern und an Jakob und alles, was damit zu tun hat.'

8. 'Aber als der Krieg zu Ende war, war ich gerade erst [. . .] ich höre das Mitleid in ihrer Stimme und werde verrückt.'

9. 'Die ganze Stadt liegt im Grünen, die Umgebung ist einzigartig, die Parks sind gepflegt, jeder Baum lädt mich ein zu Erinnerungen.'

10. 'es ist jetzt, als müßte man sich alles genau einprägen, um hinterher darüber berichten zu können. Hinterher.'

11. 'Leider werde ich mich später plump und direkt in die Handlung einmischen müssen, wenn es ans Erklären geht, denn nach Möglichkeit soll kein Loch bleiben. Die Erklärung wird es notdürftig stopfen, aber später, erst muß das Loch in seiner vollen Größe sichtbar sein.'

12. 'ich stelle mir vor, daß mancher mißtrauisch die Frage stellen wird, auf welchem Wege ich in dieses Auto gelangt sein will.' The narrator's account of his visit to West Berlin also underlines the bitter ironies of the present for it turns out that the former Gestapo man, now in possession of his denazification document, not only lives in passable circumstances but also, in contrast to the narrator, appears to experience little difficulty in salving his conscience: 'Finally, he told me that he really had to confide to me what his present thoughts were about that ill-fated time, and get all that *schmalz* off his chest by talking to someone sensible' (Zum Schluß wollte er mir unbedingt noch anvertrauen, wie er heute über diese unselige Zeit dächte, sich mal mit einem vernünftigen Menschen das ganze Schmalz von der Seele reden' – J 212)

13. 'An diesem blauen Tag bin ich der Austeiler [. . .] Dann fahren wir.'

14. 'Immerhin erzähle ich die Geschichte, nicht er, Jakob ist tot, und außerdem erzähle ich nicht seine Geschichte sondern eine Geschichte.'

15. Werner Zimmermann is thus not entirely correct when he argues that the narrator's aesthetic and political judgement is 'nicht an der Realität orientiert' (1988: 13).

16. 'Ich kann nicht hören, was Herschel redet [. . .] aber denken kann ich es mir, und das hat nichts mit vagen Vermutungen zu tun. Je länger ich überlege, um so klarer weiß ich seine Worte, auch wenn er sie mir nie bestätigt hat.'

17. 'Und der Widerstand, wird man fragen, wo bleibt der Widerstand? [. . .] gibt es in dieser elenden Stadt nur Hände, die genau das tun, was Hardtloff und seine Posten von ihnen verlangen? [. . .] Verurteilt sie, immer verurteilt uns, es hat nur solche Hände gegeben. [. . .] Ich sage, mit Ehrfurcht habe ich inzwischen von Warschau und Buchenwald gelesen, eine andere Welt, doch vergleichbar. Ich habe viel über Heldentum gelesen, wahrscheinlich zuviel, der sinnlose Neid hat mich gepackt, aber das braucht mir keiner zu glauben. Jedenfalls haben wir bis zur letzten Sekunde stillgehalten, und ich kan nichts mehr daran ändern. Mir ist nicht unbekannt, daß ein unterdrücktes Volk nur dann wirklich frei werden kann, wenn es Beihilfe zu seiner Befreiung leistet, wenn es dem Messias wenigstens ein Stückchen des Weges entgegengeht. Wir haben es nicht getan, ich habe mich nicht von der Stelle gerührt, ich habe die Verordnungen auswendig gelernt, mich strikt an sie gehalten und nur von Zeit zu Zeit den armen Jakob gefragt, was an Neuigkeiten eingegangen wäre. Wahrscheinlich werde ich nie damit fertig, ich habe es nicht besser verdient, mein ganzer privater Kram mit den Bäumen hat sicher damit zu tun und meine schlimme Rührseligkeit und die Freigebigkeit meiner Tränensäcke. Es hat dort, wo ich war, keinen Widerstand gegeben'.

18. 'Kommt mir nicht und redet von Kameradschaft und ähnlichem Zeug, wer so redet, versteht nichts von hier, aber auch gar nichts.'

19. 'Das Schlimmste, was uns hätte geschehen können, wäre ein sinnvoller Tod gewesen.'

20. 'Ich male mir die Rache für Jakob aus, denn dies ist nach meinem Willen die kühle und sternklare Nacht, in der die Russen kommen. Soll es der Roten Arme gelungen sein, die Stadt in kürzester Frist zu umzingeln, der Himmel wird hell vom Feuer der schweren Geschütze, sofort nach der Salve, die Jakob gegolten hat, hebt ein ohrenbetäubendes Donnern an, als wäre es von dem unglücklichen Schützen auf dem Postturm versehentlich ausgelöst worden. Die ersten gespenstischen Panzer, Einschläge im Revier, die Postentürme brennen, verbissene Deutsche, die sich bis zum letzten Schuß verteidigen, oder flüchtende Deutsche, die kein Loch finden, um sich darin zu verkriechen, lieber Gott, wäre das eine Nacht gewesen.'

21. 'Jakob kann tausendmal wiedererfinden, berichten, Schlachten ersinnen und in Umlauf setzen, eins kann er nicht verhindern,

zuverlässig nähert sich die Geschichte ihrem nichtswürdigen Ende. Das heißt, sie hat zwei Enden, im Grunde natürlich nur eins, das von Jakob und uns allen erlebte, aber für mich hat sie noch ein anderes. Bei aller Bescheidenheit, ich weiß ein Ende, bei dem man blaß werden könnte vor Neid, nicht eben glücklich, ein wenig auf Kosten Jakobs, dennoch unvergleichlich gelungener als das wirkliche Ende, ich habe es mir in Jahren zusammengezimmert. Ich habe mir gesagt, eigentlich jammerschade um eine so schöne Geschichte, daß sie so armselig im Sande verläuft, erfinde ihr ein Ende, mit dem man halbwegs zufrieden sein kann, eins mit Hand und Fuß, ein ordentliches Ende läßt manche Schwäche vergessen.'

22. See also Chapter 5; Wetzel 1983: 267; and Brecheisen 1993: 216.

23. 'Ich halte einen Autor für legitimiert, die Realität zu verlassen – nicht etwa, weil er sich nicht um sie kümmert, sondern in Kenntnis der Realität. Ich muß mir Realitäten beschaffen, um damit machen zu können, was ich will: nicht um sie zu reproduzieren.'

24. 'Dabei erinnert Jakob, wenn man ihn sieht, in keiner Weise an einen Baum.'

25. 'Mit seiner Trauer, seinem Zorn über diese Unempfindlichkeit, diesen erneuten Mangel an Humanität beginnt der Roman. [. . .] Nicht als eine historisch einmalige abgeschlossene und überwundene Katastrophe erscheint die Verfolgung der Juden in diesem Roman, sondern als extremer Tiefpunkt in der latent vorhandenen Gefühlslosigkeit und Brutalität der Menschen.'

26. 'ein paar belanglose Tage, [. . .] belanglos für die Geschichtsschreiber.'

27. 'Sartres Satz "Ein Toter ist ein Unglück, tausend Tote sind eine Zahl" hat großen Eindruck auf mich gemacht. [. . .] Ich hatte nie das Gefühl, daß es sich bei Beschreibungen von Leichenbergen um Literatur handeln könne, weil es keinen Schlüssel zu etwas Abstraktem gibt.'

28. 'Wenn ich mir die Frage stelle: "Wozu über Vergangenheit schreiben, wozu über Judenverfolgung, über Faschismus, über Nationalsozialismus, über Krieg schreiben?", dann ist die Antwort: "Damit die Leute wissen, was das war" eigentlich zu klein. Die übergeordnete Antwort müßte lauten: "Um das Risiko einer Wiederholung möglichst gering zu halten". Das heißt: Sinn solcher Literatur sollte und kann höchstens in einer Zunahme, in einer minimalen Zunahme von Sensibilität, von Empfindsamkeit bestehen. Vielleicht Leuten das Bewußtsein schärfen für Gewalt: was ist Gewalt, wo fängt Gewalt an, was sind Erscheinungsformen von Gewalt?'

29. 'wie ein Spaßmacher, der im entscheidenden Moment seinen Text vergessen hat. [. . .] Aber nach dem erfundenen endlich das blaßwangige und verdrießliche, das wirkliche und einfallslose Ende, bei dem man leicht Lust bekommt zu der unsinnigen Frage: Wofür nur das alles?'

30. See also Prévost 1989: 107.

31. 'Wer jetzt noch erschossen wird, so kurz vor Schluß, der hat plötzlich eine Zukunft verloren, um Himmels willen nur keinen Grund mehr geben für Majdanek oder Auschwitz, sofern Gründe Bedeutung haben, Vorsicht, Juden, höchste Vorsicht und keinen unüberlegten Schritt.'

32. 'welche Rolle dem Faktor "Hoffnung" im Leben zukommt. Die Geschichte zeigt, daß es zwar eine Bedingung, aber keine hinreichende für Leben ist.'

33. 'Alles falsch, sage ich dann, ihr könnt aufhören zu raten, ihr kommt doch nicht darauf.'

34. 'Fragt nicht nach der genauen Uhrzeit, die wissen nur die Deutschen, wir haben keine Uhren.'

35. '*Jakob* [my italics] trifft fast der Schlag. Da überwindet *man* [my italics] sich, mißachtet alle Regeln der Vorsicht und alle Vorbehalte, die ja nicht aus der Luft gegriffen sind, da macht man einen blauäugigen jungen Idioten zum Auserwählten, und was tut die Rotznase? Sie glaubt einem nicht. Und *du* [my italics] kannst nicht einfach weggehen, du kannst ihn nicht stehenlassen in seiner Blödheit, ihm sagen, daß ihn der Teufel holen soll, und einfach weggehen. Du mußt bei ihm bleiben.'

36. 'Sie setzt sich auf den freien Sessel, sehr gerade, sie legt die Hände in den Schoß, jetzt wird gewartet. Ich kann es getrost sagen, Kirschbaum kommt nach etwa einer halben Stunde.'

37. Wir atmen noch schwer, wir haben noch nie darüber gesprochen, da fragt sie mich plötzlich: "Sag mal, stimmt es daß du . . . ." / Weiß der Teufel, wer es ihr erzählt hat, ich höre das Mitleid in ihrer Stimme und werde verrückt. Ich gehe ins Bad, setze mich in die Wanne und fange an zu singen, damit ich nicht etwas tue, wovon ich genau weiß, daß es mir nach fünf Schritten leid tut. Als ich nach einer halben Stunde wiederkomme, fragt sie mich verwundert, was ich denn auf einmal hatte, und ich sage "nichts" und gebe ihr einen Kuß und mache das Licht aus und versuche einzuschlafen.'

38. '"Ich danke dir", sagt Jakob mit bewegter Stimme. Bewegt ist schon das richtige Wort, nach vierzig Jahren zum erstenmal bewegt, man bekommt nicht jeden Tag das Leben gerettet, dazu noch von einem,

den man so lange kennt und von dem man es, ganz ehrlich gesprochen, nicht erwartet hätte.'

39. 'Mischa dreht sich zu ihm um, der Anführer ist einen Kopf kleiner als er, und es bereitet ihn einige Mühe, bis zu Mischas Gesicht hinaufzuschlagen. Es sieht beinahe ein bißchen komisch aus, nichts für die deutsche Wochenschau, eher wie ein Spaß aus der Stummfilmzeit, wenn der kleine Polizist Charlie versuchte, den Riesen mit den buschigen Augen zur Strecke zu bringen, und er müht sich ab, und der Große merkt es gar nicht. Alle wissen, daß Mischa ihn hochheben könnte und in Stücke reißen. Wenn er nur wollte. Der Anführer schlägt noch ein wenig, die Hände müssen ihm schon weh tun, er schreit irgendwelches Zeug, das keinen interessiert und gibt erst Ruhe, als ein dünner Blutstrom aus Mischas Mundwinkel rinnt.'

40. 'Das Haus ist zu Ende, Jakob setzt zum Sprung an, wenige Minuten vor acht sind nahezu zwanzig Meter zu gewinnen, die Sache ist so gut wie sicher, und doch. Eine Maus müßte man sein? Eine Maus ist so unscheinbar, klein und leise? Und du? Laut Verordnung bist du eine Laus, eine Wanze, wir alle sind Wanzen, durch die Laune unseres Schöpfers lächerlich groß ausgefallene Wanzen, und wann hat sich je eine Wanze gewünscht, mit einer Maus zu tauschen? '

41. 'weil ein Spaziergang nach Feierabend so einen seltsamen Hauch von normalen Zeiten hat'.

42. 'und darum ein schwaches Glied in der ansonsten logischen Beweiskette'.

43. 'Er ist gezwungen worden, verantwortungslose Behauptungen in die Welt zu setzen, der ahnungslose Idiot da hat ihn gezwungen mit seinem lächerlichen Mißtrauen, bloß weil er Appetit auf Kartoffeln bekommen hat.'

44. 'Nicht die Posten haben geschossen [. . .] Jakob hat geschossen und ins Herz getroffen. [. . .] ganz plötzlich ist morgen auch noch ein Tag.'

45. 'Wir wissen, was geschehen wird. [. . .] Mischa wird den Mund nicht halten können'

46. 'Es hat schon einen Sinn, von der Zukunft zu reden. [. . .] gottverfluchten Zeiten, wo ganz normale Wünsche wie Ungeheuerlichkeiten klingen.'

47. 'Die großen Dinge werden sich schon irgendwie erledigen, es werden sicher bedeutende Leute kommen, die darüber wachen, fangen wir mit dem persönlichen Kleinkram an, den nimmt uns niemand ab. Rosa gerät vom Nachdenken ins Flüstern, da wäre zunächst das Haus, in dem man sich wohl fühlen soll, es könnte auch etwas anderes sein

als das Haus, wenn dir was einfällt, aber beginnen wir damit. Nicht zu klein, nicht zu groß, sagen wir fünf Zimmer, das ist nicht zuviel verlangt.'

48. 'Alte Schulden beginnen eine Rolle zu spielen, verlegen werden sie angemahnt, Töchter verwandeln sich in Bräute, in der Woche vor dem Neujahrsfest soll Hochzeit gehalten werden, die Leute sind vollkommen verrückt, die Selbstmordziffern sinken auf Null.'

49. 'Laut Radio müßte man bald das erste Geschützfeuer in der Ferne sehen, man sieht Tag für Tag das gleiche Bild, diese widerliche Trostlosigkeit.'

50. 'Oder er flieht vor den eigenen Leuten, vor ihren Nachstellungen und Anfeindungen, vor ihrer Wißbegier auch, ein Versuch, sich vor seinem Radio und seinen Folgen in Sicherheit zu bringen.'

51. 'daß Jakob die bedingungslose Kapitulation vorbereitet [. . .] ein König hat gewissermaßen abgedankt'.

52. 'Also biete ich sie zur Auswahl an, möge jeder sich den aussuchen, den er nach den eigenen Erfahrungen für den stichhaltigsten hält, vielleicht fallen dem einen oder anderen sogar noch einleuchtendere ein.'

53. 'unbekümmerten und ostentativ gemächlichen Plauderton – als ginge es nur um Selbstverständlches. [. . .] Bei einem so düsteren Thema läßt sich mit Düsterheit am wenigsten ausrichten, eher schon mit hellen und heiteren Kontrasteffekten, mit Witz und Komik. Das allerdings ist sehr schwierig und nahezu waghalsig. Aber Becker hat es geschafft.'

54. 'Die Erzählung lebt aus dem meist leisen, verhaltenen Humor seiner Sprache und aus der diskreten Komik seiner vielen Episoden.'

55. 'So also klingt seine Stimme, ich würde sagen keine sehr gelungene Premiere, ich würde sagen schwacher Bariton, man hätte sich einen angenehmeren Klang gewünscht.'

56. 'Wir stellen uns in einer Reihe auf, sehr beherrscht und ohne die geringste Drängelei. Das haben sie uns so beigebracht, unter Androhung von keinem Essen. Es muß aussehen, als hätten wir im Moment gar keinen Appetit, schon wieder dieses Essen, kaum hat man sich richtig eingearbeitet, wird man schon wieder unterbrochen durch eine der vielen Mahlzeiten.'

57. 'Jakob sieht von neuem hinaus, ob alles noch in Ordnung ist, nichts ist in Ordnung, gar nichts, auf dem Weg zurück liegt Mine neben Mine, ein Soldat kommt auf das Häuschen zu, man könnte sagen zielstrebig. [. . .] er hat noch fünf Schritte, dir bleibt jetzt nur noch das kleine ovale Loch, in ihren Mist hinein. Wozu du dich nicht

überwinden kannst, mager genug wärst du. / Der Soldat öffnet die Tür, die sich nicht sträubt, zu seinem Verdruß sieht er eine aufgeschlagene Doppelseite Zeitung vor sich, in Maßen zitternd, was aber in solch peinlichem Moment nicht weiter auffällt. / "Oh, Verzeihung!" sagt er und macht die Tür schnell zu.'

58. 'Der Geruch in diesem Haus ist anders geworden, irgendwie besser. Der Gestank von Salmiak, der früher auf den Gang gelegen hat, ist verschwunden, dafür riecht es auf unerklärliche Weise ziviler.'

59. 'In der Gegend von hundertsiebzig Pfund ist ihm das Ghetto dazwischengekommen, und seitdem geht es mit seinem Gewicht langsam abwärts.'

60. 'ich habe [. . .] beschrieben, ohne Beschönigung, so wie es wirklich war'.

61. 'daß jeder fünfte von uns im Winter erfriert, daß jeden Tag eine halbe Straße zum Transport geht'.

62. 'Ich stelle mir vor, was mit einem geschieht, der einen Ring am Finger hat und mit einem Hund nach acht auf der Straße angetroffen wird.'

63. 'Er hat versucht, mir zu erklären, wie eins nach dem anderen gekommen ist und daß er gar nicht anders gekonnt hat, aber ich will erzählen, daß er ein Held war. Keine drei Sätze sind ihm über die Lippen gekommen, ohne daß von seiner Angst die Rede war, aber ich will von seinem Mut erzählen.'

64. 'Kowalski ist himmlisch. Er hält sich für einen Fuchs und mit allen Wassern gewaschen, dabei kann sein Gesicht nichts verbergen, es ist geschwätzig. Wenn man ihn ein kleines bißchen kennt, weiß man genau, was mit ihm los ist, bevor er noch den Mund aufgemacht hat.'

65. 'ausstaffiert mit dieser und jener fragwürdigen Eigenschaft, war mißtrauisch, verschroben, ungeschickt, geschwätzig, obergescheit, wenn man alles zusammenrechnet, im nachhinein, plötzlich liebenswert'.

66. 'Kirschbaum hat nie einen Gedanken daran verschwendet, daß er Jude ist, schon sein Vater war Chirurg, was ist das schon, jüdische Herkunft, sie zwingen einen, Jude zu sein, und man selbst hat gar keine Vorstellung, was das überhaupt ist. Jetzt sind um ihn herum lauter Juden, zum ersten Mal in seinem Leben nichts als Juden, er hat sich den Kopf über sie zerbrochen, er wollte herausfinden, was es ist, wodurch sich alle gleichen, vergeblich, sie haben untereinander nichts Erkennbares gemein, und er mit ihnen schon gar nicht.'

67. 'auf dem besten Wege, ein deutscher Nationalist zu werden.' [. . .] 'weil sein Urgroßvater in die Synagoge gegangen ist und seine Eltern dumm genug waren, ihn beschneiden zu lassen.'

68. 'die bemerkenswerte Rechtsauffassung dieses komischen Volkes'.

69. 'er würde wahrscheinlich gegen das ganze Ghetto kein Wort einzu-
wenden haben, wenn sie nicht ausgerechnet ihn mit hineingesteckt
hätten.'

70. The novel's similarities with the Yiddish narrative tradition have been
established by a number of critics, notably Melvin Kornfeld (in his
introduction to the American translation), John P. Wieczorek and
Manfred Karnick.

71. 'Hätte mich meine Mutter mit einem klügeren Kopf geboren,
phantasiebegabt wie Scholem Alejchem, was rede ich, die Hälfte
würde genügen . . . [. . .] aber man ist, das ändert sich leider nie, kein
Scholem Alejchem an Erfindungsgabe'.

72. 'gute Nachrichten sind dazu da, weitergegeben zu werden.'

73. 'So ist das leider, Schmidt kennt sich nicht aus im Spiel der Andeutungen, wie gewisse Dinge nicht erwähnt werden und doch gesagt
sind, er wird sich nie auskennen, im Herzen ist er ein für allemal ein
Fremder. Ihm muß alles plump und deutlich ausgesprochen sein.'

74. 'Jakob geht weiter und entdeckt, wie er mir gesagt hat, daß er anders
geworden ist. Seine Sinne sind plötzlich viel wacher, von einem Tag
auf den anderen, er beginnt zu beobachten. Die teilnahmslose
Verzweiflung hat die Aufregungen der letzten Nacht nicht überlebt,
nichts mehr von der Dumpfheit, es ist jetzt, als müßte man sich alles
genau einprägen, um hinterher darüber berichten zu können. Hinterher.'

75. '. . . es war ein wichtiger Augenblick für ihn, hat er gesagt. Die erste
Lüge, die vielleicht gar keine war, so klein nur, und Kowalski ist
zufrieden. Das ist es wert, die Hoffnung darf nicht einschlafen, sonst
werden sie nicht überleben, er weiß genau, daß die Russen auf dem
Vormarsch sind, er hat es mit den eigenen Ohren gehört, und wenn
es einen Gott im Himmel gibt, dann müssen sie auch bis zu uns
kommen, und wenn es keinen gibt, dann müssen sie auch bis zu uns
kommen, und möglichst viele Überlebende müssen sie antreffen, das
ist es wert. Und wenn wir alle tot sein werden, dann war es ein
Versuch, das ist es wert.'

—4—

A Jew Who Became a German?
Questions of Language and
Jewish Identity in the Later Works

Language and Memory

In his last interview before his death (*Der Spiegel,* 13, 1997: 210), Jurek
Becker made the surprising declaration that his first, best-known and most
successful novel seemed to him to be linguistically inadequate, full of
'Sprachludereien', the sort of blunders and howlers which he would not
allow to get through into print today. The reason for this was quite clear
to him: it had been written in the GDR, in other words, he had mistrusted
the publishing house in which the book had first appeared in the GDR
and had consequently paid no attention to comments from the editors,
admitting that at this time he was still very much a novice in the business
of writing books. Hence *Jakob der Lügner* was basically 'ein unlektori-
ertes Buch' (a book on which no expert editorial advice had been given).
Becker branded his novel 'ein hübsches Kind, das in den Brunnen gefallen
war' (a nice project which had gone wrong); for despite the virtues of the
plot, praised by his interviewer as wonderfully imaginative, the language
was 'just not up to it' ('die Sprache [. . .] läuft nebenher').

In my view, Becker's judgement of his most successful and popular
early work is too severe because it is determined too much by his later,
very different notion of language and literature. As he admitted in the
same interview, it had been above all Arno Schmidt and Franz Kafka
who had changed his entire approach to writing, two writers whose work
he was only able really to get to know after he had left the GDR. Yet with
his first novel, it was precisely the vivid language and oral narrative
technique (and not just the imaginative plot about hopes sustained by
lies) which impressed critics in Germany and abroad. Even in November
1996, the *New York Times* praised the uniqueness of the novel when the
authorised English version was published in New York.

Yet *Jakob der Lügner* is also an exception in Becker's *œuvre.* In an earlier interview in 1984, he explained that he had written the novel in a quite specific language which he had virtually constructed for himself and could not repeat: It was not his own language but one in which he attempted to transfer some of the rules of colloquial Yiddish to High German (Pfeiffer 1984: 8). Along with these grammatical elements, a number of individual Yiddish words, too, together with Old Testament imagery are interwoven to give the language a flavour perfectly suited to conveying Becker's unique tragicomic vision of ghetto life. And through language itself he manages give us a miniature cross-section of East European Jewish culture: through, for instance, the use of individual Yiddish words, some related to religion and religious festivals ('Tscholent' – J 29; 'Chassene' – J 52; 'Schamess' [sexton] – J 68; 'Schabess' – J 70), some fairly common in general German usage ('mazzot' – J 173; 'nebbich' [shame] – J 215; 'Tinnef' [rubbish] – J 114; 'Zoress' [problems] – J 93) and others more obscure ('Chale' [*Challah*] – J 119; 'Jontefarbeit' [holiday job] – J 126; 'Hakoah' – J 28; 'Moissi' – J 41); through the evocative names of orthodox Jewish characters such as Herschel Schtamm; and through direct echoes of both Judaism ('Messias', the Messiah – J 99) and the Old Testament, both in the text ('die große Zeit der Propheten ist angebrochen', the great age of the prophets has dawned – J 83) and also in the title itself with its echoes not only of the man who deceived his brother Esau out of his rights as first-born son, but also of his namesake, for Becker's Jakob is the man who has 'a direct line to our dear God himself' (J 69).

It may well be the case that the language of Becker's first work is occasionally not as well-wrought and not as terse as that of some of his later texts. Yet it has other characteristics, other qualities, for in the person of the narrator and the other Jewish figures in *Jakob der Lügner*, Becker articulates the speaking Jew for his German readers through its narrative tone and language and through the oral narrative form of the novel, through repeated interaction between the narrator and his assumed listeners which partially reconstructs the discourse of the East European Jew.[1] As John Wieczorek has argued (Wieczorek 1990: 642), this novel, narrating the destruction of the ghetto as part of the Nazis' attempted destruction of the Jewish race and culture, is evidence that this attempt has failed, for Becker employs the very narrative techniques, vocabulary and symbolism associated with that culture in order to preserve something of the everyday life, language and ideas of the Eastern European 'Schtetl-welt' from oblivion.

Yet *Jakob der Lügner* remains the exception. True, four later works by Becker (two novels and two stories) deal with the theme 'Judentum'

('Jews and Jewishness'), but in none of them does Becker make the attempt to reconstruct a similar language. Why not? Here we must return to his biography in order to best appreciate the distinctive qualities of his later, more self-aware writing about his Jewish identity.

The fact that Jurek Becker is thought of at all as a German writer is, as he himself explained (*Die Zeit*, 20.5.94), 'die Folge einer Reihe von Zufällen' (the result of a succession of coincidences): he was born to parents 'mit jüdischem Hintergrund' (with a Jewish background), as he once put it so succinctly. In 1994, he explained his situation thus:

> And if the German army had not arrived shortly after my birth, if they had not occupied the country and stuck me and my parents in a ghetto and later in various concentration camps, if the Red Army had not liberated Sachsenhausen, the last camp I stayed in, then I myself would not have a clue what I would be and before whom I would be standing today. (*Die Zeit*, 20.5.1994)[2]

Puzzling, too, was his father's decision to move to Berlin after the war: 'Couldn't he have emigrated to Brooklyn', asked Becker,

> where perhaps I might have turned out to be an American writer? Or to Buenos Aires or, something that isn't so entirely far-fetched, to Tel Aviv? But no, he decided on what is in my eyes the most exotic of all possibilities, he stayed here, moved into a flat a few stops away from the entrance to the camp and settled down, with the result that I became a German. (*Die Zeit*, 20.5.1994)[3]

So did Becker become a German, then, just like that – a member of a people who had made the almost completely successful attempt to murder his entire family? His ironically succinct, seemingly casual statement is, of course, typical of the deceptive, mischievous stance which conceals his profound earnestness. Becker had often asked his father why they of all people, survivors of the Holocaust, had ended up at No. 5 Lippehner Straße in East Berlin rather than anywhere else in the world and why they did not at least return to Poland. But his father always maintained a stony silence until one day he answered his son's question with one of his own: 'Was it the Polish or the German anti-Semites that lost the war?'[4] His father was convinced, then, that they would be reasonably safe from persecution in Germany, and in the Eastern rather than the Western sector 'where old Nazis like Globke and Oberländer were able to make a career for themselves again'.[5] As far as the Soviet zone of occupation (and later the GDR) was concerned, his father was only interested in one thing: 'that the anti-fascists were in command there. And if anyone dared to criticise the behaviour of *his* Russians or the conditions in their bit of

Germany, then they were either a moaner or an enemy' (*Die Zeit*, 20.5.1994).[6]

Initially, therefore, Jurek Becker himself, not least through the influence of his father, was convinced of the merits of the GDR both as home and as political system, and he did become a German in a special sense, an East German, a citizen of the GDR, joining the Young Pioneers and then the Free German Youth movement. Only with the invasion of Czechoslovakia by Warsaw Pact troops in 1968 did he really fall out with the Party.

Yet the questions about his identity remained, and here, from the outset, language played a critical role. As an eight-year-old child in a strange country whose language he did not speak and whose countrymen had tried to murder him and his father a short while before, Becker was from the very start and in every way an outsider. He spoke hardly a word of German. For the first seven years of his life, he had spoken only Polish, and even his Polish was not that of a near nine-year-old, as he explained in *Warnung vor dem Schriftsteller*: 'It had got stuck within the linguistic range of a four-year-old, for at this age I was exposed to conditions in which language was as good as superfluous' (W 10).[7] In Berlin he now had to learn the language of his erstwhile oppressors – the first German words which he could remember were the commands shouted at him and his parents in the ghetto: 'Alles alle' (all of you), 'Antreten – Zählappell!' (fall in – roll call!) and 'Dalli-dalli' (at the double! – W 10). In order to encourage his young son to pick up German 'in the twinkling of an eye, as it were', Becker's father suddenly, 'from one day to the next', stopped speaking Polish with him, an experience which left the young boy literally speechless, as the author explained in 1983: 'Thus for a while I had to live literally speechless' (Heidelberger-Leonard 1992: 13).[8]

Becker, then, did not learn the German language casually in children's games, nor gradually year by year as he grew up: his acquisition of German was 'the result of organised efforts' (W 10) which meant, in effect, picking up the language as quickly as possible: 'For me, improving my German as quickly as possible was almost a matter of life or death: the sooner I eradicated the errors, the more infrequently others would discover that I was a foreigner. And if the errors dried up completely, then one day, even though mistakenly, they would even take me for one of them' ((W 10–12).[9] 'Mistakenly' – even if Becker was able to cope fairly quickly with the foreign language, then, something of the foreigner did still remain in terms of his linguistic identity, for even as a young man, at a time when those around him no longer noticed any linguistic difference from them in the way that he spoke, he still felt 'an outsider' (*Dimension:* 409).

His linguistic problems were, however, not without short-term advantages for the writer-to-be, for his way of learning German by carefully observing and following rules led with him to a 'besonders bewußten Verhältnis zur Sprache' (particularly deliberate relationship to language – W 12):

> The fact that I did not start to learn German until the age of eight could be the reason why my relationship to this language became a rather effusive one. Just as other children of my age were interested in may-bugs or racing cars, observing them from all sides, I too scrutinised words and sentences. I saw in this extremely intense preoccupation with language the only means of escaping the ridicule and disadvantages which arose from the fact that I was the only eight-year-old anywhere around who could not speak properly. (Heidelberger-Leonard 1992: 17)[10]

In the long term, though, Becker considered this a disadvantage for he later admitted that it was precisely authors like Arno Schmidt who 'contravene rules and break up language as if to see what is inside. It is not the way I do things, and if I do attempt to do it, then I get the feeling that I am just pretending' (W 12).[11] And even in 1984 (some fifteen years after the appearance of his first novel), Becker made the surprising if somewhat exaggerated assertion that he did not feel entirely at home in the German language:

> I do not feel at home in the midst of all these strange words and constructions and shades of meaning. I am not saying I feel uneasy here, no. But what I miss are familiarity and a security, which are indeed part of the feeling of 'being at home' and which I think I do observe in others now and again. Compared to them, I have to be constantly on my guard. (Heidelberger-Leonard 1992: 14)[12]

One cannot take this statement entirely at face value, though, for in 1994 he claimed that he felt no sense of 'Distanz zum Deutschen' (distance towards the German language), that he was entirely familiar with its 'facets', but also that he still had the feeling of having learnt German and hence too the memory of what was for him the 'terrible disadvantage' of having spoken German badly: 'when I said something, it was as if I had been carrying a banner above my head with the words: "I am someone different"' (*Literarische Porträts* 1992: 6).[13] All in all, then, and despite his success as a writer, German did still remain something of a foreign language for Becker, a factor which was not without consequences for his sense of identity.

As we know, the eight-year-old Becker forgot his Polish much quicker than he learnt the new (German) language. When I interviewed him in 1991, he admitted that he had now totally forgotten his mother tongue. He also claimed to have almost no memories of his earliest childhood. He believed that these memories of his experiences in the ghetto and concentration camps, 'in dieser Sprache abgespeichert' (stored away in this [Polish] language), had been forgotten along with his Polish: 'My mother tongue is Polish. All the memories that I have are Polish. I learnt German after the war and quickly forgot my Polish. By forgetting the language, I have probably forgotten a large part of the information stored away in this language' (Graf and Konietzny 1991: 5).[14] His father did not offer an alternative source of information about experiences of the Holocaust since from the outset he consistently refused to discuss the past with his son (Heidelberger-Leonard 1992: 16).

Consequently, Becker continually returned to the theme of Jewish victims of the Holocaust (the last occasion in his novel *Bronsteins Kinder* – 1986), testimony enough of his intense preoccupation with his own Jewish origins and also with his own lack of memories of experiences which largely determined the course of his life. In 1988, for instance, he commented: 'As a child I was in a concentration camp. I have hardly any memories of this, and of all my experiences it probably had the most far-reaching effect. What became of my family, of me and of a country itself has been an obsessive preoccupation of mine for a long time' (Stöhr 1988: 28).[15]

In his very last interview, too, he claimed that *Jakob der Lügner* was 'der Versuch des Hauchs einer Autobiographie' (the attempt to trace some hint of my autobiography – *Der Spiegel* 1997: 211): in the novel, he was asking the question as to where he came from since he himself was

> some sort of Kaspar Hauser: I had landed in this world at the age of eight. And apart from some very scanty information, no one told me who I was, what I was doing here and where I came from. [. . .] If you don't know where you come from, it's a bit like running around for the whole of your life with a rucksack [. . .] without knowing what's inside it. That's a very unpleasant condition, and your preoccupation with it is almost a lifelong one – my efforts to find out what is in this sack which I have on my back.'[16]

His Jewish works, then, are a search for identity via linguistic constructs, an attempt, as it were, to open the locked door of the past with the key of language itself. Works such as his first novel which relate directly to his Polish-Jewish origins are, however, not rediscovered, direct reflections of his own experiences but fictitious reconstructions. *Jakob der Lügner* is a freely invented reconstruction, based on his own research after the war, of the historical context, the Polish ghetto, which had such a far-reaching effect on Becker's life but which left no clear imprint on his memory. In his final interview, he explained one of his reasons for writing his first novel: 'I wanted to know one thing more precisely. What the ghetto was like, which of course I knew much better after the book than before it. Beforehand, the ghetto was for me something in my head, something eerie, threatening and black. And I studied it and worked on it until it became something inhabited by people, one of whom was me, that is for certain' (*Der Spiegel* 1997: 211).[17] And in stories such as 'Die Mauer' (The Wall) and 'Die beliebteste Familiengeschichte' (My family's favourite story), Becker explores conceivable versions of the past, possible dimensions of his own forgotten experiences and of his Jewish origins, through fiction, through the medium of his imagination.

The latter story is, for instance, not literally about Becker's own family, but 'frei erfunden' (freely invented), as he explained to me in 1991, for as we have noted, he had no detailed knowledge of his own family since his father consistently refused to talk about the Holocaust with him. Indeed, only through his own imagination and its expression in language was he able to overcome the 'Zustand tiefer Sprachlosigkeit' ('state of profound silence') which prevailed in such matters between father and son, as he once commented: 'I was only capable of inventing a dialogue between us, a relationship as I would have wished it to be' (Hage 1987: 331).[18]

After the appearance of his first novel in the GDR in 1969, when critics attempted to link *Jakob der Lügner* to the tradition of Jewish storytelling represented by writers such as Aleichem and Singer, Becker had been quick to reject this. An atheist, he regarded his own Jewishness as a 'Zwangs-Identität' ('enforced-identity') imposed on him by historical circumstances. In his essay in 'Mein Judentum', he explained why he got so 'aufgeregt' ('agitated') in this matter: it was 'because people have decided for me with tedious frequency who and what I am: amongst other things, a Jew of course' (Heidelberger-Leonard 1992: 19).[19] Becker firmly denied, then, any emotional or religious attachment to Judaism and agreed with his father's view of this: 'If anti-Semitism did not exist, do you think I would have felt like a Jew for even a single second?' (Heidelberger-Leonard 1992: 17).[20]

Almost without exception, though, literary critics have praised his ability as a storyteller, an ability which they see as evidence of his Jewish descent: in one of the main reference works on modern German literature, Sigrid Lüdke-Haertel and Martin Lüdke comment: 'Jurek Becker can simply tell stories well. He draws on abundant resources; the Jewish (Yiddish) tradition may be playing its part here' (Arnold 1978: 2).[21] Many consider him to be 'der geborene Geschichtenerzähler' (the born story-teller – Kalb 1983: 59–60), and in 1992, one critic came to the conclusion: 'Thus there is evidence of a characteristic element of the Jewish identity not least in the clearly oral character of Becker's work' (Heidelberger-Leonard 1992: 286).[22] Becker has himself admitted his indebtedness to the oral tradition of storytelling. However, he was exposed to this influence not within the sphere of his own Jewish family in Lodz, but only during the later stages of his childhood in Berlin after the war. In an interview in 1990, he explained how he was encouraged by his father to develop his oral storytelling technique in the presence of Jewish friends and fellow survivors of the Holocaust, who would meet every few weeks to tell stories in the district where he lived with his father. He commented:

> It is correct to say that after the war I was given some training in storytelling. [. . .] There was no large community to which I belonged and in which it would have been the usual thing to do. But my father and his friends who came to our home had been exposed to similar customs and traditions. Since childhood, oral storytelling has been important for me. (Graf and Konietzny 1991: 62)[23]

Such first-hand experience of the oral tradition is perhaps the main reason for his view that one of the most important factors in storytelling is aesthetic pleasure in words themselves and in the act of narration, for 'part and parcel of storytelling [. . .] is [. . .] a certain attitude, also a certain pleasure' (Kalb 1983: 62).[24]

'Die beliebteste Familiengeschichte'[25]

This 'Lust am Erzählen' (pleasure in storytelling) is very much in evidence in Becker's most popular novel *Jakob der Lügner* and, above all, in 'Die beliebteste Familiengeschichte', a story about the telling of a story. Its narrator retells a tale which has been retold to him over and over again by his own father, about a family tradition which both arose and disappeared before the narrator's time: in the past, each time the large Jewish family gathered to celebrate important family events, usually births, his Uncle Gideon, a Jew from Lublin, always retold the 'favourite family story' about a practical joke played upon him during a pre-war business trip to England. Invited to a fancy-dress ball by a mischievous English-Jewish business associate, Gideon arrives dressed as a clown only to discover to his embarrassment not only that his English hosts are not in fancy dress, but that he is the sole guest!

'Die beliebteste Familiengeschichte' is, though, more than just a story about the Uncle's funny story; it is a story about the storyteller's art itself as an aesthetically pleasurable activity. Becker's framework story, his story around a story, is a celebration of storytelling, an expression of pleasure in the sovereign act of narration. And this 'Lust am Erzählen' extends to a delight in the recreation of the actual storytelling situation and ritual. In so doing, Becker manages to bring alive again an aspect of Jewish family culture so important to him, a custom which is part of his own heritage but which to his annoyance, as his narrator tells us, has disappeared before his time (NZ 40). The narrator's father, the only surviving witness of this family event, has retold the story orally to his son many times, thereby passing down to his only son his sense of obligation to carry on the storytelling tradition. The narrator, however, has to overcome a certain difficulty: he too feels a sense of obligation to his father to carry on the oral tradition, but he has not inherited his father's desire literally to retell the same old story over and over again. Becker allows his narrator to find the solution to his problem in writing the story down, thereby giving it a final and enduring shape and so also paradoxically marking both the end of this oral tradition and its perpetuation, since the story will now not be told, but read again and again.

Yet although the narrator writes the story down, he retells it in a way which enables the reader to re-experience the dynamics and the humour involved in the traditional retelling of the story at family gatherings. Through his evocation of the whole family ritual of storytelling, including the usual persistent requests for the old familiar story to be retold yet again, time itself frequently appears suspended in the past, above all at the end of the story when the narrator tells how Uncle Gideon has forgotten to bring back a souvenir of London 'diesmal' (this time) and promises not to forget 'beim nächsten Mal' (next time – NZ 61).

What, though, has become of this avuncular storyteller since these happier times? Only once in the story does the narrator give the reader an indication of what has happened to Uncle Gideon, why this cheerful family custom has long since disappeared and what has taken place in the gap between the more distant past of the family gathering (*'damals'*) and the present. In the introductory framework to the story, he comments quite casually: 'Once my father said: Gideon was already a very old man when they took him off to Maidanek, but they did it just the same' (NZ 42).[26] Such laconic reference to the Holocaust is typical of the author, the single sentence providing as it were the historical frame both to the family event of storytelling and to Gideon's ensuing story, thereby giving a sinister, even eerie, undertone to the details of the humorous account of the experiences of a Galician Jew as cultural misfit in London. Even Becker himself once made the following comment about this story: 'It is a story entirely about people who were gassed in Maidanek or Auschwitz, all except me [. . .] the narrator' (Johnson 1988: 8).[27]

'The art of giving a cheerful tone to sadness and, precisely by so doing, of preserving the memory of mockery and extermination'[28] (Beisbart and Abraham 1992: 142), is, according to Peter Hanenberg, Jurek Becker's distinctive contribution to literature. One might also add that, in 'Die beliebteste Familiengeschichte', Becker succeeds in skilfully employing techniques associated both with his own family heritage and with that of Central European Jewish culture – the oral tradition of storytelling, whose exponents in his own family have perished – in order to ensure its survival at least in written form. Through his reminiscing narrator, Becker is able, too, to preserve something of the cheerful humour of traditional Jewish storytelling, even in the shadow of the Holocaust. And through the medium of the German language, the voice of the author's long since vanished East European Jewish family can still be heard.

'Die Mauer'

If 'Die beliebteste Familiengeschichte' is pure fiction, then the story 'Die Mauer' would appear to be based on Becker's experiences as a child in the Polish ghetto, for its first-person narrator is the same age as Becker was at the time and is much closer to the author than, for instance, the fictional narrator of *Jakob der Lügner* who, 'einundzwanzig geboren' (born in twenty-one – J 24), is an adult witness to events in the ghetto. Becker explained to me in 1991 that the situation in the story was indeed based on the very few extremely hazy memories of his own childhood in Lodz.[29] And when the work appeared in the collection of stories entitled *Nach der ersten Zukunft* (After the initial future), most reviewers took it to be pure autobiography, 'Kindheitserinnerungen aus dem Getto' (childhood memories from the ghetto – Werth, *Süddeutsche Zeitung*: 4.11.1980).

However, one must exercise caution here, bearing in mind Becker's frequent assertions that he had almost no memories of the ghetto and the concentration camps, and that his works set in this period are largely the product of one or two of his father's anecdotes but mainly of a combination of his imagination and his own historical research. In 1988, for instance, he explained his reasons for this research: 'I was not going to risk any clumsy mistakes; I wanted, as it were, to compose the deviations' (Hage 1988: 41).[30] The ghetto in 'Die Mauer' has, then, many similarities with Lodz and with other Polish ghettoes during the Second World War: for instance, the ghetto and the transit camp are completely enclosed (the latter by the eponymous wall), patrolled day and night by German sentries with orders to shoot any Jews (including children) approaching the boundaries (NZ 95); living conditions are insanitary (NZ 67); suicides are everyday occurrences (NZ 73); and entire Jewish families on one side of the street are suddenly ordered to leave their homes in the middle of the night (NZ 67). Yet the ghetto of the story is neither an historically exact reproduction of that in Lodz[31] nor of that in any other Polish town. It is an imaginative construction. The few particulars of the situation and the surroundings which Becker does give us reveal nothing of the horrors of the real ghettos, only the prevailing sense of threat, the bleakness and the squalor – sufficient details to evoke an inimical environment. As he once commented: 'I cannot portray the horrors, I am not an historian' (*Badische Neueste Nachrichten* 1981).[32] 'Die Mauer' is, then, a fictional reconstruction of the historical context which has exerted an important influence on Becker's life but has left no clear imprint on his memory.

He affirmed that his only 'deutliche und abrufbare Erinnerungen' (clear and retrievable memories – Heidelberger-Leonard 1992: 15) started from the point of his reunion with his father after the war. He was not sure, therefore, whether his memories of the ghetto were his own memories, those of others or even inventions. He viewed his writing about this time as an attempt to retrieve memories or even create them for himself. Commenting on an exhibition of photographs of the Lodz Ghetto, he once declared: 'I cannnot remember anything. [. . .] Nevertheless, I have written stories about ghettoes as if I were an expert. Perhaps I thought that if I wrote for long enough, then the memories would come. Perhaps at some point, too, I started regarding some of my inventions as memories.' Although Becker himself had as good as no real memories, he saw them as indispensable: 'Being without memories of your childhood is like being condemned to drag a big box around with you the whole time, whose contents you do not know. And the older you get, the heavier it seems to be and the more impatient you become finally to open the thing.' Yet no matter how hard Becker stared at the photographs from the world of his earliest childhood, they were unable to trigger off any of his memories: 'I stare at the pictures and search till my eyes are sore for the part of my life which decided everything. But I can only make out the fading lives of the others; why should I speak of indignation or pity, I would like to climb back down to them but I cannot find the way' (Loewy and Schoenberner 1990: 10).[33]

The story 'Die Mauer', along with the other work set in this period, the novel *Jakob der Lügner*, can be seen as the attempt by the author to 'climb back down' into the past and 'unlock the box' of his own memories. The retrieval of his own possible memories and of the forgotten past through words, through language, through writing, is the central though understated theme of 'Die Mauer'. It is announced, indirectly, in the opening lines as the narrator acts as if, through a sudden vivid memory which takes him by surprise, he has indeed become a child again and is experiencing the past through the eyes of a five-year-old:

> My God! I'm five years old, we Jews are our own quiet, happy selves again. Our neighbour is called Olmo again and he and his wife are shouting at each other the whole day long, and anybody with nothing better to do can stand behind the door and hear every word. And the street has its houses again, in every single one something happened to me. (NZ 62)[34]

Here Becker is articulating the voice of his own possible childhood. He goes on to tell a tale of nocturnal adventures in the ghetto as two children climb over the wall around a transit camp in order to go back and search for their toys left behind in their abandoned homes. The narrator, though, is a mixture of past and present selves: the restricted, naive viewpoint of the small child (a possible past self of the author's), for whom it is all an exciting adventure, predominates for most of the story, but occasionally, the contrasting historical perspective of the survivor (the mature Becker) intrudes when the vividness of the narrator's memories makes him feel compelled to interrupt his story at critical moments from the standpoint of the adult.

Yet Becker not only writes mostly from the child's perspective, he also deliberately employs childish language. A familiar conversational tone is achieved by the predominance of the present tense and the use of simple, colloquial language, often giving the impression that a child is speaking. The narrator's frequent use, too, of successions of short, usually main, clauses, childlike idioms and unselfconscious vulgarities similarly creates the illusion that events are being seen through the eyes of a child. The imagery is also predominantly taken from the world of childhood, for in the mind of the child, the real dangers of everyday life in the ghetto take on the terrifying yet also exciting dimensions of the world of fairy-tale and the supernatural, as the child believes he is about to be boiled alive (NZ 71) or pursued by ghosts (NZ 78), thinks he hears a signal from a raven (NZ 84), becomes a robber in the night (NZ 88), confronts a devil's face (NZ 88) and is later captured by a giant in the shape of a German soldier (NZ 95). And personification is sometimes used in order to reflect the way in which inanimate things appear to come alive in the mind of the child: 'Die Straße sieht mich kaum' (the street can hardly see me – NZ 65), he declares; he runs across the whispering courtyard (NZ 67), and tells us later that the edge of the wall has let go of his hands (NZ 87). Occasionally, however, the historical perspective breaks through the 'Kindersprache', indirectly and seemingly unintentionally: for instance, the 'child' narrator's apparently innocent use of hyperbole in his brief admission of his inability to keep a secret (he tells 'millions of people' about it – NZ 65) is an ominous reminder of the millions of Jews who died in the Holocaust. By reflecting events through the imagined filter of the mind and language of a child, 'Die Mauer' also conveys, indirectly, the horrific reality of what happened to the Jews at this time: the monstrous became 'normalised'. This is suggested perhaps most strikingly in the matter-of-fact, almost casual tone of the small boy's first reaction when, on returning to the wall at the end, he encounters a German soldier and comments: 'I have no doubt that we'll soon be shot, that was clear from the start' (NZ 95).[35]

On the occasions when, in the midst of this process of vivid recollection of the past through the eyes and experiences of a child, the historical consciousness of the mature narrator does intrude, memory itself emerges as a problem. For instance, just as he is about to describe the transit camp, the narrator makes a startling confession – that most of his story is only a story and that his memories are fictitious: 'A small part of the ghetto – and this has nothing to do with memories, it's the truth – a small part of the ghetto is like a camp' (NZ 67).[36] The narrator's view of memory in 'Die Mauer' is similar to that of the author himself. In an interview in 1988, Becker explained the way such stories came to him in terms of 'pseudo-memories': 'A third possibility is: [. . .] I remember or I think I remember, that is, I remember erroneously. Remembering things erroneously is a particularly abundant source' (*Dimension* 1988: 8).[37] Becker's erroneous memory was thus an important source of his creativity: memory was for him creative, functioning as the filter through which imagined and therefore possibly real experience was transformed into literature.

In 'Die Mauer', then, the narrator is a double persona, a mixture of past and present selves, of possible child and author, giving the story from the outset a dual narrative structure. Through the narrow perspective of the child, the author creates tension, immediacy, and vivid retrieval of the past, encouraging the reader to identify and empathise. Yet occasionally the narrator in the present also feels compelled to interrupt his story at critical moments from the standpoint of the adult. Through this dual narrative structure, Becker creates distance, avoids sentimentality, and reminds the reader of the historical dimensions of the story.

We have already noted Becker's denial of any emotional attachment to 'Judentum'. Yet for one brief moment in 'Die Mauer', the narrator returns to a collective identity as he begins his story with the words 'wir Juden sind wieder ein stilles Glück' (we Jews are our own quiet, happy selves again).[38] By placing his 'ich' (I) within a framework of the 'wir' (we) of his Jewish childhood, Becker is expressing his solidarity with his Jewish fellow-sufferers. This does not indicate, though, a reaffirmation of the narrator's (or the author's) Jewishness, for it is a 'wir' which no longer exists. Since the bridge to the world of the past consists of language and memory, the narrator is only able to recreate the 'wir' in his own mind, fictionally, for it is a 'wir' from 'damals' ('that time'), and one which no longer exists.

Der Boxer

We know that Becker's only clear memories date from the time after his father had managed to find him with the help of an American relief organisation. Unlike *Jakob der Lügner* which was purely fictitious, Becker's second Holocaust novel relates to these memories of his own experiences after the war, and the author described it as his 'most private book' (*Dimension* 1978: 411). Its plot has several autobiographical parallels, such as: the death of the mother in a concentration camp; father and son as the sole survivors of the entire family; the father's reunion with his son in a camp shortly after the end of the war via the help of an American relief agency; and the decision to resettle in East Berlin. One scene in particular stands out: the first meeting after the war between father and putative son (there is never any complete certainty about the latter's identity as his documents bear the wrong surname). The name of the fictional father is Aron Blank, and he does indeed confront a blank, stunted personality in the shape of the little boy who is unaware of his own identity: unspeakable and inexpressible experiences in the concentration camp have left him bereft of the language of normal family relationships. In this first meeting, Mark's alienation from anything associated with the family is particularly striking. Simultaneously, though, the scene poignantly illustrates how the acquisition of the language of normal, everyday human relations brings with it a sense of a new identity.

As Aron explains to Mark what the words 'father' and 'son' mean, the parallels with Becker's own life are unmistakable: specifically, the need to learn a new vocabulary, a new language, and the implications of this for the development of identity:

'If I'm your father, then you are my . . .?'

For the first time, Mark ignored the rules of interrogation; he did not answer but shrugged his shoulders. Beneath the white shirt, says Aron, which up to that point seemed to be lying empty on the bed, shoulders were moving up and down.

'Then you are my son,' said Aron. 'Do you understand?'

'No.'

For several minutes Aron was unable to grasp just what Mark could not understand about this, the woman in charge of the place had not mentioned a word about him being *barmy*. He said:

'What don't you understand?'

'That word.'

'Which word?'

'The one you said.'

'Son?'

'Yes.'

'That's quite easy,' said Aron. 'I'm your father and you're my son. Those are simply the words used. Now do you understand?'

'Yes.'

'Then say it again.'

'You are my father,' said Mark, 'and I am your son.'

'Right. But you don't have to use the "Sie" form with me; say "du". Say it again: You are my father.'

'You are my father.'

'I am your son.'

'You are my son.'

'No, that's wrong,' said Aron.

Suddenly Mark began to cry. (B 64–5)[39]

This sensitive first encounter between father and son, with its emphasis on the importance of basic family concepts for individual identity and for human relationships, stands in stark contrast to the slow disintegration of the relationship between father and son towards the end of the novel, which is largely the result of Aron's increasing inability to communicate. Motivated above all by his desire to shield his son from painful memories of the past, Aron refuses to speak about the Holocaust. His 'efforts to get rid of the past' and 'delete a bad time' (B 18) lead Aron to suppress his Jewish identity: he falsifies his date of birth in his new identity card, making himself six years younger, tries to change his appearance by dying his hair, and interchanges two letters in his first name to make Aron into Arno. Yet these desperate efforts quite literally to turn over a new leaf and acquire a new identity are doomed to failure. Not only is he continually haunted by ghosts of the past (for the camps still exist in his head –

B 103), in other respects too he is unable to deny, or indeed to escape, his Jewish identity. His reticence is that of the Jew as Holocaust-survivor and leads to the tragic breakdown of communication between both father and son, who is also later described by Aron as 'a boy with a poorly developed need to communicate' (B 268)[40] and who becomes increasingly estranged from his father, until one day he suddenly leaves home without any forewarning. From subsequent letters, it turns out that he has gone to Israel on the eve of the Six Day War. When the letters suddenly stop, Aron assumes that he has been killed. Thus, by choosing a Jewish identity for himself in the Jewish state of Israel, Mark negates his father's attempts to suppress his own Jewish identity and also to protect Mark from his own Jewishness. In this respect, Mark corresponds closely to the definition of a Jew given by Becker in his essay 'Mein Judentum' (Heidelberger-Leonard 1992: 19), when he claimed that the question of belonging to a group of people such as the Jews involved an act of individual free will, an intellectual decision. Aron himself expresses this same view as his author's at one point in a discussion with the young writer who is interviewing him:

> What does it really mean to say you're a Jew, he asks me, is it anything other than a confession of faith? Aren't we now, at last, living in an age in which everyone can decide for himself which party he wishes to be a member of, he asks? As to whether he's a Turk or a German, of course, he can't have any influence on this, but can't he have any influence on whether he's a Christian or a Jew? When it comes of age, a child of Catholic parents can freely choose whether to remain a Catholic or not. Why then, he asks me, deny the children of Jewish parents the same right? (B 298)[41]

In an essay which has had some considerable influence on Becker research,[42] Chaim Shoham (Röll and Bayerdörfer 1986: 225–36) puts forward the view that Becker is identical with his Jewish protagonist Mark: both Becker's and Mark's choice of their new language are analogous to Heidegger's definition of language as the 'Haus des Seins' (house of being). It may well be correct to argue that in this sense, as a child, Becker (like Mark) entered an empty house, as it were, and began to furnish it. For it was precisely those aspects of life which largely shape the identity of a person (the mother tongue and, associated with it, childhood memories and family traditions) which had been eradicated in his case. And Shoham is also right to argue that, in a sense, Becker's life and identity only really began when he finally settled down with his father in Berlin and adopted the German language, since the learning of the language was also the means of appropriating a new independent identity.

Yet Shoham contradicts himself, for he also claims that Becker's refusal 'to define his identity according to his biological origins and the religious faith of his parents' represents 'from a Jewish point of view [. . .] a typically assimilatory tendency' (Schöne 1986: 225).[43] For Shoham, then, Becker did indeed have a 'jüdische Identität' (Jewish identity), which he denied by trying to 'find through the act of writing a new identity in place of his old [Jewish] one which he wanted to extinguish' (Schöne 1986: 226, 228).[44] It is my view, though, that Becker's case was exactly the reverse: it was precisely through the act of writing, and indeed through the medium of the German language, that he sought to find, to rediscover that part of himself, namely the Jewish identity, which as a child he had extinguished from his memory. Shoham goes on to argue that Mark Blank is Jurek Becker's 'Doppelgänger' (double – Schöne 1986: 231) and he interprets Mark's later turning to Israel and to things Hebrew, his return to a Jewish identity, as evidence of Becker's inability to deny, to suppress his own Jewishness. Here Shoham clearly goes too far, for none of Becker's protagonists are identical with their author. One of Becker's distinguishing marks as a writer was the obvious delight which he took in quite literally playing different parts, showing great skill in adopting a multitude of different mantles. Significantly, all his 'Jewish' novels and stories (and the great predominance of the rest) have first-person narrators.

Bronsteins Kinder

The narrator and main character of *Bronsteins Kinder* (Bronstein's children) was also interpreted by most reviewers as an autobiographical parallel to Becker, for like his author himself, Hans Bronstein resists any sense of identity as victim. Like Becker, too, he is a citizen of the GDR, philosophy student and the son of Jewish parents.

The plot offers yet another example of Becker's unique inventiveness. One day, Hans is suddenly an accessory to a secret crime at the family dacha, where his father and two other Jewish survivors are holding prisoner a former guard from the Neuengamme concentration camp. Now the tables are turned for here it is the Jews who are the torturers as they try to wring confessions from Heppner, their former tormentor. As the past suddenly engulfs the present, the distraught Hans is unable to understand the actions of a father who now no longer fits the image which Hans has had of him hitherto. *Bronsteins Kinder* is, then, another novel with strong parallels to Becker's own life and above all to his own difficult relationship with his father, which is reflected in the novel's major theme: the repercussions of the Holocaust. Despite the semblance of normality in their everyday lives, the survivors remain lifelong victims, unable to communicate with their children who therefore have difficulty comprehending them. One of the central themes in both this novel and *Der Boxer* is this 'Sprachlosigkeit' (silence) between the generations, the symbol of which is a door in the Bronsteins' flat: 'Between my father's room and mine was a door which was never used and which was blocked from his side with a bookshelf and from my side with a wardrobe' (BK 218).[45]

Yet as Hannes Krauss has rightly claimed (Hermand and Mattenklott 1988: 139–46), 'Becker's "Jewish novels" are [. . .] not confessional autobiography but models with types'.[46] The autobiographical dimension is, then, not to be found at the level of facts, for 'the author gives shape to his fundamental experiences in free literary fiction' (Hermand and Mattenklott 1988: 143).[47] The stories of characters such as Hans and Mark (*Der Boxer*) represent just two of several possible situations and views of life. Yet Becker goes further than Krauss is prepared to concede, for a work such as 'Die beliebteste Familiengeschichte' is, for instance, not just a 'starting-point for reflections on his own biography' (Hermand and Mattenklott 1988: 141),[48] to which Krauss tries to limit it, but also the attempt to animate extinct Jewish family customs and to reconstruct the world of Becker's own forgotten past, and hence of intense personal significance to the author.

In many of Becker's texts, the idea of the past is integrally linked to the notion of the future, indeed, it is often the precondition both for the future itself and for free self-determination, with memory frequently playing a vital role. His novels, though, deal not with the author's own case, namely the psychological problems associated with the repression of memories, but with the related yet distinct theme of memory as an essential factor in coming to terms with past experiences. A central theme in many of his works, including those set entirely in the GDR such as *Schlaflose Tage* (Sleepless days), is the realisation that the future is dependent on the past, and that those who wish to determine their own future have to fix their gaze on the past in order to be able to leave it behind and move on. At the start of *Bronsteins Kinder*, for instance, the narrator explains his reasons for telling his story thus: 'I suspect that first of all one has to form as precise an impression as possible of events that are to be removed from one's memory' (BK 15).[49] *Der Boxer* offers a contrasting variation on this theme when Aron's American lover points out that whoever wishes to determine his own future must first face up to the past in order to be able to leave it behind: 'If we sought to forget everything else beforehand, then we'd never get round actually to living our lives' (B 45).[50]

Originally *Bronsteins Kinder* was to have the ironically sounding title 'How I became a German' ('Wie ich ein Deutscher wurde' – Hage 1988: 45). This would, though, have been too obvious a pointer to the fact that Hans, with his quintessentially German name, had apparently reconciled himself to his German identity, and Becker rejected it. Significantly, it is precisely Hans's identity as a German which is called into question through the 'Jewish' events in which he becomes embroiled, for the young narrator himself, very much against his will, occasionally feels Jewish.

In some respects Hans is the typically passive product of GDR society, as witness his following admission: 'Not a single person had taught me how to offer resistance; no one had shown me how to do what is thought to be right' (BK 85).[51] He is disturbed to see his father involved as a Jew in acts of revenge, for he wants only to integrate into 'normal' society (Werner 1996: 31). So Hans initially reacts almost as any normal German would to the situation he finds in the dacha: he tries to rationalise these terrible events and in the end decides to free the imprisoned guard in order to protect his father from the irrationality of his own actions. But before he can implement his plan he discovers the dead body of his father alongside the bed of the captive. Bronstein's heart was unable to survive the strains of the preceding weeks.

These incidents are all narrated retrospectively by Hans, for he is trying to recapitulate, and so to rationalise, the events of the previous year surrounding the death of his father. In the course of his narrative, however, it is precisely his sense of identity as a German which is undermined as he reflects on his present situation. Through this specific narrator, Becker in turn reflects on the difficulties, even so long after the event, facing children of Jewish victims of the Holocaust in adjusting to life in Germany and trying to live as 'Germans'. Despite himself, as it were, Hans develops a sense of Jewish identity above all *after* his father's death as he increasingly feels an outsider in the country in which he is a citizen. Moreover, his father's scorn for the 'deutschen Gesindel' (German rabble – BK 80) has raised certain questions to which he is unable to find answers: 'Several times during the course of this year I have been preoccupied with the question as to whether the people around me are really as terrible as father had claimed that time at Schwanenteich. [. . .] I still don't know the answer today' (BK 83).[52] Ultimately Hans feels compelled to admit that he himself is perhaps 'doch ein Opfer des Faschismus' (a victim of fascism after all) and simply 'will es nicht wahrhaben' (won't admit it – BK 224). Occasional irrational outbursts linked to his Jewishness are a characteristic of his behaviour before the death of his father too: when he strikes out at an unpleasant schoolfellow who is pressurising him, one of the sort 'die gern peinigen' (who like tormenting you), this bully with the 'aufseher-haften Blick' (look of a prison guard) becomes one in his mind with the other, earlier tormentor of the Jews in his father's dacha (BK 43). He is disturbed at the thought that his action in hitting this schoolboy might be a symptom of the same condition which has reached an advanced stage in his sister: Elle suffered so terribly during the war years that she later makes seemingly random, unmotivated attacks on strangers (men and women but never children) and has been committed to a psychiatric hospital. Hans's crisis of identity is deepened, too, by the remarks made by his ex-girlfriend Martha, also Jewish, as she points quite unambiguously to the reason for his peculiar behaviour: he is literally dumbfounded as far as the subject 'Judentum' is concerned:

> 'I've known for a long time that one can't discuss a certain subject with you', she said. 'Hardly does a word begin with "J" and you break out in a sweat. The real victims want continually to have commemoration days and put on memorial weeks and you want people to keep quiet about it. You imagine perhaps it's the opposite, but I'm telling you, it's to do with the same self-consciousness.' (BK 211)[53]

It is also never explained to the reader how Hans comes to have a Jewish girlfriend. During the course of the novel, then, the question of his possibly suppressed Jewish identity becomes increasingly apparent, above all in view of the silence and secrecy which prevails between father and son at critical moments.

There are, though, moments of sudden revelation of facts hitherto withheld which catch the reader by surprise, nowhere more so than on the evening when Hans returns to his room in the family appartment and hears the unusually loud voices of his father and his fellow abductors through the concealed, unused door between his own room and his father's (BK 218), of which Hans has made no mention up to now. He pushes a chest of drawers away from the door, lies on the floor. listens through a tiny gap between the door and its frame and discovers to his surprise that his father, Arno, can speak Yiddish:

> The first words that I heard made it clear why they did not need to speak quietly: they were speaking in Yiddish. It was incomprehensible to me that father could make himself understood in this language. I tried to make myself believe it was a stranger sitting there with father's voice. Not only had he avoided speaking Yiddish in my presence up to now, he had never even intimated that he was capable of speaking it. He spoke without any clumsiness, without stuttering, as if the language had flown to him from one moment to

the next. I found that dreadful, I felt betrayed. He spoke louder than the others so that I wondered whether he was probably counting on my listening and wanted to betray his secret to me in this way. Never before was I so against him. (BK 221)[54]

Though Hans himself knows a handful of Yiddish words from the few which his father and his friends have used now and again, the idea of using them himself in conversation would be entirely alien: 'Scattering a few Yiddish words in a conversation would have seemed to me like some intrusive kind of folklore' (BK 222).[55] Yet as he listens, he makes another, even more astonishing discovery: that with a little effort, he can gradually understand it. However, it is a process not of acquisition but rather of breaking down resistance to something already inherent in him:

> I found the sound of the language unpleasant, not simply just strange as is normally the case with foreign languages; this one bordered on the comprehensible, and I continually had the feeling of only having to strain myself a little to grasp the sense. Perhaps they were speaking Yiddish together because they believed that this language was particularly appropriate for the matter concerning them.
>
> I needed some time to get used to overcoming my resistance to the inelegant, ugly sounds; then I was surprised how many of the words were comprehensible. At first I did not pay attention to the coherence of the words; I let them flow past and just registered the ones easily understood. I did not begin actually to understand until the distance between these became smaller.
>
> The result astounded me: they were not talking about the abduction, they were talking about the past, about the war and the camps. (BK 222)[56]

This is the moment in the text when suddenly and momentarily the Jew within Hans surfaces through the language of the Jews. It is a language which, in this situation in post-war Germany, be it east or west, marks the speakers out as both Jews and victims, for significantly, the subject which they are discussing is not (as Hans expects) the abduction of the camp-guard, but a topic about which his father is usually silent, namely the past. This change in his father's usual behaviour 'baffles' Hans, for normally his father cannot stand 'Lagergeschichten' (tales about the camps – BK 223). Is it language itself, then, which is capable of modifying the identity of the speaker? This is a question neither directly posed nor confronted by Hans, of course: his assertion that he is too weary for the subject of their conversation (BK 223) betrays his need immediately 'to feel like the German he has always believed himself to be' (Gilman 1991: 266), for sleep turns out to be not a natural succumbing to weariness but a conscious decision to escape from the 'Potpourri der Leiden' (potpourri of suffering) in the next room which Hans can still hear in bed: 'I fell asleep, but not by mistake: I decided in favour of the better alternative' (BK 223).[57]

On other occasions, too, the Bronstein in Hans is in the ascendancy. When he first learns who Heppner is, his prejudgement of the concentration camp guard is betrayed in his observation that Heppner's face 'miraculously' conceals the evidence of the horrors in which he has taken part (BK 24). His latent aggression towards Heppner comes out when the latter expresses regret but no feeling of personal responsibility for the horrific events of the past, and Hans tightens the leather strap around his ankles 'with all his might' (BK 103). And when Heppner finally tries to offer him his life savings as a bribe to release him, Hans relishes the thought of Heppner's money justly going to the son of a Jewish victim, which almost tempts him to accept (BK 105). There are even moments when Hans wishes to 'belong', to be one of the three Jewish accomplices (BK 187), with his confusion about his identity nowhere more apparent than in the final scene of the novel when he goes to set Heppner free and is torn between 'entgegengesetzten Wünschen' ('diamatrically opposed desires' – BK 296), between those of the Jew in him who wants to keep Heppner manacled, and those of the German who wants to set him free and be rid of the Jewish past. His actions reflect the psychological *impasse*: even though he knows that there is a key in his dead father's pocket, he uses a file first on the seemingly indestructible steel handcuffs and then on the heavy iron bedpost to which they are attached.

Hans's attempt at 'Vergangenheitsbewältigung' (overcoming the past) ultimately fails, for his goal of remembering with precision in order to be able to 'remove the past from his memory' (BK 15) proves an impossible one. This failure is anticipated in two incidents which take place during the year after his father's death, both of which demonstrate that the past can never be eradicated. The first features an image employed elsewhere by Becker as a metaphor for memory (in: Heidelberger-Leonard 1992: 25): when sorting out a box of family mementoes, Hans poses the question whether starting a new life entails destroying the box and its contents, but has to answer in the negative, for this would simple perpetuate 'das alte Leben' (his old life – BK 255). The second incident involves an old school exercise-book into which Hans has copied details about Heppner from the latter's own notebook just a few days before his father's death and which, after some deliberation, Hans does destroy, tearing it into the tiniest shreds, but to no avail for he is unable to destroy the information in his own head (BK 256). Though he wants only to be rid of Heppner (BK 261), he realises that he cannot obliterate the man simply by destroying the things with which he is associated (BK 261).

Do these major themes, the inescapable repercussions of the past, Hans's denial of his Jewishness and his confusion about his identity, point, then, after all to central characteristics of Becker's own complex psyche? Is Hans really Becker in disguise, as several critics have suggested? Here the answer must still be no, because despite several parallel autobiographical features, Becker is not speaking through his character Hans. As we have established above, a character such as Hans represents just one of various possible views of life, not the author's own. Indeed, in terms of age, Hans's sister Elle is much closer to Becker. Exactly twice Hans's age (thirty-eight), his mentally disturbed sister represents another variation on the theme of Jewish-German identity. In the novel, Elle serves as a foil for the tensions between father and brother and makes her presence felt through her letters which, printed in full, are 'a syntactically eccentric mixture of insight and whimsical delusion and provide oblique and eerie comment on the central events of the novel' (Kane 1991: 172). In her letters, Becker indulges in linguistic outbursts of a poetic intensity absent in his work both hitherto and hereafter. For Hannes Krauss, these letters are 'a pointer to the secret desires of the author which this character transports' (Hermand and Mattenklott 1988: 144).[58] More specifically, they represent Becker's attempt to indulge in the linguistic experiments of an Arno Schmidt, yet not directly for, as we noted above, with such attempts he usually had the feeling that he was 'just pretending' (W 12). He could only permit himself such poetic outbursts in the German (foreign?) language via a fictitious character such as Elle, via one of the many roles which he played with such sovereign mastery in his novels and stories.

Notes

1. Sander Gilman argues, surely erroneously, that Becker creates the impression of the speaking Jew for the German reader 'through the conscious absence of any Yiddishisms' (Gilman 1991: 259).

2. 'Und wenn nicht bald nach meiner Geburt die deutsche Wehrmacht gekommen wäre, wenn sie das Land nicht besetzt und meine Eltern und mich in ein Ghetto und später in verschiedene Konzentrationslager

gesteckt hätte, wenn die Rote Armee nicht das Lager Sachsenhausen, wo ich zuletzt weilte, befreit hätte, dann möchte ich selber nicht wissen, als was und vor wem ich heute stehen würde.'

3. 'Hätte er nicht nach Brooklyn auswandern können, wo aus mir vielleicht ein amerikanischer Schriftsteller geworden wäre? Oder nach Buenos Aires oder; was ja nicht ganz an den Haaren herbeigezogen ist, nach Tel Aviv? Aber nein, er entschied sich für die in meinen Augen exotischste aller Möglichkeiten, er blieb hier, bezog eine Wohnung wenige S-Bahnstationen vom Lagereingang entfernt und richtete sich so ein, daß ich Deutscher wurde.'

4. 'Haben die polnischen Antisemiten den Krieg verloren oder die deutschen?'

5. 'wo alte Nazis wie Globke und Oberländer wieder Karriere machen konnten.'

6. 'daß die Antifaschisten dort das Kommando hatten. Und wenn jemand es wagte, das Verhalten *seiner* Russen oder die Zustände in ihrem Stück Deutschland zu kritisieren, dann hielt er ihn entweder für einen Nörgler oder für einen Feind.'

7. 'Es war im Sprachumfang eines Vierjährigen steckengeblieben, denn in diesem Alter wurde ich Umständen ausgesetzt, in denen Sprache so gut wie überflüßig war.'

8. 'gleichsam im Handumdrehen [. . .] von einem Tag zum nächsten. [. . .] So mußte ich einige Zeit buchstäblich sprachlos leben.'

9. 'das Resultat einer organisierten Anstrengung'. [. . .] 'Es war für mich beinahe eine Existenzfrage, so schnell wie möglich mein Deutsch zu verbessern: Je eher ich die Fehler ausmerzte, um so seltener würden die anderen darauf gestoßen, daß ich ein Fremder war. Und wenn die Fehler ganz und gar aufhörten, würden sie mich eines Tages, wenn auch fälschlicherweise, sogar für einen der ihren halten.'

10. 'Der Umstand, daß ich erst mit acht Jahren Deutsch zu lernen anfing, könnte verantwortlich dafür sein, daß mein Verhältnis zu dieser Sprache ein ziemlich exaltiertes wurde. So wie andere Kinder meines Alters sich für Maikäfer oder Rennautos interessierten und sie von allen Seiten betrachteten, so drehte ich und wendete Wörter und Sätze. In einer extrem intensiven Beschäftigung mit der Sprache sah ich das einzige Mittel, dem Spott und den Nachteilen zu entkommen, die sich daraus ergaben, daß ich als einziger Achtjähriger weit und breit nicht richtig sprechen konnte.'

11. 'Regeln verletzen, die Sprache zerbrechen, wie um nachzusehen, was drin ist. Das liegt mir nicht, und wenn ich es doch versuche, habe ich das Empfinden, mich zu verstellen.'

12. 'Ich komme mir nicht zu Hause inmitten all dieser merkwürdigen Wörter und Konstruktionen und Andeutungen vor. Ich will nicht sagen, daß ich mich unwohl darin fühle, das nicht. Doch es fehlen mir Vertrautheit und eine Sicherheit, die zum "Zu-Hause-Sein" wohl gehören und die ich dann und wann bei anderen zu bemerken meine. Ich dagegen muß ständig auf der Hut sein.'

13. 'wenn ich etwas gesagt habe, war's, als hätte ich ein Transparent über dem Kopf getragen: "ich bin ein Anderer." '

14. 'Meine Muttersprache ist Polnisch. Alle Erinnerungen, die ich habe, sind Polnisch. Ich habe nach dem Krieg Deutsch gelernt und Polnisch schnell vergessen. Wahrscheinlich habe ich mit dem Vergessen der Sprache einen Großteil der Informationen, die in dieser Sprache abgespeichert waren, vergessen.' Becker offered a different explanation of his lack of memories in his earlier essay 'Mein Judentum': 'First of all, the unusually late start of my memories must have something to do with repression. A protective mechanism, the presence of which is certainly a stroke of good fortune, might be separating me from a dreadful period and thus be protecting me from it' ('Zum ersten muß der eigenartig späte Beginn meiner Erinnerungen etwas mit Verdrängung zu tun haben. Ein Schutzmechanismus, dessen Vorhandensein wohl ein Glück ist, könnte mich von einer schlimmen Zeit trennen und so in gewisser Weise vor ihr bewahren') (Heidelberger-Leonard 1992: 16).

15. 'Ich war als Kind in einem Konzentrationslager. Ich habe kaum Erinnerungen daran, und es handelt sich wohl um die einschneidendste unter allen meinen Erfahrungen. Das, was daraus geworden ist, aus meiner Familie, aus mir und aus einem Land, hat mich lange auf obsessive Weise beschäftigt.'

16. 'irgendwie Kaspar Hauser: ich war in diese Welt gefallen mit acht Jahren. Und keiner hat mir erzählt, bis auf ganz dürftige Informationen, was ich für einer bin und was mit mir los ist und wo ich herkomme. [. . .] Wenn du nicht weißt, wo du herkommst, ist es ein wenig so, als ob du ein Leben lang mit einem Rucksack rumläufst [. . .], ohne zu wissen was da drin ist. Das ist ein sehr unangenehmer Zustand, und die Beschäftigung damit ist fast schon eine lebenslängliche Beschäftigung – die Bemühung rauszukriegen, was in diesem Sack drin ist, den ich auf dem Rücken habe.'

17. 'Ich wollte etwas genauer wissen. Was das Ghetto für ein Ding ist, das wußte ich nach dem Buch natürlich viel besser als vorher. Vorher war das Ghetto für mich ein unheimliches, bedrohliches, schwarzes Ding in meinem Kopf. Und ich habe mich so lange damit beschäftigt,

bis das etwas geworden ist, wo Leute drin gewohnt haben, von denen mit Bestimmtheit ich einer gewesen bin'.

18. 'Ich wurde nur fähig, einen Dialog zwischen uns zu erfinden, ein Verhältnis, wie ich es mir gewünscht hätte.' The dialogues between the paternal Aron and the young writer who interviews him in *Der Boxer* touch on the issues which Becker's own father refused to discuss.

19. 'weil schon so lästig oft über meinem Kopf entschieden wurde, was und wie ich bin: unter anderem eben Jude.'

20. 'Wenn es keinen Antisemitismus geben würde – denkst du, ich hätte mich auch nur eine Sekunde als Jude gefühlt?'

21. 'Jurek Becker kann einfach gut erzählen. Er schöpft aus dem Vollen; die jüdische (jiddische) Tradition mag da mit hereinspielen.'

22. 'So bewährt sich in der prononcierten Mündlichkeit von Beckers Werk nicht zuletzt ein prägendes Element jüdischer Identität.'

23. 'Richtig ist, daß ich nach dem Krieg auf Erzählen getrimmt worden bin. [. . .] Da war keine große Gemeinde, der ich angehört hatte, in der das so Gang und Gäbe gewesen wäre. Aber mein Vater und seine Freunde, die nach Hause kamen zu uns, waren ähnlichen Gewohnheiten und Traditionen gefallen. Das mündliche Erzählen spielte für mich, seit ich ein Kind war, eine Rolle.'

24. 'Zum Geschichtenerzählen [. . .] gehört [. . .] eine bestimmte Haltung, auch eine bestimmte Lust.'

25. The story was written in 1978 in the USA (letter to me, 15.12.1993).

26. 'Einmal sagte mein Vater: Gideon war schon ein sehr alter Mann, als sie ihn nach Maidanek brachten, aber trotzdem.'

27. 'Das ist ja eine Geschichte, die von lauter Leuten handelt, die in Maidanek oder Auschwitz vergast worden sind, bis auf mich [. . .] den Erzähler.'

28. 'Die Kunst, der Trauer einen heiteren Klang zu geben und gerade darin die Erinnerung an Verhöhnung und Vernichtung zu bewahren.'

29. In the story, the child's mother has 'kein Gesicht mehr [. . .] nur noch eine Stimme' (no face any longer [. . .] just a voice – NZ 63). Becker said that he himself had no recollection of his mother's face, only 'akustische Erinnerungen [. . .] das jüngere Kind in der Geschichte war ich' (acoustic recollections [. . .] the younger child in the story was me – personal interview, 1991).

30. 'Es sollten mir keine plumpen Fehler unterlaufen, ich wollte die Abweichungen sozusagen komponieren.'

31. See the Introduction and also my edition, *Jurek Becker Five Stories* (1993). The evacuation of the family in 'Die Mauer' echoes the fate

of the Jews in most ghettos, but not in Lodz, where families were split up and most children deported in a barbaric way. See also Loewy and Schoenberner 1990: 280. Annegret Mannion is therefore not strictly correct when she speaks of a 'five-year-old boy living in a camp near Lodz' ('fünfjährigen Jungen, der in einem Lager bei Lodz lebt'), in: Graf and Konietzky 1991: 11.

32. 'Ich kann die Greuel nicht darstellen, ich bin kein Historiker.'
33. 'Ich kann mich an nichts erinnern. [. . .] Dennoch habe ich Geschichten über Gettos geschrieben, als wäre ich ein Fachmann. Vielleicht habe ich gedacht, wenn ich lange genug schreibe, werden die Erinnerungen schon kommen. Vielleicht habe ich auch irgendwann angefangen, manche meiner Erfindungen für Erinnerung zu halten. [. . .] Ohne Erinnerungen an die Kindheit zu sein, das ist, als wärst du verurteilt, ständig eine Kiste mit dir herumzuschleppen, deren Inhalt du nicht kennst. Und je älter du wirst, um so schwerer kommt sie dir vor, und um so ungeduldiger wirst du, das Ding endlich zu öffnen. [. . .] Ich starre auf die Bilder und suche mir die Augen wund nach dem alles entscheidenden Stück meines Lebens. Aber nur die verlöschenden Leben der anderen sind zu erkennen, wozu soll ich von Empörung oder Mitleid reden, ich möchte zu ihnen hinabsteigen und finde den Weg nicht.'
34. 'Mein Gott, ich bin fünf Jahre alt, wir Juden sind wieder ein stilles Glück. Der Nachbar heißt wieder Olmo und schreit den ganzen Tag mit seiner Frau, und wer nichts besseres zu tun hat, der kann sich hinter die Tür stellen und jedes Wort hören. Und die Straße hat wieder ihre Häuser, in jedem ist etwas geschehen mit mir.'
35. 'Ich habe keinen Zweifel, daß wir bald erschossen werden, das war uns klar von Anfang an.'
36. 'Ein kleiner Teil des Gettos – und das hat mit Erinnerung nichts zu tun, es ist die Wahrheit – ein kleiner Teil des Ghettos ist wie ein Lager.' Although the narrator claims this detail to be the truth, there is no historical record of such a transit camp in the Lodz Ghetto – the closest recorded parallel was a special camp for the gipsies located at the edge of the Jewish Ghetto (cf. the introduction to Dobroszycki 1984).
37. 'Eine dritte Möglichkeit ist: [. . .] Ich erinnere mich oder ich verinnere mich, d.h. ich erinnere mich falsch. Das falsche sich Erinnern ist eine besonders reiche Quelle.'
38. In her otherwise excellent essay, Irene Heidelberger-Leonard overlooks this earlier example of Becker's 'Solidaritätsbekenntnis zu seinen jüdischen Leidensgenossen' (profession of solidarity with his Jewish fellow-sufferers (Arnold 1992: 20)).

39. 'Wenn ich dein Vater bin, dann bist du mein . . .?' / Zum erstenmal mißachtete Mark die Regeln eines Verhörs, er antwortete nicht, sondern zuckte mit den Schultern. Unter dem weißen Hemd, sagt Aron, das bis dahin leer auf dem Bett zu liegen schien, bewegten sich die Schultern auf und ab. / 'Dann bist du mein Sohn', sagte Aron. 'Verstehst du?' / 'Nein.' / Für Minuten war es Aron unbegreiflich, was Mark daran nicht verstehen mochte, die Direktorin hatte mit keinem Wort erwähnt, daß er auch *meschugge* war. Er sagte: 'Was verstehst du nicht?' / 'Dieses Wort.' / 'Welches Wort?' / 'Was Sie gesagt haben.' / 'Sohn?' / 'Ja.' / 'Das ist ganz leicht', sagte Aron. 'Ich bin dein Vater, und du bist mein Sohn. Das sind einfach die Worte dafür. Verstehst du jetzt?' / 'Ja.' / 'Dann sag es noch einmal.' / 'Sie sind mein Vater,' sagte Mark, 'und ich bin Ihr Sohn.' / 'Richtig. Aber du mußt nicht Sie zu mir sagen, sondern du. Sag noch einmal: Du bist mein Vater.' / 'Du bist mein Vater.' / 'Ich bin dein Sohn.' / 'Du bist mein Sohn.' / 'Nein, das ist falsch', sagte Aron. / Plötzlich begann Mark zu weinen.

40. 'ein Junge mit schwach ausgeprägtem Mitteilungsbedürfnis'.

41. 'Was das überhaupt sei, fragt er mich, ein Jude, was denn anderes als ein Glaubensbekenntnis? Ob wir nicht endlich in einer Zeit lebten, fragt er, in der jeder für sich allein entscheiden könne, in welcher Partei er Mitglied zu sein wünsche? Ob er Türke sei oder Deutscher, darauf habe er natürlich keinen Einfluß, aber auch nicht darauf, ob er Christ sei oder Jude? Ein Kind katholischer Eltern könne mit Beginn der Volljährigkeit frei entscheiden, ob es ebenfalls Katholik sein wolle oder nicht. Warum man, fragt er mich, den Kindern jüdischer Eltern das gleiche Recht verweigere?'

42. See, for instance, Volker Wehdeking, '*Der Boxer* und die übermächtige Vergangenheit', in Heidelberger-Leonard 1992: 227.

43. 'seine Identität nach seiner biologischen Herkunft und dem Glauben seiner Eltern zu definieren [. . .] aus jüdischer Sicht [. . .] eine typisch assimilatorische Tendenz'.

44. 'durch den Schreibakt eine neue Identität zu finden, [. . .] anstelle seiner alten, die er auszulöschen wünschte'.

45. 'Zwischen meines Vaters und meinem Zimmer gab es eine nie benutzte Tür, die von seiner Seite mit einem Bücherregal und von meiner Seite mit einem Kleiderschrank verstellt war.'

46. 'Beckers "Judenromane" sind [. . .] nicht bekenntnishafte Autobiographie, sondern Modelle und Typisierungen.'

47. 'Grunderfahrungen des Autors werden in freier literarischer Fiktion gestaltet.'

48. 'Ausgangspunkt fürs Nachdenken über die eigene Geschichte'.

49. 'Ich vermute, daß man sich von Ereignissen, die aus dem Gedächtnis entfernt werden sollen, zunächst ein möglichst genaues Bild machen muß.'

50. 'Wenn wir alles andere vorher vergessen wollten, würden wir nie mehr zum Leben kommen.'

51. 'Kein Mensch hatte mich gelehrt, Widerstand zu leisten, niemand hatte mir gezeigt, wie man das macht, was man für richtig hält.'

52. 'Manchmal in diesem Jahr hat mich die Frage beschäftigt, ob die Leute um mich herum tatsächlich so furchtbar sind, wie Vater damals am Schwanenteich behauptet hatte. [. . .] Noch heute weiß ich keine Antwort.'

53. 'Ich weiß seit langem, daß man über ein bestimmtes Thema mit dir nicht reden kann', sagte sie. 'Kaum fängt ein Wort mit Jot an, bricht dir der Schweiß aus. Die wirklichen Opfer wollen andauernd Gedenktage feiern und Mahnwachen aufstellen, und du willst, daß geschwiegen wird. Du bildest dir vielleicht ein, das wäre das Gegenteil, aber ich sage dir: es handelt sich um dieselbe Befangenheit.'

54. 'Die ersten Worte, die ich hörte, machten mir klar, warum sie es nicht nötig hatten, leise zu sein: sie redeten Jiddisch. Es war unfaßbar, daß Vater sich in dieser Sprache verständigen konnte, ich wollte glauben, dort säße ein Fremder mit Vaters Stimme. Er hatte es bisher nicht nur vermieden, in meiner Gegenwart Jiddisch zu sprechen, er hatte auch nie angedeutet, daß er dazu imstande war. Er redete ohne Unbeholfenheit, ohne Stocken, von einem Augenblick zum nächsten war ihm die Sprache zugeflogen. Ich fand das schaurig, ich fühlte mich betrogen. Er redete lauter als die anderen, so daß ich mich fragte, ob er wohl mit meinem Lauschen rechnete und mir auf diese Weise sein Geheimnis verraten wollte. Nie zuvor war ich so gegen ihn.'

55. 'Jiddische Vokabeln in eine Unterhaltung einzustreuen, das wäre mir wie eine aufdringliche Art von Folklore vorgekommen.'

56. 'Der Klang der Sprache war mir unangenehm, nicht einfach nur fremd wie bei gewöhnlichen Fremdsprachen; diese bewegte sich dicht an der Grenze zum Verständlichen, und ich hatte fortwährend das Gefühl, mich nur ein wenig anstrengen zu müssen, um den Sinn zu erfassen. Vielleicht redeten sie deshalb Jiddisch miteinander, weil sie glaubten, diese Sprache paßte zu ihrer Angelegenheit besonders gut. / Ich brauchte eine Eingewöhnungszeit, um meinen Widerstand gegen die anmutlosen, verwachsenen Töne zu überwinden; dann wunderte ich mich, wie viele der Wörter verständlich waren. Zunächst achtete ich nicht auf den Zusammenhang, ich ließ die Wörter vorbeiziehen

und registrierte nur die sinnfälligen. Erst als deren Abstand immer kürzer wurde, begann ich mit dem Verstehen. / Das Resultat verblüffte mich: sie sprachen nicht von der Entführung, sie sprachen von ihrer Vergangenheit, von Krieg und Lager.'

57. 'ich schlief ein, doch nicht versehentlich: ich entschied mich für die bessere Möglichkeit.'

58. 'ein Hinweis auf verborgene Wünsche des Autors, die diese Figur transportiert'.

After the Initial Future: Becker's GDR Writing and his Break With the GDR

From Loyalty to Recalcitrance

Even in the early 1970s, Jurek Becker still saw his future as a writer lying in the GDR. At that time he was a convinced socialist and firmly believed in the notion of a socialist literature whose role was to improve GDR society through constructive criticism: 'to consolidate the GDR and make the socialism which we practise more practical' (*Deutsche Zeitung*, 15.3.1974).[1] Yet his GDR works of the 1970s increasingly gave the lie to this belief, with Becker himself acknowledging to me in 1991: 'My texts are more intelligent than I am';[2] and in an interview shortly before his death, he expressed his doubt as to whether he had 'ever been a GDR writer' in the truest sense, adding: 'In the GDR, I was very politically involved as a person, but I never saw my books as vehicles for transporting my views to the reader' (Riordan 1998: 20).[3]

During his early years in the GDR, Becker's positive response to the society around him, what he described as his 'feeling of being involved in a venture which I considered rewarding', was hardly surprising, considering his experiences during his early childhood and youth. By 1992, though, he was of the opinion that he had 'considered this venture rewarding for too long' (Heidelberger-Leonard 1992: 108).[4] Yet his original socialist convictions are entirely understandable and attributable above all to the influence of his father. The sole adult survivor of a once 'unübersehbare' (vast) Jewish family, as Becker described it in 'Mein Judentum', his father had been liberated from Auschwitz by the Soviet army, and until his death in 1972 he consequently held to his view of the Soviet liberators of Auschwitz as 'the goodies, the bringers of salvation. I was brought up by him with this background' (Heidelberger-Leonard 1992: 106),[5] commented Becker in 1992.

Reunited with his father by the relief organisation UNRAA, the little boy was to become, by the mid-1970s, one of the most prominent of a younger generation of GDR writers, and certainly one of the most well known internationally. In 1973 he was elected to the executive committee of the Writers' Union and won the GDR National Prize in 1975. Both his novel *Jakob der Lügner* and its extremely successful film version had established his international reputation, winning him several prizes in both East and West, as we have seen.

Then in 1976 things suddenly changed: Becker's name became associated with opposition to hard-line trends in GDR cultural policy. In October 1976 he had been one of the few prominent GDR writers to speak out in public on behalf of Reiner Kunze, after the latter had been expelled from the Writers' Union for committing the cardinal sin of publishing in West Germany a work which was highly critical of the GDR (*Die Wunderbaren Jahre*, The wonderful years – 1976). Becker was also one of the twelve leading intellectuals who signed the open letter to Honecker protesting against the expatriation of Wolf Biermann. Becker became one of the most vociferous sympathisers with Biermann and was consequently ejected from the SED and from the Executive of the Berlin Writers' Union, to which he had also been elected. Far from indulging in public self-criticism, an action which would probably have led to his reinstatement, he rounded on the Party and then resigned from the Writers' Union in spring 1977 as a further act of protest. His next novel, *Schlaflose Tage*, was rejected by the censors: Klaus Höpke, Deputy Minister for Culture, justified this action by arguing that in his novel the author had dealt with the Western theme of midlife crisis and also broken a sacred GDR taboo by having his heroine attempt to escape from the GDR. In response to this official rejection of his latest work, Becker applied to leave the GDR and received a special visa, valid up to 1990, which allowed him to travel freely between the GDR and the Federal Republic. He was thus one of a very small number of privileged GDR citizens who were able to cross the border between East and West unimpeded.

Becker's statements written after the demise of the GDR, though, clearly indicated that over the years he had been moving slowly but surely towards the ultimately critical stance which he adopted *vis-à-vis* 'actually existing' socialism in the GDR. In 1992 (Heidelberger-Leonard 1992: 108–12), for instance, he explained that the seeds of his disillusionment dated back to 1956 when was in the National People's Army, where he acquired an aversion to the sort of blind obedience which he later lampooned in stories such as 'Allein mit dem Anderen' and 'Der Fluch der Verwandtschaft'. He was also expelled from university in 1960 for getting into trouble with the Party after petitioning for a lecture course to be discontinued, only to discover that the professor who gave the course was a member of the Central Committee of the SED. Yet he still remained publicly loyal to the Party in the early years, and he regarded any disagreements with the Party as problems to be 'kept to ourselves', difficulties experienced by those of like mind which were not for public consumption beyond the confines of the Party meeting (Arnold 1992: 9). He did, though, have the courage to protest at actual Party gatherings where fierce arguments often took place, but later realised that this was all a 'Ventil' (release-valve) deliberately permitted by the Party.

As with other former GDR writers, the first critical point in Becker's relationship with the GDR came, eight years before the Biermann episode, with the invasion of Czechoslovakia by Warsaw Pact troops, an event which brought about a severe crisis in relations between many writers and the state. Suddenly Becker's loyalty was overtaken by these political events, which he described as a 'sort of caesura' in his relationship with the GDR (Arnold 1992: 9), feeling that any basis for loyalty had now been severely damaged if not destroyed (Heidelberger-Leonard 1992: 112). Any previous acquiescence in an intolerant system gradually changed into a position of critical defiance, and the following eight years were a period of 'perpetual nagging and moaning', as he put it, during which Becker, in the relatively protected position which his international reputation gave him, felt increasingly obliged to 'open his mouth' and speak out on controversial issues (Heidelberger-Leonard 1992: 112).

Jakob der Lügner as a Subversive Novel

The signs of his later recalcitrance are visible. though, even in his earliest novels, which increasingly called into question the sacred cows of GDR ideology. Indeed, in an interview in 1992, Becker implied that his own writing was, from the outset, motivated by discontent and disagreement: 'I am convinced that the most important impetus for writing literature is dissatisfaction, some sort of disagreement with things. That was of course no different in the GDR than it is anywhere else in the world' (Arnold 1992: 8).[6]

We have noted Becker's suspicion that he may have written his first novel *Jakob der Lügner* partly in reaction to the 'resistance literature' in fashion in the GDR, which he regarded as an historical distortion since examples of actual resistance were the exception to the rule. This becomes an actual theme in the novel as the narrator looks back on Buchenwald and Warsaw 'mit Ehrfurcht' (with great respect), having to admit of his own ghetto: 'I will probably never come to terms with this. [. . .] Where I was, there was no resistance' (JL 99).[7] And, significantly, *Jakob der*

Lügner was initially criticised in the GDR for its defeatist tendencies, by Werner Neubert, for instance, in his article 'Wahrheitserpichter Lügner' (the liar keen on the truth) in *Neues Deutschland* (14.5.1969) : it was considered out of line with the anti-fascist tradition which required writing about the National Socialist period to feature heroic resistance against Nazi oppression as a main theme.

On the other hand, some West German critics have tended to share Peter Hanenberg's view that the narrator of *Jakob der Lügner* is himself a hero when the novel is considered in the context of the place and time of its narration (namely, the GDR of the late 1960s), 'because he knows how to narrate: [. . .] and resist the repressive mechanisms of two German societies, one of which preferred to hear nothing, whilst the other was only prepared to hear of things heroic from that particular time' (in: Beisbart and Abraham 1992: 143).[8] Indeed, Becker has emphasised on several occasions that in writing *Jakob der Lügner* he was not interested in history, in fascism itself, but in its relationship to the present:

> I have to say, however, that fascism as a subject *per se* has never been of interest to me, nor just the history of the ghettoes. [. . .] A work of art has no point if its ideas start and end in the past. What is being narrated, regardless of whether it is taking place thirty or three hundred years ago, has to relate somehow or other to the present. (*Sonntag. Kulturpolitische Wochenzeitung*: 20.4.1975)[9]

The very title of the short story 'Die Mauer' (The wall), for instance, suggests historical parallels between the GDR and the Nazi period – the wall in question turns out not to be the one that German readers might have expected, but a wall which surrounds a transit camp in a Jewish ghetto.[10] In *Jakob der Lügner* and 'Die Mauer', the watch-towers, the closely guarded barbed-wire ghetto-fences and walls, and not least the orders to shoot on sight, evoke uncomfortable similarities with the state-borders of the GDR.

Becker suggested similar parallels between the past and the present when he commented in an interview in the USA in 1983 that the novel *Jakob der Lügner* could be viewed as a 'parable about the role of literature in our society' (*Seminar* 1983: 290), implying that, for Becker, literature itself, writing and storytelling, could function as a form of resistance in the GDR too, for he claimed that *Jakob der Lügner* was a novel about resistance, but not in the conventional GDR sense. Asked what he understood by resistance, he spoke about the importance of mental as well as physical survival: 'a lot of people I would say died mentally'; and, evoking Orwellian images of the totalitarian super-state, he argued that mental survival implied the need to 'practise resistance [. . .] not to do what they want you to do. Not to behave in the way that Big Brother wants.' Jakob Heym himself, then, practises resistance, but his weapons are not guns but just words, as he explains to Professor Kirschbaum in answer to the latter's accusation that Jakob is irresponsibly exposing his fellow-Jews to danger by spreading his 'radio-news': 'And all that still isn't enough for you? And when I am trying to exploit the very last opportunity to keep them from just lying down and dying – with words, do you understand? I'm trying to do it with words! Because that is all I have!' (JL 194).[11] His fictitious radio is invented to supply the source of further life-sustaining fiction – stories, lies, which give hope to his desperate fellow-Jews and courage to resist Nazi oppression by not succumbing to its aim, their mental and physical destruction. And though physical resistance to physical oppression may be absent, Jakob counters psychological oppression with his own brand of psychological resistance. Lies, that is fiction, that is literature itself, thus take on the power to change and so transform reality in so far as Jakob's lies have their direct effect on life in the ghetto.

With its provocative parallels between Jakob's role within the ghetto community in relation to his fellow-Jews and the role of the narrator within the novel in relation to the reader,[12] *Jakob der Lügner* is thus a fundamentally subversive novel, as Oliver Sill has observed: 'The subversity of a work, which is directed at all forms of repressive state power, remained undetected by the censors' (Arnold 1992: 75).[13] As Irene Heidelberger-Leonard correctly comments, the main theme of the novel is also in accord with Becker's own biography and 'his existential difficulties: both the power and the impotence of the word, the power of literature, the power of narration. Narration as a strategy for survival' (Heidelberger-Leonard 1992: 197).[14]

Two Critical Novels

Becker's next two novels, *Irreführung der Behörden* (Misleading the authorities – 1973) and *Der Boxer* (The boxer – 1976), were written during the period of relaxed restrictions after 1971 under Honecker after he had declared that he wanted a literature without taboos. Though both are set in the GDR, both move emphatically away from Socialist Realism in content and form in a manner which disturbed some GDR critics. *Irreführung der Behörden* takes an ironical and critical look at aspects of cultural life in the GDR in the early 1970s and tackles a new theme for GDR literature: the author gradually exposes the insidious pressures on

Gregor Bienek, a young writer of some potential and originality, to conform. In order to get on at all as a writer, he has increasingly to produce the kind of literature which the Party wants, and the more Bienek unwittingly sacrifices his integrity to his career, the more he dishes up, as his wife puts it, 'old hat [. . .] which you polish up in your workshop with a bit of talent' (IB 248).[15]

New, too, and a challenge to the conventions of GDR Socialist Realist literature is the emphasis on aesthetic problems and on the subjective nature of human experience in both form and content. Thematically, the latter is announced at the start of the novel, when Bienek produces a story about a funeral, focusing on the mourners' divergent memories of the deceased: 'And what is more, it turned out that each one of them had buried a different man, for each had a different image of him in their memory, and you could no longer reconstruct any of them and say it was the right one' (IB 13).[16] The story is, of course, rejected by the publisher's editor because, he is told, 'the tracks which a person leaves behind are concrete and can be read unambiguously' (IB 13).[17] In certain ways, the frustrations which Gregor experiences with the 'authorities' mirror those of his author in the 1960s: Becker explained (letter to me: 4.8.1993) that three of Gregor's humorous stories (about two young lovers Toni and Rita who accept that Romantic dreams must inevitably become humdrum reality; about a man who sacrfices his unique assets to the common good but becomes 'toothless' in the process; and about three criminals whose frenetic road-building work in preparation for their next crime ironically turns them into socialist worker-heroes) were based on three of his own film scripts which had recently been turned down by the powers that be.

In *Irreführung der Behörden*, Becker also focuses the reader's attention on the form of the novel and on aesthetic problems through the constant interruptions of the first-person narrator and the provocative interpolation, between two lengthy 'Geschichten' (stories), of a very short diary-section headed 'Roman' (novel). Though the novel made an impact on its GDR readers, many orthodox GDR critics were predictably negative in their reaction to the idea of narration, the production of literature, becoming its own subject, and Klaus-Dieter Hähnel even accused Becker of demonstrating 'a tendency towards loss of reality', whereby 'the fictitious reality of art and the artist moves very far away from the real world' (Hähnel 1974: 149),[18] a criticism convincingly refuted by Philip Manger in his essay of 1981 (*Seminar*, 17: 147–63). On the other hand, seen from a Western point of view, it is precisely the qualities to which Hähnel and others objected which make the novel an early example of what Wilhelm Emmerich, in his history of the literature of the GDR, calls 'die neuere

DDR-Literatur' (modern GDR literature – Emmerich 1997: 239), which emerged in the early 1970s when writers broke with the convention of unconditional affirmation of 'actually existing socialism', criticising the repressive structure of GDR society and employing for this the techniques of European Modernism.

Der Boxer (see also Chapter 4), written in the form of a protocol of a series of interviews, gives an account of the ultimately insurmountable difficulties which a Jewish survivor of the concentration camps encounters in trying to lead an ordinary life again. The author explained his main reasons for writing about this particular theme in an interview which he gave in 1977: 'At the time, I had a desire to write a book about an outsider in my society, about someone indifferent to the goals of this society, whose relationship to it is neither intimate nor cool but completely non-existent' (Schwarz 1990: 125–6).[19] The novel not only gives the lie to naive assumptions that all outsiders could be integrated into the socialist society of the GDR; the author also casts doubt on the legitimacy of his young socialist narrator who interviews the Holocaust survivor, with the aim 'Aron Blank zu erkunden' (to find out all there is to know about Aron Blank – B 7), a favourite phrase with Socialist Realist writers. The latter resists the writer's attempt to categorise him and fit his unique experiences into some preconceived social-historical pattern, Aron's sarcastic comments recalling the notion of false images ('falsche Bilder') in *Andorra* by Max Frisch: 'I'm not telling you the history of the post-war period, I'm telling you what happened to me. [. . .] I can understand that you have a specific image of this and that you are concerned about similarities. But that's your problem' (B 93).[20] The narrator's final product, written down in five notebooks, is therefore rejected by Aron as the inadequate, over-simplified version of the life story which he has been telling him over the previous two years, and he points out 'That [. . .] what I tell you is one thing, and what you write, another' (B 10).[21] The aesthetic hegemony of Socialist Realism, with its claim to portray reality in a concrete, non-subjective way comprehensible and accessible to all, is firmly called into question as a narrative strategy inadequate for this particular 'material', namely the unique individuality of Aron Blank, who tells the young writer: 'If you really are hell-bent on being objective, then go and describe a football match' (B 32).[22] And Becker's anti-hero and social misfit Aron Blank is a challenge, too, to the typical, conventional exemplary heroes of Socialist Realism, such as Frau Traugott, the 'resettler' from the Sudetenland in Franz Fühmann's early story, 'Böhmen am Meer' (Bohemia by the sea), who, despite her mental scars from the past, finds her true home in the GDR, her 'Bohemia on the Baltic'.

Becker's Break with the GDR

The aforementioned works were, for all their controversial aspects, all published in the GDR, though *Irreführung der Behörden* only just made it, as Becker later confirmed (Graf and Konietzny 1991: 51). His next and fourth novel, though, was rejected for publication in the wake of the Biermann affair, which was the final 'Funke, der in einen Heuhaufen fiel' (spark which dropped into the haystack), as Becker stated some fourteen years later (he was unable to express such a view in 1977 for obvious tactical reasons): 'After that I saw only a very limited future for me in the GDR – but that is only a quarter of the truth. I saw not much future for me because I saw hardly any future for the whole country any more' (Heidelberger-Leonard 1992: 112).[23] Although these words were uttered in 1991 with the benefit of hindsight, the title of Becker's collection of short prose works *Nach der ersten Zukunft* (After the initial future), most of which were written between 1977 and 1979, evinces a similar sentiment, announcing in almost programmatic fashion the disappearance of his utopian hopes for the GDR – the implied 'second future' presumably lay elsewhere, for during the final years which he spent in the GDR, he had been 'a prisoner, entirely given up to being ruled by the pressure of people's expectations' (Graf and Konietzny 1991: 51).[24] The hero of *Schlaflose Tage* (Sleepless days) experiences a sudden awakening which he calls 'Lust auf Zukunft' ('desire for the future' – ST 27): this is a desire to overcome habitual ways of thinking and mechanical behaviour, to break out of his rigid conformist shell and enter into a dynamic state of constant change through self-reflection and then decision-making – implying, ultimately, a radical rejection of socialism as it actually exists in a society which the title suggests is 'asleep'.

Becker finally left the GDR in December 1977 after *Schlaflose Tage* had been rejected by the censor, never to appear in print in the GDR. The main reason for this was the fact that the author refused to make the necessary modifications to specific details required by the Ministry for Culture: as Uwe Eberhardt of Hinstorff Verlag explained to me (letter: 23.4.1994), there had been considerable political argument about several passages in the manuscript text:

> Thus it did not appear to be acceptable that the author allowed one of the characters in his novel to say that she had tried to escape from the GDR via Hungary because she believed that they would not be ready to open fire as quickly on Hungary's borders as they would in the GDR. This was evidently the main hurdle unable to be cleared at that time, because the author steadfastly refused to alter this and also other allegedly disparaging passages.[25]

Yet what interests the reader of today about *Schlaflose Tage* is not the business of spotting the details which led to the controversy with the censor, but the evidence that Becker's writing was undergoing a distinct change at this time. Indeed, Becker himself claimed in an interview in *Der Spiegel* in July 1977 'that in the last seven or eight months [his] identity [had] changed in some way or other'[26] after he, like several other GDR writers, had perceived the 'Verdrängungsmechanismus' (repressive mechanism) within himself and, as he put it, 'amputated' it (*Der Spiegel* 31, no. 30, 1977: 133); now any previous acquiescence in an intolerant system was replaced by an attitude of critical defiance, discernible in the unmistakably ironic tone of the explanation of his *impasse* with the GDR which he gave at the time:

> I want to stay in this country as someone who is able to publish what he writes; for in the long run, that is the only practicable method which a writer has to butt in and have his say. Mind you, if it is a question of keeping my mouth shut, then I prefer to keep my mouth shut in the Bahamas.[27]

A change of approach is discernible in his controversial novel *Schlaflose Tage* and particularly in the collection of shorter prose works *Nach der ersten Zukunft*,[28] in which the author gives us what Günter de Bruyn has called 'DDR-Innenansichten' (interior views of the GDR): Becker now focuses his gaze primarily on the psychology of his protagonists, the way they think, the minutiae of their inner lives, their 'Verdrängungsmechanismus' (repressive mechanism), as he called it. We witness their psychological reactions, as external constraints become internalised; thus we experience their fears, their feelings of guilt and repression, their crises of identity, but also their hopes and dreams. Hence, too, this inner life of individuals reflects the external influences to which they are exposed in the world outside – rigidly inflexible, oppressive GDR norms, strong socio-political compulsions, the constant pressure to conform.

In *Schlaflose Tage*, for instance, Becker demonstrates how external walls quite literally create internal walls, barriers within the mind. When, in the case of the schoolteacher Karl Simrock, intimations of mortality in the form of a mild heart tremor shortly after his thirty-sixth birthday trigger off a radical reappraisal of his existence, he becomes aware for the first time of his own internal captivity. He begins to question the easy existence which he has led hitherto and in which everything has already been decided for him by others. This GDR anti-hero speaks not only of breaking 'den Ring um mich herum' (the ring around me – ST 56), he discovers this 'ring' of constraints within himself, and feels the need to 'investigate whether a cleverly devised system of misjudgements, anxiety, idleness and self-deception is blocking access to the borders. Like a wall in the interior' (ST 28).[29]

The Influence of Kafka: Interior Views of the GDR

When I interviewed Jurek Becker in 1991, he admitted that he had been working on the novel and the stories at a time time when he was also making an intensive study of the work of a writer who had for many years been proscribed in the GDR: *Schlaflose Tage* and some of the stories had been written very much under the influence of Franz Kafka, as can be discerned not only in the narrative perspective of *Schlaflose Tage* (as Wieczorek 1990 has demonstrated), but also in thematic and structural elements of the novel and of some of the stories. The latter, for instance, echo in various ways Kafka's evocation of situations which leave no way out to people who nevertheless persist in efforts to escape. The pattern of Becker's plots also recalls those of Kafka: in 'Allein mit dem Anderen', for instance, an initial 'Störung' (disruption) triggers off a chain of events which follow a logic all of their own. And Kafka's influence is in evidence above all in Becker's approach to his subject-matter, the increasing emphasis on minute details already noted above. For Becker, the distinguishing characteristic of Kafka's writing is 'his proccupation with minutiae which other authors do not consider worth the trouble. And sometime or other, I realised that these minutiae were the real subject of literature' (Heidelberger-Leonard 1992: 102).[30] He found in Kafka, too, 'the profoundest, most astonishing insights into the true nature of a society, into the secret motives of human behaviour, into the way in which the individual is at the mercy of the many' (W 14).[31]

In many of the stories written in this period immediately before and just after he left the GDR, the influence of Becker's perceived Kafka model is discernible. The nature of the society in which the individuals live is reflected in the hidden motives of their behaviour, which is shown as being directly conditioned by the external social and political pressures to which they are exposed. The stories 'Allein mit dem Anderen' and 'Der Verdächtige', for instance, demonstrate the psychological dangers which threaten individuals who succumb to the pressures to conform. These dangers are usually loss of identity and an attendant sense of guilt. Yet Becker's characters are not Kafkaesque victims, for they succumb to states of anxiety which are brought on by their own timidity and cowardliness (the adjectives 'ängstlich', timid, and 'feige', cowardly, recur frequently) and which threaten them with internal disintegration. And by focusing on this disintegration of the individual personality in typical conformists and opportunists, Becker points in turn to the society of which they are representative as being, if not yet at a terminal stage, then at least in a state of serious decline. These narrative situations which he depicts are, then, concrete presentiments of the collapse of the GDR which ensued some ten years later.

A brief examination of these two stories will illustrate these points. Both have first-person narrators, with Becker adopting the roles of conformists in order to expose their cowardly mentality from the 'inside'. 'Allein mit dem Anderen' is a portrayal of a fragmented personality and demonstrates the individual's potential for psychological self-mutilation. A high-ranking state official explains how his cowardly subservience to the system has caused him to become divided against himself. His story is, in fact, a confession written from the point of view of one side of himself, the conformist side. This anxious conformist ascribes his feelings of 'Lustlosigkeit' (listlessness – NZ 211) precisely to his need always to fit in with what is expected of him and to his inability to behave in accordance with his own wishes. Feeling guilty about his hypocritical and contemptible behaviour, he decides that matters might be improved if he could actually increase the external pressures on him to behave in this way, for then he would no longer feel responsibility for his own actions and his sense of guilt would vanish. After an incident when he is robbed at gun-point, he realises that the weapon itself provides the tangible threat which he needs. He therefore steals a revolver from a police officer friend and uses it to compel himself to continue to act in a manner which he finds distasteful. He explains to the reader that he is able to do this thanks to his split personality, which enables him to play the part of others so comprehensively that his own self becomes virtually obliterated. The role-playing side of himself ('der Andere', the other one) now takes over completely from his normally dominant side and becomes the 'Befehlsgeber' (issuer of commands – NZ 218) in him. Despite a sense of oppression and anxiety (NZ 218), he believes that he has achieved a state of inner equilibrium, because he now has no option but to behave in the despicable way he does, otherwise he will be shot; this gives him peace of mind for a while. Moreover, being a 'yes-man' leads swiftly to promotion from middle- to high-ranking official, demonstrating how the socio-political system around him rewards dishonest behaviour.

After about a year, however, he begins to experience problems of identity which are rooted in his confusion about free will. Hence he fails to realise that his objective – to establish a situation in which he controls, but is not responsible for, his own behaviour – is not sustainable. His peace of mind lasts as long as the 'other' side of himself orders him to do what he does not really want to do but must do in order to get on. The trouble starts when the hitherto controlling side of himself suddenly loses control – without warning, the 'other' side of himself rebels, driving him to obey 'die unsinnigsten Befehle' (the most ridiculous commands – NZ 221) and to perform acts of insubordination. The 'other one', then, plays all sorts of comical pranks on him which lead to him to the verge of disaster, such as the command to write a report describing 'the entire department as useless and to suggest, indeed to demand, its liquidation' (NZ 223).[32] On the brink of career-threatening chaos, though, the 'other one' tells him to tear up the letter, explaining that it was all only a joke. 'Our views of humour were miles apart',[33] comments the narrator (NZ 225).

By the end of the story, the two opposing wills within him have led to stalemate and a feeling of helplessness. The official is now standing at the edge of a lake with the gun to his head, the situation 'ein auswegloses Verhängnis' (a disaster with no way out – NZ 226). The previously dominant side of the official tries to rid himself of the 'revolver-man', as he calls this side of himself, by getting rid of his weapon, but is unable to act for fear that his *alter ego* will pull the trigger before he can throw the revolver in the lake – because the 'other one' has precise knowledge of his every thought, he is no longer able even to think without terrible consequences: 'But before I've had a chance to think in the way that I'd like to, I've had it' (NZ 226).[34] He is trapped, physically as well as mentally, but has at least recognised that his imprisonment is self-inflicted, as he admits at the start of his story: 'I'm the victim of my own behaviour and nobody has forced me' (NZ 211).[35]

As well as focusing on the intricacies of the protagonist's psyche, Becker is questioning two key concepts of Marxist thought in 'Allein mit dem Anderen': freedom and alienation. The entire story revolves around a contradictory notion which had become an everyday saying in the GDR: 'freiwilliger Zwang' (voluntary compulsion), an ironic echo of Engels's idea of 'Einsicht in die Notwendigkeit' (insight into necessity) in his definition of the 'Dialektik von Notwendigkeit und Freiheit' (dialectic of necessity and freedom – *DDR Handbuch* 1979: 706). In his story, Becker exposes the psychological implications of this view for the individual: the narrator's confusion about the notion of free will leads to loss of identity and alienation.

Moreover, Becker demonstrates that the other related contributory factor in causing the individual to become divided against himself and so lose his sense of identity is subservience to the very system which is meant to eradicate alienation. The narrator's alienation has its roots in the public function which he performs within the system. Even in private moments, the role which he plays is so difficult to discard that he loses sight of his true self: 'When I finally turn the light out in the evening and tell myself I don't need to play-act any more until tomorrow morning, then sometimes I don't even know myself how I am to be' (NZ 212).[36]

In the other story, 'Der Verdächtige', Becker shows us another character completely alone with himself, and now, in a state whose former head Ulbricht once boasted 'Bei uns bleibt niemand allein' (in our country no one is alone), the state itself is the cause of his isolation, for the external pressure in question to which this character is exposed is the obsession of the authorities with 'die Sicherheit des Staates' (the security of the state – NZ 259). When a loyal servant of the state becomes convinced that, in all probability, he himself is under surveillance by the 'Auge des Staates' (eye of the state – NZ 259), as he calls it, he attempts to become inconspicuous and so avoid arousing any further suspicion. In this way, too, he hopes he may 'remove' the original suspicion: 'then it would have to be abandoned owing to lack of sustenance' (NZ 261–2).[37] His efforts, though, lead him to withdraw so completely from the society around him that he ceases to exist as a social being. The necessary defensive stance thus leads to isolation and a breakdown in social communication, and the protagonist is actually reduced to a mental state which he describes as 'a pleasantly gentle state, hardly distinguishable from sleep' (NZ 265).[38]

The atmosphere of threat and suspicion to which even this self-avowed 'überzeugter Bürger' (convinced citizen – NZ 258) falls victim points to a general truth of which the majority of GDR citizens were only too aware, even at this time: that as a fundamental principle, the state distrusted its subjects, even its loyal ones. As Becker commented in 1980:

> I grew up in the Soviet zone of occupation and in the GDR, in an environment in which the tracking down of enemies was considered one of the most important functions of the state, and by those, too, who were the heads of that state. This took place with a thoroughness [. . .] and in a manner which seems to me today as if dictated by persecution mania. So many people were deemed to be pests, and threatened and punished, that many who were well-meaning, indifferent or merely sitting on the fence actually turned into enemies. (*L80. Politische und literarische Beiträge*, 1980: 81)[39]

In the story, this state-wide neurosis spreads downwards, infecting its citizens: in his impossible situation, as he stops answering the telephone in order to avoid giving any grounds for suspicion but then realises that this (in)action is in itself suspicious, Becker's 'suspect' comes to the tormenting realisation that he 'has to decide between one thing and its opposite; I can't take both to be equally suspicious, otherwise I would have to go mad' (NZ 263).[40] In the novel *Schlaflose Tage,* Simrock's insight into his dilemma is another variation on this theme: 'whoever suffers because things seem inevitable, he said to himself, inevitably ends up neurotic' (ST, 24).[41]

Yet Becker's otherwise bleak stories do not end entirely bleakly: at the end of 'Der Verdächtige' there is, for instance, a glimpse of an admittedly faint ray of light pointing towards the future as the 'suspect' resolves to change his ways: 'I lay down in bed to reflect on my future: I already felt determined not to live yet another year like this' (NZ 268).[42] Yet we suspect that things will not change for him, for his attitude remains conformist as he seeks further reasons to justify the behaviour of the 'protectors' of the state in his own case. And in 'Allein mit dem Anderen', the light in all the gloom is provided by the official's rebellious *alter ego*: the 'other one' even offers resistance, defying the pressures to conform, though again, even here, future prospects would appear to be limited, given the situation of *impasse* at the end of the story.

Psychological Malaise

In *Irreführung der Behörden*, the film script written by the young writer Gregor Bienek is criticised by the typical Party man Bungert for portraying characters who are 'too isolated from the environment around them' and just 'left to stew in their own juice', seeking solutions to their problems in 'their own bitter thoughts'[43] without any help 'von außen' (from outside – IB 229). Their 'private Bereiche' (private domains) are not sacrosanct as far as Bungert is concerned; indeed they represent a threat for the typical communist whose attitudes are the product of a state which sought total control of its subjects' lives. This is why in *Schlaflose Tage,* Antonia's longing for a society in which there are 'genügend Inseln der Abgeschieden-heit vorhanden' (enough islands of seclusion available – ST 74), shocks even her lover, Simrock, who at this point in the novel only wishes to reform the way communism is practised.

That the threat offered by such convictions was a systemic one is underlined by the following statement made in 1992 by Hermann Lübbe with reference to the GDR and its demise: 'Totalitarian systems are internally fixed in their subjects, otherwise they disintegrate.'[44] In his stories and novels about the GDR, though, Becker demonstrates that Lübbe's 'otherwise' could equally well be replaced by an 'and'. For Becker shows that such systems can break down and disintegrate, even when they appear 'fixed' in the mentality of individuals, when they are threatened by 'Störungen' (disruptions) which suddenly intrude, creating tension and confusion within them between feelings and thoughts. For instance, the loyal servant of the state in 'Der Verdächtige' carries out his defensive 'plan' (NZ 261) for survival with a frighteningly logical consistency, but then out of the blue he suddenly experiences 'Sehnsucht [. . .] nach der alten Zeit' (a longing for his life as it used to be) which leads this recluse to change his behaviour and go out again, with his heart beating 'wie lange nicht mehr' (in a way that it had not done for a long time – NZ 267).

The man in 'Allein mit dem Anderen', too, has what he calls a 'method' (NZ 217) which becomes affected by 'malfunctions', suggesting a machine-like, systematic mentality similar to that of the man under surveillance with his logical 'plan' which ultimately backfires. Both stories can be read as satires on the mentality of the arch-bureaucrat and on a system which rewards conformist 'yes-men' who function with predictable, clockwork regularity. Beyond the satire, however, Becker points to existential and psychological problems: 'Sehnsucht' (longing) and 'Störungen' (disruptions) are the spontaneous rebellion of the repressed, instinctive side of the self against the attempt of the rational, socially conditioned self to impose a straitjacket on existence. Moreover, despite the confusion within himself, the protagonist in 'Allein mit dem Anderen' is made aware that he has only himself to blame, that he is the victim of his own 'behaviour which, of my own free will, I considered to be right' (NZ 211),[45] and that it is his subservience to the system which underlies his psychological problems.

Becker's stories and novels thus anticipate, at an early stage, something of the state of mind, the psychological malaise, which eventually culminated in events of some ten years later in October and November 1989: the demise of the GDR. In a statement which he made in 1992 which is very reminiscent of themes in his earlier stories such as 'Der Verdächtige', Becker claimed that his former country had indeed been destroyed by its own 'persecution mania': 'If the GDR had been a person, it would have had to have been sent to see the psychiatrist' (*Bild am Sonntag*, no. 46, 15.11.1992).[46] In *Schlaflose Tage*, 'Der Verdächtige' and 'Allein mit dem Anderen', then, Becker pillories the cowardice, the same 'Anpassung' (conformity) and 'Unterwerfungsbereitschaft' (submissiveness), which he attacked twelve years later in August 1990 in his polemic against former citizens of the GDR, 'Zum Bespitzeln gehören zwei. Über den Umgang mit der DDR-Vergangenheit' (For spying you need two. On ways of dealing with the GDR past, see Heidelberger-Leonard 1992: 74–80). These were, for Becker, the very characteristics which former GDR citizens were now attempting to deny: 'The special zeal with which the Stasi-harassments are now being denounced and pursued seems to me like an attempt on the part of many people to deny the reality of their own submissiveness' (Heidelberger-Leonard 1992: 77).[47]

Questioning the Communist Ideology

In his review of the novel *Schlaflose Tage* (*Times Literary Supplement*, 20.10.1978: 1236), Peter Graves saw Simrock as one of a line of East German literary figures from Christa Wolf's Christa T. onwards who, whilst disturbed by some of the dehumanising aspects of the GDR, are fundamentally in sympathy with its Marxist basis and do not question the communist ideology itself. This interpretation may well still be correct as far as it goes, and it is certainly consistent with the impression which critics had of Jurek Becker at that time, for in an interview with Wolfram Schütte, the author had declared himself a convinced socialist who was simply dissatisfied with the form which socialism had taken in the GDR: 'The GDR seems to me to be like an outline of a socialist state, according to which the proper picture still has to be painted in' (*Frankfurter Rundschau*, 6.9.1977).[48]

Thus, like his author, Becker's hero Simrock, despite his radical reassessment of his life in his quest to discover his identity, still wishes to relate to the ideology of the society around him, as the narrator informs us: 'He wanted a more intimate relationship to communism' (ST 66).[49] Yet his attempts to achieve this by putting theory into practice and testing out communism and its slogans in his everyday life meet with failure at every turn. He reaches the critical stage in his relationship to the state after his lover commits the crime of 'Republikflucht' (illegal emigration): she attempts to escape to Austria via Hungary because she thinks 'that they're probably not as quick to open fire here' (ST 112).[50] At first Simrock calls her action 'empörend und rücksichtslos' (outrageous and callous), but on reflection feels compelled to accept it as 'rechtmäßig' (legitimate – ST 115): 'He considered it quite right for her to go wherever she wanted to go' (ST 114).[51]

Moreover, his lover, Antonia, emerges as the truly subversive character in the novel and a forebear of Becker's more recent rebellious GDR outsider-figure, Amanda, in the novel *Amanda herzlos*. From a young woman on her way to becoming, as she says, 'eine Sozialistin aus dem Bilderbuch' (a picture-book socialist – ST 73), Antonia has been turned by experiences of GDR hypocrisy into what Simrock calls 'das reaktion-ärste Frauenzimmer' (the most reactionary female – ST 75) with whom he has ever slept. For in the GDR she has experienced the fundamental incompatibility between her need to express 'ihr wahres Wesen' (her true self – ST, 73) (which is what Simrock himself is now seeking to do), and the collectivist, conformist demands of 'der hiesigen Gesellschaft' (this society here – ST 74). Furthermore, she rejects not only the state, but also its ideology. Simrock, adopting his author's view at the time, tries to persuade her that 'ein gescheiter Sozialist' (a sensible socialist) should not be put off by the particular form which socialism has taken 'um uns herum' (roundabout us). But Antonia's answer indicates that experience has taken her beyond such arguments: 'I'm just a sensible person, for they've scared me so much that the cause itself no longer interests me' (ST 74).[52] Antonia's position was one her author himself was not prepared to adopt at the time, only to envisage, as it represents a fundamental rejection of everything which the GDR stood for. And Simrock's reaction to Antonia's apostatic 'Glaubensbekenntnis' (confession of faith) may well also have been that of many GDR readers at the time, had they been in possession of an illicit copy of the novel: 'Once, without being asked, she made a sort of confession of faith which made Simrock's hair stand on end' (ST 73).[53]

Aesthetic Misgivings

Despite the broadly positive reception of the novel in the West, Becker later admitted that he himself did have aesthetic misgivings about works such as *Schlaflose Tage*, fearing the inappropriate yet inevitable intrusion of political issues:

> At that time, during the years 1976, 1977 and 1978, I was involved in a fierce political argument which was not only very exciting but also very excited. When I look at the texts I wrote at that time, they do not correspond to my own notion of what good literature is. [. . .] I don't think a barricade is a good place to formulate sentences. It's a place to come up with stirring slogans, a place for acclamatory gestures, but not for literature. (Heidelberger-Leonard 1992: 92)[54]

Becker even came close to admitting, albeit indirectly, that *Schlaflose Tage* was too GDR-specific to be of lasting literary value, when he argued in his essay 'Die Wiedervereinigung der deutschen Literatur' (The reunification of German literature) that much GDR literature fulfilled only a political 'Ersatzfunktion' (substitute function), providing a forum for the sort of debate which was not permitted in the press or elsewhere in the GDR. The following comments, written in 1990, appear to have been made with *Schlaflose Tage* in mind:

Jurek Becker

> Suddenly, real life in the GDR is full of the stuff which, in the past, was only
> to be found in novels. [. . .] If in the past I read a book dealing with how the
> schools are bringing children up to be hypocritical, then today I participate in
> a parents' action group at my childrens' school, demanding the dismissal of
> hypocritical teachers. (Arnold 1992: 82)[55]

Becker's judgement, however, hardly applies to stories such as 'Allein
mit dem Anderen', 'Der Verdächtige', 'Das Parkverbot' and 'Das eine
Zimmer' (The one room) which, though all having features, ideas and
dimensions which GDR readers will have recognised as specific to the
GDR, contain no clear-cut topographical references and no clearly defined
political context. Such stories go beyond the confines of East Germany
in their significance. For instance, in 'Der Verdächtige', the narrator's
references to 'ein bestimmtes Amt' (a certain bureau – NZ 259) and an
'Amt für Überwachung' (bureau for surveillance – NZ 260) would have
been read in both East and West as a reference to the 'Stasi', the hated
'Ministerium für Staatssicherheit' (Ministry for State Security). Yet many
of the features having particular significance for GDR readers, such as
the servile mentality of the bureaucrat in 'Allein mit dem Anderen', the
red tape in 'Das ein Zimmer' and the intrusiveness of the state in 'Der
Verdächtige', were not unfamiliar to residents of West Germany. The fact
that this intra-German ambiguity was not entirely unintentional can be
seen from the following provocative remark made by Becker after a
reading of 'Der Verdächtige' in Stuttgart in 1980: 'The practices of the
Federal Criminal Investigation Agency are no better than those of the
GDR State Security Service' (*Schwäbisches Tageblatt*, 13.12.1980).[56]

Indeed, the reason why the social and political context in which the
events of the stories happen is often left open or at least ambiguous is
precisely because Becker wishes to direct his readers' attention beyond
narrow political issues. The central themes in many of his stories are thus
ultimately universal in their appeal. For instance, it is true that, super-
ficially, 'Das eine Zimmer' treats the problem of the lack of housing which
was very much a concern of everyday life in the GDR. In the light of the
contrast between the shortage of living-accommodation and the seemingly
absurd request of the young man in the story, GDR readers are likely to
have read the story as a satire on specific features of their own system.
Yet the 'Probierzimmer' (test-room) which the man requests, in which
the couple can exercise their 'fantasy', can also be seen as a metaphor
for a freedom of thought which radically deviates from all conventions
and hence, too, for that inviolable privacy, those 'islands of seclusion',
as Antonia in *Schlaflose Tage* so aptly puts it, which are the right of every

individual. In this portrayal of a young couple who are even prepared to sacrifice living together for 'dieses eine Zimmer' (this one room – NZ 238), the story is making a political statement which transcends narrow GDR issues.

Notes

1. 'die DDR zu konsolidieren, den Sozialismus, den wir praktizieren, praktikabler zu machen.'
2. 'Meine Texte sind intelligenter, als ich es bin.'
3. 'Ich war in der DDR ein sehr engagierter Mensch, aber ich habe Bücher niemals als Vehikel betrachtet, um meine Ansichten zum Leser zu transportieren.'
4. 'Empfinden, an einer Unternehmung beteiligt zu sein, die ich für lohnend hielt. [. . .] diese Unternehmung zu lange für lohnend gehalten.'
5. 'die Guten, die Heilsbringer. Mit diesem Hintergrund bin ich von ihm erzogen worden.'
6. 'Nach meiner Überzeugung ist der wichtigste Antrieb zum Schreiben von Literatur Unzufriedenheit, eine Art von Nichteinverständnis. Das war wohl in der DDR nicht anders als in aller Welt.'
7. 'Wahrscheinlich werde ich nie damit fertig. [. . .] Es hat dort, wo ich war, keinen Widerstand gegeben.'
8. 'weil er zu erzählen versteht: [. . .] gegen die Verdrängungsmechanismen zweier deutscher Gesellschaften, von denen die eine lieber nichts und die andere nur Heroisches aus jener Zeit zu hören bereit sein wollte.'
9. 'Ich muß aber sagen, daß mich nie das Thema Faschismus für sich interessiert hat, nie die Ghetto-Geschichte pur. [. . .] Ein Kunstwerk wird überflüssig, wenn sein gedankliches Ende in der Vergangenheit liegt. Das, was erzählt wird, unabhängig davon, ob es vor 30 oder 200 Jahren spielt, muß in irgendeiner Korrespondenz zur Jetztzeit stehen.'
10. Becker remarked to me in 1991 that the choice of the title of his story involved 'an unavoidable historical coincidence'!
11. 'Das alles reicht noch nicht aus? Und wenn ich versuche, die allerletzte Möglichkeit zu nutzen, die sie davon abhält, sich gleich

hinzulegen und zu krepieren, mit Worten, verstehen Sie, mit Worten versuche ich das! Weil ich nämlich nichts anderes habe!'

12. These parallels have been impressively analysed by White and White 1978.

13. 'Verborgen blieb der Zensur die Subversität eines Werkes, die gegen jede Form repressiver staatlicher Machtansprüche gerichtet ist.'

14. 'seinen existentiellen Nöten: die Macht, bzw. die Ohnmacht des Wortes, die Macht der Literatur, die Macht des Erzählens. Das Erzählen als Überlebensstrategie.'

15. 'alte Hüte, [. . .] die du in deiner Werkstatt mit ein bißchen Talent aufpolierst'.

16. 'Dabei stellte sich heraus, daß jeder von ihnen einen anderen begraben hatte, denn jeder hatte ihn anders im Gedächtnis, und es ließ sich nicht mehr rekonstruieren, wessen Version die richtige war.'

17. 'die Spuren, die ein Mensch hinterläßt, konkret und eindeutig lesbar sind.'

18. 'eine Tendenz zum Realitätsverlust' [. . .] 'wobei die fiktive Kunst-Künstlerwirklichkeit sich recht weit von der wirklichen Welt entferne.'

19. 'Ich verspürte damals Lust, ein Buch zu machen über einen Außenseiter in meiner Gesellschaft, über jemand, dem die Ziele dieser Gesellschaft gleichgültig sind, der weder eine intime noch ein kühle Beziehung zu ihr hat, sondern überhaupt keine.'

20. 'Ich erzähl dir nicht die Nachkriegsgeschichte, ich erzähl dir was mir passiert ist. [. . .] Ich versteh schon, daß du ein bestimmtes Bild hast und dich um Ähnlichkeiten sorgst. Aber das ist dein Problem.'

21. 'Daß es die eine Sache ist [. . .] was ich dir erzähle, und eine zweite, was du schreibst.'

22. 'Wenn du unbedingt objektiv sein willst, dann geh und beschreib ein Fußballspiel.'

23. 'Danach sah ich in der DDR nur noch wenig Zukunft für mich – aber das ist nur die Viertelwahrheit. Ich sah für mich wenig Zukunft, weil ich dem Ganzen kaum mehr Zukunft beimaß.'

24. 'ein Gefangener, [. . .] fixiert, einem Erwartungsdruck zu folgen'.

25. 'So schien nicht goutierbar, daß der Autor eine seiner Romanfiguren sagen ließ, sie habe den Versuch zur "Republikflucht" aus der DDR deshalb in Ungarn unternommen, weil sie glaubte, daß an Ungarns Grenzen nicht so schnell geschossen würde wie eben in der DDR. Das war offenbar die hauptsächlichste Hürde, die damals nicht genommen werden konnte, weil der Autor sich standhaft weigerte, diese und auch andere angeblich diskriminierende Passagen zu verändern.'

26. 'daß sich in den letzten sieben, acht Monaten meine Identität auf irgendeine Weise verändert hat'.

27. 'Ich will in diesem Land bleiben als jemand, der das veröffentlichen kann, was er schreibt; denn auf die Dauer ist das für einen Schriftsteller die einzige praktikable Methode, sich einzumischen. Wenn es allerdings darum geht, den Mund zu halten, dann halte ich den Mund lieber auf den Bahamas.'

28. Twenty-one of the fifteen prose pieces appeared six years later in the GDR under the title *Erzählungen* (Stories).

29. 'untersuchen, ob ein ausgeklügeltes System aus Fehleinschätzungen, Angst, Bequemlichkeit und Selbstbetrug den Zugang zu den Grenzen versperrt. Wie eine Mauer im Landesinnern.'

30. 'seine Beschäftigung mit Winzigkeiten, die andere Autoren nicht für der Mühe wert halten. Und ich habe irgendwann begriffen, daß diese Winzigkeiten das eigentliche Thema der Literatur sind.'

31. 'die tiefsten, erstaunlichsten Einsichten über das Wesen einer Gesellschaft, über die geheimen Beweggründe menschlichen Handelns, über das Ausgeliefertsein des einzelnen an die vielen'.

32. 'die ganze Behörde als unnütz zu bezeichnen und ihre Liquidierung vorzuschlagen, ja, zu verlangen'.

33. 'Unsere Ansichten von Humor klafften weit auseinander.'

34. 'Kaum aber denke ich, wie ich gerne möchte, ist es aus mit mir.'

35. 'Ich bin das Opfer meiner Handlungsweise, zu der mich kein Mensch gezwungen hat.'

36. 'Wenn ich am Abend das Licht endlich lösche und zu mir sage, daß ich mich bis zum nächsten Morgen nicht mehr zu verstellen brauche, dann weiß ich manchmal selber nicht, wie ich zu sein habe.'

37. 'dann würde er mangels Nahrung aufgegeben werden müssen.'

38. 'einen angenehm sanften Zustand, der kaum von Schlaf zu unterscheiden war'. This paradoxical notion of existing in a somnambulistic state in everyday waking life also recurs in other works, the most prominent example being the title of the novel *Schlaflose Tage*, which suggests that, unlike most of their fellow citizens, only certain individuals such as Simrock and his lover, Antonia, are really awake to the problems of the GDR.

39. 'Ich bin in der Sowjetischen Besatzungszone und in der DDR aufgewachsen, in einer Umgebung, in der das Aufspüren von Feinden für eine der wichtigsten Funktionen des Staates gehalten wurde, und zwar von denen, die dem Staat vorstanden. Dies geschah mit eiserner Gründlichkeit [. . .] und es geschah auf eine Art und Weise, die mir heute wie von Verfolgungswahn diktiert vorkommt. So viele wurden

für Schädlinge gehalten und bedroht und bestraft, daß aus vielen Gutwilligen, Gleichgültigen oder Abwartenden tatsächlich Feinde wurden.'

40. 'müsse sich entscheiden zwischen einem Teil und seinem Gegenteil; ich könne nicht alles beides für gleich verdächtig halten, ansonsten bliebe mir ja nur, verrückt zu werden.'

41. 'Er sagte sich, wer unter dem Unabänderlichen leidet, der lande zwangsläufig in der Neurose.'

42. 'Ich legte mich ins Bett, um über meine Zukunft nachzudenken; ich spürte schon die Entschlossenheit, nicht noch ein zweites Jahr so hinzuleben.'

43. 'zu isoliert von ihrer Umwelt [. . .] in ihrem eigenen Saft schmoren [. . .] aus ihren eigenen verbitterten Gedanken'.

44. 'Totalitäre Systeme sind in der Innerlichkeit ihrer Subjekte befestigt, oder sie lösen sich auf.' Quoted in Schütz 1992.

45. 'Handlungsweise, [. . .] die ich aus freien Stücken für richtig hielt'.

46. 'Wäre die DDR eine Person gewesen, man hätte sie zum Psychiater schicken müssen.'

47. 'Der besondere Eifer, mit dem die Stasi-Schikanen nun angeprangert und verfolgt werden, scheint mir für viele wie ein Versuch, die eigene Unterwürfigkeit ungeschehen zu machen.'

48. 'Die DDR kommt mir wie eine Skizze für einen sozialistischen Staat vor, nach der das richtige Bild erst gemalt werden muß.'

49. 'Er wünschte zum Kommunismus eine innigere Beziehung.'

50. 'daß sie hier wahrscheinlich nicht so leicht schießen'.

51. 'Er hielt es für ihr gutes Recht, dorthin zu gehen, wohin sie gehen wollte.'

52. 'Ich bin nur ein gescheiter Mensch, denn man hat mich so erschreckt, daß mich die Sache nicht mehr interessiert.'

53. 'Einmal legte sie ungefragt eine Art Glaubensbekenntnis ab, daß Simrock die Haare zu Berge standen.'

54. 'Ich war in jener Zeit, in den Jahren 76, 77, 78, in eine heftige politische Auseinandersetzung verwickelt, die nicht nur sehr aufregend war, sondern auch sehr aufgeregt. Wenn ich mir die Texte ansehe, die ich in jener Zeit geschrieben habe, so entsprechen sie nicht meiner eigenen Vorstellung von guter Literatur. [. . .] Ich glaube nicht, daß eine Barrikade ein guter Platz ist, um Sätze zu formulieren. Es ist ein Platz, um Aufrufe zu verfassen, ein Platz für Akklamatorisches, aber nicht für Literatur.'

55. 'Plötzlich ist die DDR-Wirklichkeit voll von dem Stoff, der in der Vergangenheit nur in den Romanen zu finden war. [. . .] Wenn ich

bisher ein Buch gelesen habe, das von der Erziehung zur Heuchelei in den Schulen handelte, beteilige ich mich heute an der Schule meiner Kinder an einer Elterninitiative, die die Entlassung heuchlerischer Lehrer fordert.'

56. 'Die Praktiken des Bundeskriminalamtes sind nicht besser als die des Staatssicherheitsdienstes.'

−6−

A Socialist Writer in the West

Becker as Political Commentator

When Jurek Becker moved to the West, he was already a prominent figure in the East–West German cultural and political arena as a result of his defiant stance over the harsh treatment of Wolf Biermann by the GDR authorities, and he soon soon acquired a high political profile in the West, too, in his new-found role as commentator on the political and cultural scene in East and West Germany. And although he frequently gave expression to his often forthright views in numerous newspaper articles, essays, speeches, and television- and radio-interviews both before and after unification, Becker's stance remained fairly consistent right up to his death.

As early as 1974, whilst still resident and publishing in the GDR, Becker spoke out in the journal *Neue Deutsche Literatur* (New German Literature) against the pressures exerted on GDR writers by Western critics to write certain types of books, defending his right to write whatever he wanted, a concern not without relevance to his position in the GDR at that time (*Neue Deutsche Literatur* 1974: 59). These very sentiments were echoed some eighteen years later in his novel *Amanda herzlos*, published in 1992, when Rudolf, the fictitious *alter ego* of the dissident writer Fritz Hetmann, claims 'that writers should write the way they want to, not the way others want them to' (A 205).[1]

Whilst Becker was still living in East Berlin, he was generally very much on the defensive *vis-à-vis* West German critics of the GDR. But as we saw in the previous chapter, he had professed himself to be a socialist who was dissatisfied with the 'actually existing' form of socialism being practised in the GDR, and so after leaving the country he took the opportunity afforded by two interviews with *Spiegel* (in 1977 and in 1980) to explain the reasons for his break with the Party and with the Writers' Union: his previous preparedness to debate controversial issues 'unter uns' (amongst ourselves) had given way to the desire to speak out, particularly in view of the way he was being treated by the Party: 'After being dealt with in a way which I can no longer approve of, I can no longer see any sensible motive anywhere for concealing my views because of the fact that they are not in accordance with the current line of my former party' (*Der Spiegel*, no. 30, 1977: 30–2).[2]

In the West, Becker's dislike of labels of any kind soon became apparent. In his essay 'Mein Judentum' (My Jewishness, 1978) he expressed his anger at his 'Zwangs-Identität', an identity imposed on him by others in specific historical circumstances when people persisted in trying to decide who and what he was, classifying him as a Jew (Heidelberger-Leonard 1992: 19). When he was asked in 1980, in 'Sieben Antworten auf Fragen der *Frankfurter Allgemeinen Zeitung*' (Seven answers to questions from the *Frankfurter Allgemeine Zeitung*), what had been his biggest disappointment since coming to the West, he replied: 'I am suddenly compelled to feel like a Jew, which was virtually of no importance to my life in the GDR'[3] and which he attributed to 'Äußerungen von Antisemitismus' (expressions of anti-Semitism – Heidelberger-Leonard 1992: 53).

In subsequent years, he published a number of articles in *Die Zeit*, criticising first authoritarian, then later fascist tendencies in both East and West Germany. The 1983 polemic 'Über den Kulturverfall in unserer Zeit' (On the decline of culture in our time), for instance, casts a critical eye at conformist, opportunistic behaviour, rewarded in both East and West. His article 'Gedächtnis verloren – Verstand verloren' (Loss of memory – loss of sense), which appeared in *Die Zeit* in November 1988, was a sharply critical retort to Martin Walser's 'Über Deutschland reden' (Speaking about Germany), published in the same newspaper two weeks previously. At a time when it still seemed a very remote possibility, Becker attacked Walser's case in favour of unification for coming dangerously close to revanchism and for being impervious to, as Becker put it, 'Faschismus-Reste, [. . .] von denen ich mich umzingelt fühle!' (vestiges of fascism which I feel surrounded by – *Die Zeit*, 18.11.1988: 61). In September 1989, in the *Allgemeine Jüdische Wochenzeitung* (General Jewish Weekly Newspaper), Becker again drew attention to 'faschistoider Tendenzen in der Jetztzeit' (fascist tendencies in present times) in an interview published under the title 'Die Republikaner sind ja nicht vom Himmel gefallen' (The Republicans have not just appeared overnight).

In the wake of unification and the events leading up to it, Becker's output in terms of articles, speeches and interviews increased considerably, and again, his criticism of both sides, East and West, is consistently in evidence. I cite just a few examples. In September 1989, in an interview published in *taz*, he commented on the reasons why young people were fleeing the GDR in droves: the answer was simple – because they did not want to become like their parents 'who have been pliant for thirty or forty years, either out of putative loyalty or out of cowardice' (Mehr 1989: 12).[4] On the reaction of the SED to Gorbachev's reforms, Becker commented: 'With horror, we witness the GDR uncoupling itself from the developments in Eastern Europe and forming an actually existing socialist enclave, raising a new wall around the wall which is around it' (Mehr 1989: 12).[5] His reflections on the future of socialism were published in October 1989 in a '*Zeit* Umfrage zum Thema "Ist der Sozialismus am Ende?"' (*Zeit* opinion poll on the topic 'Is socialism finished?') and also in a short piece with the self-explanatory title 'Über die letzten Tage. Ein kleiner Einspruch gegen die große deutsche Euphorie' (On the last few days. A minor objection to the great German euphoria) which appeared in *Neue Rundschau* in early 1990. Whilst welcoming the collapse of 'actually existing' socialist states, Becker lamented the demise of his remaining hopes for socialism and its promise of a more humane form of society in the face of Western societies which offer no real alternatives because they lack goals or objectives and are driven only by consumerism.

In August 1990, on the other hand, he produced a polemic against former citizens of the GDR, 'Zum Bespitzeln gehören zwei. Über den Umgang mit der DDR-Vergangenheit' (see Chapter 5), attacking the lack of resistance, the cowardice, the same conformity and submissiveness which he had already pilloried in his earlier novels and stories, and which he ridiculed most grotesquely in *Amanda herzlos* (1992) in the words of the cynical West German lawyer Kraushaar, who explains how he had the misfortune to marry an East German, for: 'these people are spoiled for life in the wild. They are used to living in enclosures, anything unexpected makes them panic. There is something cow-like about them, they chew their cud, gape at the horizon and want to be milked punctually' (A 299).[6]

In the aforementioned essay, Becker also asserted that former GDR citizens were now attempting to deny their submissiveness. The old opportunists were still at work, he added, and now it was the past which they were manipulating: 'That's probably what the opportunists like so much: the fact that their obedience has been forgotten overnight and that they appear as victims who have had an insuperable power breathing down their neck. This power was indeed breathing down their neck, and it was also mighty, but was it really *insuperable*?' (*Die Zeit*, 3.8.1990: 36),[7] he asked. Hence Becker saw the GDR of the 1980s essentially in terms of 'a communal work': 'Actually existing socialism was a communal work, created by the Party leadership, their henchmen and the many who obeyed them' (*Die Zeit*, 3.8.1990: 36).[8]

In 1990 he also published his three 'Frankfurter Vorlesungen' (Frankfurt lectures), *Warnung vor dem Schriftsteller* (Warning against writers), where he compared the respective literary scenes in East and West Germany, attacking West German literature for being primarily a 'Wirtschaftszweig' (branch of industry) and GDR literature for the extent to which it owed its influence to the existence of the censor: 'The books of authors [. . .] who pick arguments with the censor are even read by people who would usually never pick up a book' (W 16).[9] A variation on this sentiment appears in the novel *Amanda herzlos* in the reference to the Russian journal *Sputnik*, proscribed in the GDR: 'prior to this not a soul knew it, now everyone is missing it' (A 379).[10]

From 1991 onwards, several lengthy interviews with Becker on the subject of his relationship to the former GDR were published. He brought together many of these observations in the essay bearing the ironic title 'Die Wiedervereinigung der deutschen Literatur' (The reunification of German literature, 1992). In this provocative piece, he expounds at some length his views on the nature of literature in the former GDR, predicting rather dismal prospects for former GDR writers after unification. Literature in the GDR, he argues, had taken on a substitute function, becoming the only public domain where real political debate could take place; hence almost all works of literature written and published there had become vehicles for transporting the political concerns of their authors, which in turn made the public 'avid for books, to be more precise – for books by writers who deviated' (Arnold 1992: 78).[11] Becker claims that the existence of the censor determined the second peculiar characteristic of GDR literature: every work published, regardless of its subject-matter and its author's intentions, was 'zugleich eine Reaktion auf die Zensur' (simultaneously a reaction to the censor). For Becker, one of the direst consequences of censorship was the fact 'that all literature not banned has to exist with the odour of having been permitted' (Arnold 1992: 79),[12] and he did not shy away from acknowledging that this applied to his own GDR works too, some of which he was dissatisfied with in aesthetic terms, as we have seen: 'I have myself written books which were permitted' (W 30),[13] he admitted. Such literature would no longer sell in the West since many GDR authors owed their fame and success to a combination of the censor and the existence of a second, hostile German state, where the West German public, like the East German one, was, as Becker put it, 'auf das Dissidentische scharf' (keen on things dissident – Arnold 1992: 80). For this reason, books were often judged according to ideological rather than aesthetic criteria, with the result 'that the banning of a book often brought its author greater fame than normal publication would have done' (Arnold 1992: 80).[14] The writer Fritz Hetmann in Becker's novel *Amanda herzlos* is just such an author: his rival, the 'loyal' GDR journalist Ludwig Weniger, describes him as 'one of those writers who have made a profession out of their hostility towards our state' (A 98),[15] and we later learn of Hetmann giving deliberately provocative interviews in order to attract attention to his latest book (A 323). It comes as no surprise, therefore, to learn that Hetmann has considered going over to the West, but has rejected the idea: 'He can't do that, of course,' comments the West German narrator, 'he will be on his guard against becoming a formerly proscribed author who will soon be forgotten' (A 292).[16] And in 'Die Wiedervereinigung der deutschen Literatur', Becker posed the teasingly provocative question: 'Is it ultimately not appropriate, however macabre it may sound, to mourn the censor?' (Arnold 1992: 82).[17] For he added that the disappearance of the censor with the demise of the GDR would have several implications: former GDR writers, without this 'Orientierungshilfe' (help with their bearings), 'Wegweiser' (signpost) and 'Kompaß' (compass), would be left to their own devices and have to adapt to market forces. GDR literature would thus suffer the same fate as East German industry. What is left of it would carry on 'unter neuem Firmennamen' (under a new company name), surviving not as 'German', but as 'West German' literature (Arnold 1992: 83) whose state Becker found 'depressing', for with few exceptions, he saw as its dominant characteristics: 'currying favour, craving for admiration, vociferous marketing and simplicity of ideas' (Arnold 1992: 85).[18]

To the end of his life, Becker continued to cast a critical eye over post-unification Germany. In 1993, in his article entitled 'Der Defekt ist der Normalfall' (Defects are the norm, *Der Spiegel*, 1993: 86–8), he suggested that, given similar historical circumstances, the behaviour of the West Germans would have been just as 'würdelos' (lacking in dignity) as that of the majority of East Germans. Indeed, in the figure of a West German resident of East Berlin, the reporter Stanislaus Doll, Becker demonstrated in *Amanda herzlos* that opportunism and conformity were not exclusively GDR characteristics, for Doll, too, has to admit that he is a 'Krämerseele' ('petty-minded little man') compared to Amanda, his East German lover, when he guiltily keeps quiet about an approach made to him by the Stasi, knowing full well that she would have vociferously 'sent them packing' (A 343).

In May 1994, in perhaps his bleakest essay, 'Mein Vater, die Deutschen und ich' (My father, the Germans and me – *Die Zeit*, 20.5.1994), Becker also returned to the question of the upsurge of right-wing extremism throughout the new Germany, relating it to his own experiences as a survivor of the ghetto and concentration camps, and suggesting several reasons for it, not least the vacuum left by the demise of the only alternative system to capitalism combined with the 'Mißmut' (sullenness) and 'Bitterkeit' (bitterness) of most East Germans stemming from their disillusionment with Western values. Becker saw right-wing extremism resulting, too, from a mixture of the new and the old: on the one hand, there was the prevalent 'Gesellschaftszustand' (state of society) which was characterised by 'Zukunftsangst, Perspektivlosigkeit, Endzeitstimmung' (fear of the future, lack of prospects, an apocalyptic mood); and on the other, there were 'Nazibestandteile', fascist elements which had survived, above all in the West, where they were never really eradicated after the Second World War, but also in the East: 'As we, the people of the GDR, never really dealt with our past in a *self*-critical way, we lost sight of what was fascistic about our own conditions and in our own behaviour.'[19] It was, then, not the fall of the Wall, he concludes, which spread the 'bacillus' to the new Federal States: 'German unification was at very least also the unification of potential right-wing radicals with those already active.'[20]

A Writer in the West

Surveying Becker's writing as commentator, we note recurrent themes and also a number of constants in the stances which he adopted on the various issues. Above all, as Oliver Sill has correctly argued, the notion of Jurek Becker as political commentator can only be appreciated when one understands it as a 'consequence of his conception of himself as a writer' (Arnold 1992: 70).[21] A brief examination of what Becker understood as the purpose of his writing and as his role as a writer reveals that his views here also remained fairly constant and hardly changed in terms of fundamentals. He expounded them most extensively in *Warnung vor dem Schriftsteller* (1990), where he pinpointed his basic position as a writer: 'I suspect that from the very beginnings of literature, the most fundamental motive for writing has been the need to state a view of things, the need to protest' (W 13).[22] In nearly every work of any significance, says Becker, the author 'tells [. . .] of some misfortune, [. . .] some concern or dissatisfaction that he feels. Doubt or despair. His disagreement with something that exists' (W 14).[23] For Becker, therefore, one of the most important themes in literature was what he called 'the frenzy of social conditions and disparities' (W 53);[24] whereas, when an author attempts the opposite and writes 'to give expression to his feelings of well-being, his bliss, his affirmation', then the end-product is almost invariably 'trivial literature' (W 14).[25]

However, when Becker speaks of 'the need to state a view of things' and 'the need to take sides' ('Parteinahme' – W 51), we must be careful not to mistake this as a call to understand literature as a vehicle for political protest or as a plea for writers with a message, since he had often expressed his distaste for this kind of writing: 'I have an aversion to any prose which is half way between *belles-lettres* and essay. I take exception to lectures interpolated in novels' (Graf and Konietzny 1991: 60).[26] Indeed, Becker emphasised on several occasions that serious works of literature could not be vehicles for transporting the ideas of their authors (W 41), citing Marcel Proust's *bon mot*: 'Books in which you can read authors' opinions resembled articles which still had their price-tags hanging on them' (W 58).[27] He was, therefore, always at pains to separate his journalistic writing from his literary works; asked, for instance, whether he regarded himself like Max Frisch as a sort 'Notwehrschriftsteller' (writer out of self-defence), he retorted: 'No, this is not one of my motives. Maybe I am a journalist out of self-defence. I may attempt to deal with some urgent need by writing an article or an essay. But [. . .] momentary annoyance cannot be for me the starting point for a book' (Arnold 1992: 11).[28]

Back in 1984, though, and still in the wake of his GDR upbringing which had shaped his view that literature should have a social purpose, Becker commented: 'I cherish the hope that literature is something which can contribute to making a society in which it takes place more sensitive. More sensitive means more sensitive to disfigurement, more sensitive to violence, more alert to injustice' (Pfeiffer 1984: 17).[29] This hope faded somewhat in the light of his experiences in the West, particularly post-unification. In *Warnung vor dem Schriftsteller*, for instance, he admitted: 'Even if it is true that my views were considerably influenced by reading books, I do not rate the influence of literature very highly' (W 15);[30] and in 'Die Wiedervereinigung der deutschen Literatur' he warned GDR writers of the danger of self-delusion in this matter: 'It may have been self-deception if they believed hitherto that they were able to exert an influence on societal developments through their texts; but even more absurd is the hope that they will be able to do this in future when all around them will be the West' (Arnold 1992: 85).[31]

Yet for all his later scepticism about the influence of literature, he still held to the related view that writers can influence their readers in so far as they can encourage the latter to become active. This idea remained constant to his thinking, with certain modifications – in *Warnung vor dem Schriftsteller*, for instance, he again laid stress upon the active role which the reader should be encouraged to play by the writer, but now he put the emphasis on the shaping of opinions: 'With literature, it is essential for *readers* to form opinions when reading, their *own* opinions, and in a way which they would not have found possible without reading' (W 58–9).[32] The importance which he attached to his readers stemmed from his own experiences: one reason why the young Becker's attitude to the socialist society around him became increasingly critical was the fact that his father had encouraged him to become an avid reader (Heidelberger-Leonard 1992: 109).

From the outset, therefore, Becker adopted various narrative strategies in his novels and stories in order to encourage readers to shape their own opinions. We have noted, for instance, that the narrator of *Jakob der Lügner* interrupts his story on several occasions in order to allow himself to 'chat' with his readers and thereby encourage them to reflect on the reasons for the often light-hearted narrative stance which he adopts in spite of his potentially depressing subject; and that in many of Becker's first-person narratives, such as the stories written in the period immediately before he left the GDR, he adopts the roles of conformists in order to expose their subservient mentality from the 'inside'. He still used this technique in the first part of his last novel *Amanda herzlos* (1992), where the first of three narrators, Ludwig Weniger, is exposed through the falseness of his own words: the more he appeals to the reader's understanding and sympathy, the more the actual text in its context speaks out against him. For instance, after Amanda has mocked him for his obsequious behaviour, he poses a rhetorical question which rebounds on him: 'If the price for a nice quiet existence consists in keeping certain thoughts to oneself and refraining from certain actions, and if one pays this price – is that supposed to be obsequious? Amanda is clearly of the opinion that it is' (A 29).[33] Through his own words, Weniger is gradually exposed as being totally subservient to the state and sexist in his relationship with his wife, Amanda. Thus, through irony, the author gradually establishes a sense of complicity between himself and his readers at the expense of Weniger, the narrator, thereby encouraging the sort of critical awareness and self-reflection in his readers which he considered such an important part of the literary experience.

Amanda herzlos, though, is more complex in structure than the earlier stories and has three independent first-person narrators in the shape of Amanda's ex-husband and her two subsequent lovers: part 1 ('Die Scheidung', The divorce, 1977–80) is a report written by the 'yes-man' Ludwig Weniger, a journalist, to his lawyer, in which he builds up his side of the case in preparation for the ensuing divorce proceedings against Amanda; part 2 ('Die verlorene Geschichte', The lost story, 1980–7) is an account by the dissident writer Fritz Hetmann of how a novella, based on his relationship with Amanda and which he had been writing on his computer, has been mysteriously wiped off the floppy disk: he attempts to reconstruct it, alternating between the third and first person ('er' and 'ich'), between what he can remember of the details of the story, set against the real events on which the fiction is based; in part 3 ('Der Antrag', The application, September 1987–January 1989), Stanislaus Doll, a West German journalist based in East Berlin, keeps a diary about his affair with Amanda and their eventually successful application to leave the GDR.

This structure and the specific manner in which Becker focuses on his subject enable him to give expression to the complex, ambivalent, highly subjective nature of individual experience. Both this theme and the approach, always discouraged in the old GDR, had already been exemplified in the simpler form of a single first-person narrator in Becker's earlier novel *Irreführung der Behörden* (1973). Now, though, the story of Amanda is told through the various, varied and mutually relativising perspectives of three narrators. Becker thereby denies his readers any sovereign overview of the subject, encouraging them to experience reality as multi-faceted. Of the three different perspectives on Amanda he is reported to have said in a newspaper interview: 'All three are "distorted images" from whose uniformly biased narration a clear image is possibly created in the reader's mind' (*Stuttgarter Zeitung*, 7.11.1992).[34] Indeed, one episode alone is retold from three different perspectives: the first narrator, Weniger, relates his encounter in his own flat with the second narrator, Hetmann, who in turn recounts the incident on two different levels, the fictional and the real (A 98 and 141ff.). *Amanda herzlos,* like many of Becker's works, is thus a novel in which the act of writing becomes thematic, a novel which at one point reflects its own aesthetic process in the words of the second narrator, Hetmann, who is himself in some ways a caricature of his author and utters the sentiment close to Becker's own heart: 'On the other hand, writing is nothing other than an endless series of doubts which in the end have to be overcome in favour of a sentence' (A 143).[35]

The pluralistic narrative technique of his last novel is reminiscent of a statement which Becker made in an interview in the USA in 1978 shortly after he left the GDR, expressing a view which he held to consistently. He argued 'that the literature of a given country can be of interest only when different and conflicting points of view are presented within it; and not when a "superior author" supplies the acceptable opinion'

(*Dimension* 1978, no. 3: 412). Here lies one of the reasons for the striking predominance of first-person narrators in his works: Becker seemed to have an instinctive distrust of the anonymous omniscient narrator sitting authoritatively in judgement on characters and events, since such narrators provided the clear ideological, political message in many works of Socialist Realism in the GDR.

It would, then, be a mistake to view Becker as a novelist who had a political axe to grind, even though, as we have noted above, the two central concerns of Becker's literary *oeuvre* – his Jewish background and his life in the GDR – were also broadly central to his political writings. Indeed, political developments and historical events remain very much in the background in all his novels and stories, and nowhere more so than in the two novels with non-Jewish themes which he wrote in the West, *Aller Welt Freund* (A friend to all the world) and *Amanda herzlos*. Yet it was probably for this very reason that both works met with controversial reception, disappointing those reviewers who approached them with specific expectations resulting from their familiarity with Becker's political profile.

Aller Welt Freund (1982), for instance, was criticised by many in West Germany for its political vagueness and its lack of topographical refer-ences. Reviewers complained that the context in which events occur was so opaquely drawn that they were unable to decide whether it was set in East or West Germany. Becker's answer to such criticisms points to his desire to direct his readers' attention beyond narrow political issues (his comments apply equally well to many of the stories discussed in the previous chapter):

> It is left open as to which country this book takes place in. It even remains open whether this book takes place in the GDR or in the Federal Republic. [. . .] I want to prevent people reading it and being relieved at the thought that it is taking place on the 'other side', beyond the border; that's wrong. It is taking place precisely where they are living. (Pfeiffer 1984: 15–16)[36]

The political dimensions of the novel are, then, global, raising questions about the ideological rigidity of all social systems and inviting readers of all political persuasions to seek effective answers.

With dry humour which rescues his account from the deadly earnest-ness of its subject, the first-person narrator, a thirty-year-old journalist called Kilian, tells of his own suicide attempt which has failed as a result of two bizarre coincidences: a comic accident in which he breaks his arm falling from a chair which he has placed on the kitchen-table in the assumption that the gas from the taps which he has turned on will take effect more quickly; and the unexpected return of his landlady due to fog at the airport. He summarises his new dilemma with the words: 'Step by step, bleedin' mankind is committing suicide, in accordance with the craftiest system ever devised, but when someone would like to carry out The Thing for himself, on his own account so to speak and beforehand, then the largest obstacles are created for him' (AWF 18).[37] The despair which led to his bungled suicide attempt was triggered off by his job in the news agency where he had to report on a whole catalogue of catastrophes, from famine to wars and horrific accidents: 'the many wars are making straight for one another: they are getting closer and closer, they have chosen me as their focal point and are devouring their way towards me from all sides' (AWF 108).[38] 'I can't take any more news' (AWF 109),[39] he tells his boss who, like everyone else, misses the point and tries to solve Kilian's problem by transferring him to the sports page. Those around him are thus unaware of his acute sensitivity and unable to share his painful private perceptions. They are bewildered by their own inability to find a convincing explanation for what they see as his eccentric act. And Kilian himself is forced to recognise his complete isolation, from his mother, his lover, his friends, his colleagues, and even from his twin brother Manfred. With his central theme of individual isolation related to global pessimism, treated with wry humour and a mildly satirical edge, Becker struck a new and original note with *Aller Welt Freund*, a work which the author considered to be amongst his best (personal interview 1991), yet one which puzzled many of his readers who expected a novel about his experiences in East and/or West Germany.

Reactions were similar with the publication of his last novel, *Amanda herzlos*, in 1992, for most reviewers and readers were expecting *the* novel of the post-unification period. After all, here was a writer who, perhaps more so than any of his contemporaries, had occupied a unique vantage-point in terms of East–West German relations during the late 1970s and the 1980s. It is hardly surprising that many critics, familiar with Becker's polemical writing, were disappointed, for had they not read in *Warnung vor dem Schriftsteller* that 'narrative literature always [has] a good period when social conflicts take place or are imminent, when great changes are heralded' (W 51)?[40] True, his novel begins at the point shortly before Becker left the GDR in 1977, certainly a time of great upheaval, but it ends before the momentous events began – on 3 January 1989, a time heralding the great changes which were subsequently to follow in the GDR; and, together with his essays, it forms a main part of Becker's representation of what he really understood the GDR to be: he claimed 'that [in it], I wrote down the GDR years that I missed' (*Süddeutsche Zeitung*, 30.7.1992).[41]

Though greeted with much interest, a huge success in terms of sales, widely reviewed, and praised by many, the novel was the object of a scathing attack by a number of prominent critics, notably Marcel Reich-Ranicki who had been one of the first to draw attention in the West to the talents of the young writer of *Jakob der Lügner* back in the early 1970s. He condemned *Amanda herzlos* as a piece of 'Trivialliteratur' (trivial literature) which said nothing about the disintegration of the GDR in the 1970s and 1980s, and for this reason dismissed its three narrators as 'Drei Idioten' (three idiots – *Frankfurter Allgemeine Zeitung*, 19.9.1992)! Becker gave a direct answer to this criticism in an interview some months after this:

> I think his criticism is unseemly, I find it incomprehensible for one quite specific reason: a settling of old scores with the GDR takes place today on every other television programme, on every other radio programme and in every third book you read. Why does he demand of me something that everybody else is doing? Or to put the question another way: why does he want a book that he knows already? I cannot understand it. As to myself, I find it much more exciting to read books which I am not yet familiar with. (*Die Weltwoche*, 14.1.1993)[42]

Some critics praised but others criticised, too, Becker's frequently light-hearted treatment of the period immediately before the 'Wende', accusing him of 'Verharmlosung' (playing down) an inhuman regime (*Jakob der Lügner* had been both praised and condemned for the very same reason when it first appeared in 1969). Many, expecting *the* novel of the 'Wende', were disappointed. The reviewer in the *Times Literary Supplement* (9.10.1992), for instance, concluded that the novel must have been completed before the Wall came down, that Becker was reacting to the old GDR he had left fifteen years previously, and that much of the political comment seemed irrelevant in 1992. Yet, as we have seen from his essays, Becker appears to have been very much in touch with events; and up to 1989, he had continued to make good use of his special visa, visiting the GDR (usually friends in East Berlin) at least once a month to see his two sons from his first marriage, as he explained to me in a letter (18.2.1993). His choice of the date for the ending of the novel, January 1989, surely marks a quite deliberate refusal to write the 'Wende-Roman' of epic proportions which many expected of him.

Yet Irene Heidelberger-Leonard is surely mistaken when she argues: 'Jurek Becker [. . .] is here making a statement by not making a statement on the most recent events' (Heidelberger-Leonard 1992: 302).[43] For the political developments of the late 1980s, 'die Unruhe im Land' (the unrest in the country – A 276), as it is referred to at one point, do form the backdrop to the novel which, set during the final twelve years of the GDR, takes the form of a 'Liebesroman' (romantic novel) whose plot, whilst focusing on three lovers, is an ironic mirror of the broad historical backcloth: Amanda's unhappy first marriage to the 'East' (with the rigidly doctrinaire GDR-conformist Weniger) is followed by her affair with a fellow-dissident (the writer Hetmann) and the novel ends with her second marriage, this time to the 'West' (in the shape of the ever-adaptable and appropriately named Doll for whom love can conquer all). The plot, then, anticipates the political events which were to follow beyond the time-frame of the novel. Dreams of material fulfilment and happiness in this new union are ironised by Becker in his parody of both the conventional happy ending and ensuing unification itself, with 'bananas' becoming the ironic symbol of the transitional period leading up to German unification. In her attempt to reassure her little son Sebastian that he has nothing to fear about life in the West, Amanda describes, in the final two sentences of the novel, the cornucopia of delights which awaits him: 'And did you know that you can buy bananas on every corner? So that's not so bad, is it?'[44]

Notes

1. 'daß Schriftsteller so schreiben sollten, wie sie und nicht andere es für richtig hielten.'
2. 'Nachdem auf eine Art und Weise mit mir verfahren wurde, die ich nicht mehr billigen kann, sehe ich weit und breit kein vernünftiges Motiv mehr, meine Ansichten zu verbergen, aufgrund der Tatsache, daß sie der heutigen Linie meiner ehemaligen Partei nicht entsprechen.'
3. 'Plötzlich bin ich gezwungen, mich als Jude zu fühlen, was in meinem Leben in der DDR so gut wie keine Rolle gespielt hat.'
4. 'die sich seit dreißig oder vierzig Jahren verbiegen, entweder aus vermeintlicher Loyalität oder aus Feigheit'.
5. 'Man sieht mit Grauen, wie die DDR sich von der Entwicklung in Osteuropa abkoppelt und eine realsozialistische Enklave bildet, um die Mauer, die um sie herum ist, eine neue Mauer zieht.'

6. 'diese Leute sind für ein Leben in freier Wildbahn verdorben. Sie sind es gewohnt, in Gehegen zu existieren, alles Unerwartete versetzt sie in Panik. Sie haben etwas Kuhiges, sie malmen ihr Gras, glotzen den Horizont an und wollen pünktlich gemolken werden.'

7. 'Das könnte den Opportunisten so gefallen, daß ihre Fügsamkeit über Nacht vergessen ist, daß sie als Opfer dastehen, denen eine unüberwindliche Macht im Nacken gesessen hat. Im Nacken saß ihnen diese Macht wohl, und stark war sie auch, aber *unüberwindlich*?'

8. 'Der real existierende Sozialismus war ein Gemeinschaftswerk der Parteiführung, ihrer Handlanger und der vielen Gehorsamen.'

9. 'Die Bücher der Autoren [. . .], die sich mit dem Zensor anlegen, werden selbst von denen gelesen, die sonst nie ein Buch in die Hand nehmen würden.'

10. 'kein Mensch kannte sie vorher, jetzt vermissen sie alle.'

11. 'begierig auf Bücher, genauer – auf die Bücher der Abweichler'.

12. 'daß alle nicht verbotene Literatur mit dem Geruch existieren muß, erlaubt zu sein'.

13. 'Ich selbst habe erlaubte Bücher geschrieben.'

14. 'daß das Verbot eines Buches dem Autor oft eine größere Bekanntheit einbrachte, als die normale Veröffentlichung es getan hätte'.

15. 'einer jener Schriftsteller, die aus ihrer Feindseligkeit gegenüber unserem Staat einen Beruf gemacht haben'.

16. 'Natürlich kann er das nicht tun, er wird sich hüten, ein ehemals verbotener Autor zu werden, der schnell vergessen ist.'

17. 'Ist am Ende, wie makaber das auch klingt, Trauer um die Zensur gebracht?'

18. 'Anbiederung, Gefallsucht, Marktschreierei und Schlichtheit der Gedanken'.

19. 'Da wir, die DDR-Menschen, uns nie *selbst*kritisch mit unserer Vergangenheit beschäftigt haben, ging uns der Blick für das Faschistoide an unseren eigenen Verhältnissen und in unserem eigenen Verhalten verloren.'

20. 'Die deutsche Vereinigung war jedenfalls auch die Vereinigung der potentiellen mit den bereits praktizierenden Rechtsradikalen.'

21. 'Konsequenz seines Selbstverständnisses als Schriftsteller'.

22. 'Ich vermute, daß seit den Anfängen der Literatur der wesentlichste Antrieb zum Schreiben das Bedürfnis nach Stellungnahme gewesen ist, also nach Widerspruch.'

23. 'erzählt [. . .] von einem Unglück, [. . .] von einem Unbehagen, von einer Unzufriedenheit. Von Zweifel oder Verzweiflung. Vom Nichteinverstandensein mit etwas, das ist.'

24. 'das Toben der gesellschaftlichen Verhältnisse und Mißverhältnisse'.
25. 'um seinem Wohlbehagen Ausdruck zu geben, seiner Seligkeit, seinem Einverständnis, [. . .] Trivialliteratur'.
26. 'Ich habe eine Abneigung gegen Prosa, die ein Mittelding ist zwischen Belletristik und Essay. Mich stören an Romanen die eingeschobenen Vorträge.'
27. 'Bücher, in denen die Meinungen der Autoren zu lesen seien, glichen Gegenständen, an denen noch die Preisschilder hingen.'
28. 'Nein, dieses Motiv habe ich eigentlich nicht. Ich bin vielleicht ein Notwehrjournalist. Einer schnellen Not versuche ich mit einem Artikel oder mit einem Essay beizukommen. Aber [. . .] ein momentaner Ärger kann für mich nicht Ausgangspunkt eines Buches sein.'
29. 'Ich habe die Hoffnung, daß Literatur etwas ist, was dazu beitragen könnte, eine Gesellschaft, in der sie stattfindet, sensibler zu machen. Sensibler bedeutet, sensibler für Verunstaltung, sensibler für Gewalt, aufmerksamer für Unrecht.'
30. 'Auch wenn es wahr ist, daß meine Ansichten durchs Bücherlesen wesentlich beeinflußt wurden, schätze ich die Wirkung von Literatur nicht sehr hoch ein.'
31. 'Es mag Selbsttäuschung gewesen sein, wenn sie bisher glaubten, mit ihren Texten Einfluß auf gesellschaftliche Entwicklungen nehmen zu können; noch absurder aber ist die Hoffnung, daß ihnen dies in Zukunft möglich sein wird, da alles um sie herum Westen wird.'
32. 'Unverzichtbar ist der Literatur, daß *Leser* sich beim Lesen Meinungen bilden, *ihre* Meinungen, auf eine Weise, wie es ihnen ohne die Lektüre nicht möglich wäre.'
33. 'Wenn der Preis für eine gute und ruhige Existenz darin besteht, daß man gewisse Gedanken für sich behält und gewisse Handlungen unterläßt, und wenn man diesen Preis zahlt – das soll unterwürfig sein? Amanda ist eindeutig dieser Ansicht.'
34. 'Alle drei seien "Zerrbilder", aus deren durchwegs unobjektiven Erzählungen möglicherweise ein klares Bild im Kopf des Lesers entstehe.'
35. 'Andererseits ist Schreiben nichts anderes als eine endlose Reihe von Zweifeln, die zugunsten eines Satzes schließlich überwunden werden müssen.'
36. 'Es bleibt [. . .] offen, in welchem Land dieses Buch spielt. Es bleibt sogar offen, ob dieses Buch in der DDR oder in der Bundesrepublik spielt. [. . .] ich will verhindern, daß jemand es liest und sich beruhigt bei dem Gedanken, das findet auf der "anderen Seite" statt, das findet

jenseits der Grenze statt; das ist falsch. Es findet genau dort statt, wo man lebt.'

37. 'Schritt für Schritt bringt sich die Scheißmenschheit um, nach dem schlausten System, das je ersonnen wurde, doch wenn einer Die Sache für sich selbst erledigen möchte, auf eigene Rechnung sozusagen und vorneweg, dann werden ihm die größten Steine in den Weg gelegt.'

38. 'die vielen Kriege streben aufeinander zu: sie kommen näher und näher, sie haben mich zu ihrem Mittelpunkt erkoren und fressen sich von allen Seiten auf mich zu'.

39. 'Ich kann Nachrichten nicht mehr ertragen.'

40. 'erzählende Literatur immer dann eine gute Zeit [hat], wenn gesellschaftliche Auseindersetzungen stattfinden oder bevorstehen, wenn große Veränderungen sich ankündigen.'

41. 'daß ich [in *Amanda Herzlos*] die DDR-Jahre, die mir fehlen, aufgeschrieben habe.'

42. 'Ich halte seine Kritik für unziemlich, ich verstehe sie nicht, und zwar aus einem ganz bestimmten Grund: Die Abrechnung mit der DDR-Vergangenheit findet heute in jeder zweiten Fernsehsendung, in jeder zweiten Rundfunksendung und in jedem dritten Buch statt, das ich lese. Warum verlangt er von mir, daß ich das tue, was alle tun? Oder anders gefragt: Warum will er ein Buch, das er schon kennt? Das begreife ich nicht. Ich für meine Person finde es viel aufregender, Bücher zu lesen, die ich noch nicht kenne.'

43. 'Jurek Becker [. . .] nimmt hier Stellung, indem er zu den allerletzten Ereignissen nicht Stellung nimmt.'

44. 'Und weißt du, daß es an jeder Ecke Bananen zu kaufen gibt? So ein Unglück ist das ja auch nicht.'

New Modes of Portrayal?
Scriptwriting for Television

Liebling Kreuzberg

In the previous chapter, we noted Jurek Becker's doubts about the implications and effects of the 'Wende' on the role of writers, the words of warning which he issued to former GDR writers in this respect, and his attack on West German literature for its dependence on market forces. When we consider Becker's own career, though, we wonder perhaps whether he himself may have been guilty of the very things which he was criticising in the new German situation after unification, for Becker himself was and still is known to the wider (West) German public not for his literary works, but for his two extremely successful television series, the long-running *Liebling Kreuzberg* (Darling Kreuzberg, first shown in 1986) and *Wir sind auch nur ein Volk* (We are after all just a people, shown in 1994). The viewing figures for the first six episodes of *Liebling Kreuzberg* back in 1986 reached 47 per cent and it is still running today (January 1999), though later series have been taken over by other scriptwriters, including fellow GDR novelist Ulrich Plenzdorf. Becker's success with his television scripts is not limited to the realms of popular acclaim: fellow TV scriptwriter Wolfgang Menge declared *Liebling Kreuzberg* to be the best series which he had seen on television (cited by Durzak in Heidelberger-Leonard 1992: 313); it was awarded the Adolf Grimme Prize in 1987; and Keith Bullivant has even asserted that posterity will indeed remember Becker more for his brilliant television scriptwriting than for his novels and stories (Bullivant 1994: 107). How is one to reconcile, then, Becker's scathing criticism of the cultural scene in West Germany with his success in television, the most commercial of all capitalist media and also the one most subject to market forces, itself a 'Wirtschaftszweig' (branch of industry) and for many the home of the very 'Marktschreierei' (vociferous marketing) which Becker lambasted in his criticism of West German literature?

Is Becker perhaps guilty of the worst sort of hypocrisy? For even though he was no longer a communist, he had been quick to reiterate his sympathy with the socialist cause when the Wall came down in 1989. Like most critical writers in the GDR, Becker had been broadly supportive of the socialist ideology, even after leaving the GDR in 1977, though loyalties had been increasingly strained during the late 1970s and 1980s. He may have welcomed the breakdown of the SED regime and other 'actually existing' socialist states in 1989; yet at the same time, as we have seen, he lamented the disappearance of his hopes for a more humane form of society in the face of what he saw as the empty capitalism and consumerism of Western societies (Heidelberger-Leonard 1992: 59).

Is this a case, then, of the incorrigible socialist trying to have his capitalist cake and eat it? The issue is further complicated by the fatefully interconnected relationship between serious literature and a select elitist readership which persists above all in Germany, whereby bestsellers appear automatically dubious not only to such readers but also often to their serious authors themselves (Durzak in Heidelberger-Leonard 1992: 312). And often even more compromising in Germany is success which comes the way of serious authors in the most popular of the mass media, television.

Is Becker then to be regarded as a sort of Brechtian chameleon, one of the few former GDR writers to have successfully adapted to the harsher climate of market forces by employing a different medium of production – evidence, perhaps, that the only means of survival for former GDR writers in the new Germany involves a lowering of their sights and standards in order to aim at the lowest popular common denominator? Such an assumption, however, overlooks the element of continuity in his *œuvre* – the fact that Jurek Becker, as we have seen and like several other prominent GDR writers such as Günter Kunert and Ulrich Plenzdorf, had begun his career as a scriptwriter for DEFA, the nationalised East German film company. Indeed, we have noted that Becker's most successful novel, *Jakob der Lügner*, would never have been written if his original project in the form of a film script had been accepted by the censors at the time. In the GDR, he wrote no less than eleven film scripts (most of them comedies), five for television and six for the cinema, before leaving for the West where he was involved in scriptwriting for seven more films, apart from the two television series discussed here (see Bibliography). When Becker died, Hollywood had already begun work on a new production of *Jacob the Liar*, with Robin Williams in the main role.

Moreover, after living in West Germany for several years, Becker certainly had no illusions about television, expressing his dislike of this medium at the time that he was writing *Liebling Kreuzberg* and admitting that the only television programmes which he actually watched himself were live sports programmes (Schmitt in Heidelberger-Leonard 1992: 178).[1] Why, then, did he turn to writing for television once again? Two good reasons which Becker conceded back in 1987 were: first, the difficulties he was currently experiencing in writing prose, stemming from his fear of the danger of simply contributing to the trivia he saw all around him in every bookshop he entered; and second, the related feeling that he only had a small number of books within him: 'Increasingly, I have problems writing prose. Not for fear of lack of ability but of possibly contributing myself to all the superfluous literature that surrounds me now, today, in every bookshop. Some authors are only good for three or four books' (Heidelberger-Leonard 1992: 178).[2] In substantiation of this point, he later acknowledged that the sense of having produced something worthwhile was always greater with the film scripts for *Liebling Kreuzberg* than with his novels, where he had invariably been unsure as to whether he had managed to achieve his artistic intentions (Durzak in Heidelberger-Leonard 1992: 315).

What distinguishes *Liebling Kreuzberg* from all other lawyer series such as America's *Perry Mason* and *L.A. Law* or even the German ZDF programme *Ein Fall für Zwei* (A case for two), and also a main reason for its popularity, is the unorthodox character of Becker's central character, the lawyer Liebling, who is an idiosyncratic yet realistically drawn individual, and like some of the other main characters in Becker's novels, he is a nonconformist *par excellence* with his own little whims and quirks. The part was tailor made by Becker for the actor Manfred Krug, an old friend of the author's from his GDR days (not only did they live together as students in the 1950s, they also both left the GDR in the wake of the protests about Wolf Biermann's expatriation). Krug's powerful personality and physical presence are a distinguishing feature of the series. Becker later pointed out how working with Krug had been mutually productive: never before had Krug, a notoriously lazy learner of acting parts, managed to sustain a role so effortlessly, and never before had Becker, with his enormous talent for writing natural-sounding dialogue in his novels, been able to try it out straight away on someone whom he knew so well (Schmitt in Heidelberger-Leonard 1992: 180).

Liebling is the opposite of the stock TV-lawyer of American ilk with the flashily smooth image. That he is a humorous figure is signalled in his name, which is often the cause of comic misunderstanding on the telephone, exemplified in his irate words to a female public prosecutor: 'Hallo, Darling speaking. [. . .] No I'm not giving you the come on, it's my name!' (Heidelberger-Leonard 1992: 180).[3] Hooked on 'Götterspeise' (fruit jelly), he is often bad-tempered, goes around unkempt and half-shaven (definitely not a case of designer stubble), and takes off his shoes whenever he can. His scruffy appearance is perfectly complemented by his fat cigars and his 'flower-power' ties which always hang loosely from his collar. This liberal timekeeper pretends to be busy when he is not and can afford to be choosy about his clients as he has inherited a real-estate business and so he even has time to play at being the philanderer, easy-riding his way around Berlin on his motorbike. He delegates any unpleasant tasks to his guileless young colleague Arnold. Like his author, he is not a man of many words, but when he does open his mouth, he is a straight-shooter in his dealings with ordinary folk and he has the ability to explain complicated legal procedures in a direct, accessible way. He is, though, despite his dry, sometimes gruff, humour and brash tone of voice, not a comic character in the usual sense, but a recognised yet unorthodox figure of considerable authority, and his opponents underestimate his talents at their peril. He is, then, quite unlike his one-dimensional rationalist counterparts in American TV-series who, like pale relatives of Sherlock Holmes, solve their cases through intellectual brilliance and deductive logic. And though he is a Berliner born and bred, Liebling's success comes from characteristics which he shares with several of Becker's Jewish characters which come together in a potent mixture: he has the nous, cunning and craftiness of an Aron Blank (*Der Boxer*) and the quick inventiveness and tenacity of the courageous, inspired liar Jakob Heym (*Jakob der Lügner*), allied to his own special brand of chutzpah and rough humour.

As Manfred Durzak has pointed out (in Heidelberger-Leonard 1992: 319), Becker has thus managed to dismantle the falseness and artificiality of the American model, not least by demythologising the stock lawyer-hero, and it is this, together with the earthy Berlin humour and the fresh authenticity of the Kreuzberg setting with all its social heterogeneity that gives his script its special quality. The authenticity appears to be something which Becker was specifically aiming at, for when he was asked about his reasons for writing the series for television, he commented on his desire to avoid the artificiality so characteristic of many television series: 'What I do know, or what I hope, is that – apart from the dialogues and the actors and so on – perhaps one merit of this series was the absence of falseness. There was a certain degree of falseness missing which is usually accepted on television, particularly in series, as being commonplace' (Graf and Konietzny 1991: 68).[4] Thus as the author pointed out, the plots are concerned with everyday trivia, with market vendors who have lost their licences rather than with serial killers (Heidelberger-Leonard 1992: 181). According to Becker, the series is about: 'Modest, proletarian, everyday things [. . .] They aim to be run-of-the-mill stories, but not cheap, mass-produced items' (Heidelberger-Leonard 1993: 179).[5]

Moreover, the cases which Liebling deals with are themselves authentic, based on real ones encountered by the prominent Berlin lawyer Nicolas Becker (no relation to the author) who acted as adviser on legal matters and became for the legal layman Jurek Becker 'a superb guide-dog through this maze of snares' (Heidelberger-Leonard 1992: 179).[6] Real life is thus adapted and transformed by Becker into television drama, which itself throws light back onto real life by underlining the potential impotence of ordinary individuals in the face of inscrutable modern legal bureaucratic systems which have taken on a life of their own. It is the wily Liebling, of course, who helps them overcome this impotence: in his little explanatory asides to his clients and his assistants, he reveals, as Uwe Schmitt neatly puts it, 'his own miniature philosophy of law with laconic Berlin humour' (in Heidelberger-Leonard 1992: 181).[7] And so Liebling explains 'that you can expect a verdict from the courts, but not justice, [. . .] that it has to be a question of proof, not of guilt' (Heidelberger-Leonard 1992: 181).[8] The series is thus also distinguished from its lesser peers by a certain didactic dimension. Becker did not actually set out with any didactic intention; he was simply interested in writing a good story-line, as he commented in an interview: 'I have written a few stories which I considered justifiable in terms of my own taste – it was no more than that' (Graf and Konietzny 1991: 68).[9] Yet with the benefit of hindsight, he did recognise that, in effect, there was 'more than that' when reflecting on the question as to whether his series had had any influence on its viewers:

> Perhaps it has reinforced people's awareness just a little that it is not pointless to put up a fight. It really is important not to see legal events in a country as some fate which suddenly befalls one, but to see oneself as a participant in these legal events, as a subject and not as an object. But I would be lying if I told you that I had this didactic intention when I wrote it. (Graf and Konietzny 1991: 68)[10]

Wir sind auch nur ein Volk

With *Liebling Kreuzberg*, then, Becker became an established household name in Germany. But what about the later series *Wir sind auch nur ein Volk*, written after German unification? What were his motives for returning to television scriptwriting again after completing the best-selling novel *Amanda herzlos*, and had Becker meanwhile, in some way, modified his views on television as a medium?

Despite having been in the West for almost twenty years, Becker had found it difficult to write about life in the West in his prose works, and his novels and short stories written in the 1970s, 1980s and even in the 1990s, as we have seen, focused on his GDR experiences. Asked in a *Spiegel* interview in 1994 whether one of his recent characters, a writer from the West, was identical with his author, he retorted that the figure in question, Steinheim, was a man from the West, and that he had to invent people from the West since up to now he had not managed to be one himself (*Der Spiegel* 12.12.1994: 195). Becker described his seventeen years in the West as a transitional period and admitted that he had not managed to write prose which was set in the West, because he was unable to get rid of the feeling that here he was interfering in the 'Gelegenheiten fremder Leute' (affairs of strangers – *Der Spiegel* 12.12.1994: 195). Becker remained convinced that the experiential differences of people in the two Germanies would separate them for some time to come, and even in 1994, he was still referring to the East as the GDR: 'I say the GDR because I am convinced of the fact that what people associate with these three letters will be there for a long time to come' (*Der Spiegel* 1994: 195).[11]

Becker may have restricted the concerns of his prose writing to life in the GDR, yet he did confront the issue of the new Germany through the medium of television in his series *Wir sind auch nur ein Volk*. Why television? One reason was, of course, the most obvious one of all: the financial rewards ensuing from success in television, which in Becker's case were eventually considerable. And who can begrudge Jurek Becker the fruits of this success? He was aware of its positive potential as a medium, and his work for television hitherto had not involved any artistic compromise, any lowering of aesthetic standards. Only once had he wavered in this respect, admitting that during the writing of the first series of *Liebling Kreuzberg* he had been under considerable political pressure to rewrite the last episode, which dealt with the alleged but unproven maltreatment of an individual in police custody. After a protracted battle with the television company, Becker had given in with a heavy conscience. When he signed the contract for the second series, he made sure that he would not be vulnerable to such pressure again (cf. Heidelberger-Leonard 1992: 181). Indeed, that he was now more than ever on his guard against such dangers is illustrated in his defensive comments made during an interview given shortly after the first showing of *Liebling Kreuzberg*: 'I am not doing this work with my eyes closed. I cannot write better dialogues or scenes than the ones I am doing here. Not in any other story, or for any other payment' (Heidelberger-Leonard 1992: 176).[12] Moreover, Becker's integrity as a writer had been demonstrated only too well in the reasons behind his leaving of the GDR: as we have seen, he had been prevented from earning his living as a writer after his novel *Schlaflose Tage* had been rejected by the censor when Becker steadfastly refused to make any of the necessary modifications to specific details required by the Ministry for Culture.

The main reason, though, for Becker's turning to a different mode of portrayal does relate to his GDR upbringing, which shaped his earlier view of literature. In the early 1980s, as we have seen, he still held the view that literature had a social purpose, helping to make a society more sensitive, but this hope had faded somewhat after unification, with Becker now having serious doubts about the ability of writers to influence society through their books. Yet there was an alternative: television.

We have noted that when he set out to write *Liebling Kreuzberg* back in the mid-1980s, he did not have any overtly didactic intentions, yet by 1990, Becker had recognized the didactic potential. Television now appeared to him to be the one medium in the new Germany where writers could actually have a direct influence on their public, a view substantiated both by the popularity of his own series and by the considerable influence on public opinion in Germany exerted by Erich Loest's *Nicolaikirche* (St Nicholas's Church) in 1995, when the novel was adapted for television by Frank Beyer (Soldat 1997: 145).[13] Explaining his reasons for writing *Wir sind auch nur ein Volk* in an interview, Becker acknowledged not only his desire to entertain but also a more serious intention: to open people's eyes (particularly in the West) to the realities of the new Germany:

> Quite a few things are said and shown which appear to me to be appropriate with regard to our German situation. [. . .] The fact that so many West Germans are convinced that the GDR would not have been possible if they had been there; that their characters are so steadfast and their spines so rigidly constructed that the authorities over there would never have been able to bend them as they did the people in the GDR. Or I would like to open people's eyes to the fact that the different views and behaviour of East and West Germans will exist for as long as the conditions in which they live are so different. (*Der Spiegel* 12.12.1994: 96)[14]

These points were underlined by Otto Meissner, the producer, in his short summary of the series where he commented that they were interested not so much in the theme of reappraising the GDR past, but more with the questions as to how Germans from East and West might be able to find common ground again after forty years' separation and how to convey to West Germans some idea of the everyday lives of former citizens of the GDR: 'We were preoccupied with the question of conveying to the majority of the 60 million West Germans, in an amusing, entertaining way, some idea of the everyday lives of former citizens of the GDR' (Meissner 1994: IV/3).[15]

The title of Becker's TV series, *Wir sind auch nur ein Volk*, is of course yet another (this time ironic) modification of the famous phrases of November 1989, when the original opposition slogan of the 'sanfte Revolution' (gentle revolution), 'Wir sind das Volk' (we are the people), became the nationalistic 'Wir sind ein Volk' (we are one people). Becker explained his own variation thus: 'The title is intended to indicate that the author is making a plea for a more sober approach: he is saying that the elation of celebrating unification is past. Get your feet back on the ground, that's the best place to be!' (*Der Spiegel*, 12.12.1994: 200).[16] Whilst the title is an indication of the author's light-hearted approach to the subject, with his desire to deflate any remaining euphoria, it signals, too, a vein of humour far removed from the harsh, mocking satire of 'Motzki' and 'Trotski', the two controversial German television sitcoms featuring stereotypical characters: the West German Friedhelm Motzki, a 'foul-mouthed bigot in the Alf Garnett mould' (Rinke 1995: 236), and the East German antidote with the telling surname, Herbert Trotski. For all the laughter that they evoke, Becker's characters are, without exception, all allowed to retain their dignity.

The plot focuses directly on 'German–German' issues and their representation in the media, for *Wir sind auch nur ein Volk* is a television series within a television series. Self-referentiality and the representation of events between truth and fiction via the medium of television become central themes of Becker's series.[17] One of the directors of ARD television decides that it is time to put on a 'Serie zur Einheit' (series on unification) (also the self-referential title of the first episode of Becker's script): it will be a series about everyday life in a typical East German family which will be 'our contribution to furthering the mutual understanding of the people in East and West' (V 11).[18] 'Let's not kid ourselves,' he goes on, 'It is the sense of strangeness that separates us, and until we've overcome this, it will not be possible carry out the act of true union.' 'That sounds like a disgusting thing to do' (V 11),[19] thinks another director to himself, as Becker keeps his own feet firmly on the ground by amusingly deflating overblown aspirations not so far removed from his own in writing this series, one of numerous examples of authorial self-irony in the script.

Becker also thematises belletristic prejudices about television as a medium. For instance, the directors of ARD insist on commissioning the successful novelist Steinheim who, unlike Becker, has never written for television before, and his elitist wife immediately turns her nose up at the mere sound of the word 'Fernsehserie' (television series – V 37). The West German Steinheim, though, is attracted by the fee offered and easily overcomes such reservations. But he has to admit one seemingly insurmountable problem: not only has he never been to East Germany, he has never even met an 'Ossi' and declares, with his author's tongue firmly in his cheek, 'It is a bit of a problem writing about something you haven't got a clue about' (V 33).[20] He accepts the contract, however, on condition that the television company find a typical East German family for him to observe at close quarters: 'I would need a typical family in the East in whose house I could live for a while – a mouse-hole, as it were. And who would initiate me into the mysteries of the East, without feeling disturbed by my presence' (V 35).[21] Yet he is not optimistic for they would have to be in the position to offer him something different from the depressing stuff which appears in the newspaper every day and he concludes: 'In a word – such a family does not exist at all' (V 35).[22] The film producer knows better, however, pointing out that the East is 'voll von typischen Ostfamilien' (full of typical Eastern families), and encounters no difficulty in finding the 'Grimm family'. The Grimms consist of four members, three unemployed males and one working female: Benno is an unemployed 'Dispatcher', a GDR 'profession' which baffles all the 'Wessis' ; his wife Trude is a teacher, who explains that she is one of the few teachers at her school not to lose their job: 'I'm considered to be uncriminated, whatever that means' (V 49);[23] their son Theo, like his author, is a former student of philosophy; and Grandpa Blauhorn is a pensioner. The Grimms agree to be used as guinea pigs 'zu Studienzwecken' (for the purpose of study), despite Theo's misgivings about the venture: 'I suspect that in this television thing, we are supposed somehow to play the role of insects that somebody wants to look at under a magnifying glass, and I don't feel very happy about it. But if it pays well . . .' (V 52).[24]

The theme of discrepancies between representation and reality becomes a main source of comedy as Steinheim's putative empirical observation distorts its own results. For instance, after a couple of visits from the writer, the Grimms overhear a telephone call in which Steinheim informs his wife that the TV-people will have to get him a more inspiring family: instead of being supplied with the material for 'wahnsinnig originelle Geschichten', (incredibly original stories), he is merely 'Zeuge von tausend Alltäglichkeiten' (witness to a thousand commonplace events).

Afraid to jeopardise their fee for 'das Sich-beobachten-lassen' (having themselves watched), the family decide to spice up Steinheim's 'studies' in order to sustain his interest in them, and a series of comical episodes ensues, designed to initiate their guest from the West into many of the mysteries of life in the former GDR. One of the best of these occurs when Steinheim expresses the desire to meet a real, live former Stasi-collaborator. The Grimms, uncertain which of their acquaintances were definitely working for the Stasi, employ an actor-friend to play the role, and the latter, lamenting the absence of a script, gives an inspired performance, an on-the-spot improvisation of the 'authentic' Stasi-man that Steinheim expects.

It is interesting to compare Becker's literary treatment of the Stasi issue, his wry, humorous approach, with Wolf Biermann's advice on how to come to terms with the real life experience of betrayal. For the latter, the only way is to do it via a brutal literary treatment, 'with an aesthetic cosh': 'The only way you can still strike these rogues dead is with the aesthetic cosh and in alliance with the muses'.[25] Biermann offered the following advice to Karl-Heinz Jakobs on how best to respond to the revelation that a friend had spied on him for years: 'In my opinion you should write a great novel on this theme. That would be the only possible way to boot it into touch. [. . .] Your fiasco with this fellow Dahnke is as banal and cosy as a well-farted-on farmhouse chair which only becomes exciting when Van Gogh paints it. [. . .] Write it down in durable language – and floor the bastard' (cited by Wallace 1994: 126–7).[26] This is strong and no doubt therapeutic medicine as far as Jakobs is concerned, but is it a recipe for serious literature? I think not. Becker, on the other hand, as critics' favourable responses would indicate, managed to bridge the gap between 'Literatur und Unterhaltung' (literature and entertainment) precisely by eschewing the sort of literary hatchet job called for by Biermann. Becker's weapon was a gentle one, namely comic irony. And by giving the Stasi issue and other problems humorous treatment, he deterred such above-cited indulgence in bitter revenge, whilst also avoiding the sort of 'Ostalgie' (nostalgia for East Germany) prevalent elsewhere, which was losing sight of the reality which was the GDR.

The situation which Becker created in *Wir sind auch nur ein Volk* afforded him the opportunity to focus on realities, on the difficulties facing East Germans in the new political situation, but also to expose prejudices and false assumptions of 'Insektenforscher aus'm Westen' (insect-researchers from the West) as Theo Grimm, with humour typical of his author, calls them. As in Loest's *Nicolaikirche*, a family situation is employed to reflect social and political problems at first hand, but through delicate irony, Becker gives both the conventional family model, and the wider problems that it reflects, humorous treatment, thereby avoiding Loest's occasional tendency to cliché. For instance, during his stay in the East German household, Steinheim, for all his wit and culture, is ultimately exposed as the typically naive West German, unversed in the circumstances and sensibilities of the former GDR and its people, and all too frequently concealing his own ignorance under his air of easy superiority. Even the seemingly sophisticated scriptwriter, then, needs considerable time and effort before he is able to come to a balanced, realistic appreciation of these 'ordinary' Ossis. His initial impression, for instance, leads him to the assumption that an East Berlin family is no different from any other, be it in Hesse, Bavaria or Thuringia! Such naive oversimplifications are soon corrected, as Becker himself commented: 'Later he realises that this is wrong. The difference ensues from the fact that the Grimms are from the acceded area, not the old federal states. They have to find their feet in a completely new situation. The place where they have always been living is now suddenly the West' (*Der Spiegel* 12.12.1994: 195).[27]

Yet the strength of Becker's script lies not so much in the plot and the central themes set against the backcloth of East–West German problems, as in the sensitively drawn characters themselves who really do come alive, and in the humour which they generate. And even if, for the various reasons cited above, the author from the West is unable to experience the 'close up' of this family that he demands, 'with its cares, its joys, its dreams, its farts and its belches too' (V 30),[28] we, the TV audience do. Indeed, Becker lamented the lack of literature in Germany which deals simply with the ordinary and the everyday, a fault which may lie in the pressurising expectations of influential critics who hold court in the press and on television: 'In Germany more frequently than elsewhere, authors suffer the constraint of being expected to investigate the ultimate and most dreadful mysteries of life. Too seldom do they try to write just a book, too often the book to end all books. It seems to me that they lack the courage to be more commonplace' (*Der Spiegel* 1994: 197–8).[29] The strength of Becker's scriptwriting lies in the fact that he is more interested in stories about people than in historical and political events, as he commented in 1992, albeit with reference to his novel *Amanda herzlos*: 'My concern is not with the GDR but with stories I want to tell' (*Süddeutsche Zeitung*, 30.7.1992).[30] And Becker admitted that it was his move to the West which had changed him in this respect: 'Without a doubt, since I have been living here in the West, I have become more private. To the extent that I previously considered myself to be a social being, I now consider myself more and more to be a separate individual, of course with social interests and aspects too, no question about that' (Arnold 1992: 12).[31] Thus Becker now tended to focus his gaze even more than he had previously on private experience rather than socio-political circumstances, giving us even more of what Günter de Bruyn had called 'DDR-Innenansichten' (interior views of the GDR – de Bruyn 1992: 155). In his stories from the late 1970s, he had exposed the extent to which individuals in the GDR had internalised authoritarian character traits, and in his works written in the 1990s, the broader picture of social and political issues is gradually reflected through the fine details of people's everyday lives and experiences, as two critics have observed of *Amanda herzlos*: 'As if quite by the way, the reader learns more and more about everyday life in the GDR' (Köpf 1992);[32] 'It is precisely the casualness with which he introduces numerous facets of GDR history which makes his depiction credible and impressive' (Dobrick 1992).[33]

One year after the demise of the GDR, a country where many writers had felt obliged to wield a political axe, the prominent GDR novelist Christoph Hein commented that literature was starting to return to 'ihre eigentlichen Aufgaben' (its real tasks – Hein 1990: 23), employing a discourse rooted in personal, individual experiences of the ordinary and the everyday, and moved not by what Hein called the 'Mantel der Geschichte' (mantle of history), but by 'das Hemd der Geliebten' (the lover's shirt – Hein 1990: 5). It may well be the case that works such as Becker's television scripts *Liebling Kreuzberg* and *Wir sind auch nur ein Volk*, as well as his novel *Amanda herzlos*, all of which focus on these 'Innenansichten', will be recognised as particularly appropriate vehicles for probing the complex business of coming to terms with the new Germany.

Notes

1. The medium that he had loved since his later childhood was the radio. His first reward from his father for success at school had been his own radio, which, as he explained, became in one respect a substitute for the all the aunts and uncles whom he had lost: it supplied the stories which fired his imagination. He was extremely critical of the decline in standards of the state-owned radio stations in Germany in the 1990s (*Der Spiegel*, 49, no. 2, 1995).

2. 'Ich habe zunehmend Probleme mit dem Prosaschreiben. Nicht aus Furcht vor mangelnder Fähigkeit, sondern davor, zu dem Überflüssigen, das mich heute schon in jedem Buchladen umzingelt, womöglich selbst etwas beizutragen. Manche Autoren sind vielleicht nur gut für drei, vier Bücher.'

3. 'Hallo, Liebling hier. [. . .] Nein, ich will Sie nicht anmachen, ich heiße so!'

4. 'Was ich weiß, oder was ich hoffe, ist, daß – von Dialogen und Schauspielern und so weiter abgesehen – ein Vorzug dieser Serie vielleicht das Abhandensein von Verlogenheit war. Es fehlte ein gewisses Maß an Verlogenheit, wie es im Fernsehen, vor allem in Serien, als alltäglich gilt.'

5. 'Bescheidenes, Proletarisches, Alltägliches. [. . .] Es wollen Dutzendgeschichten sein, aber keine Dutzendware.'

6. 'ein unübertrefflicher Blindenhund durch dieses Gewirr von Fallstricken'.

7. 'eine kleine kritische Rechtsphilosophie mit lakonischem Berliner Humor'.

8. 'daß von Gerichten ein Urteil, nicht Recht erwartet werden darf, [. . .] daß es um Beweise, nicht um Schuld gehen muß.'

9. 'ich hab einige Geschichten erzählt, die ich mit meinem Geschmack für vertretbar hielt – mehr ist das nicht gewesen.'

10. 'Vielleicht hat sie ein wenig das Bewußtsein gestärkt oder geweckt, daß es nicht sinnlos ist, sich zu wehren. Ist ja eine bedeutende Sache, das Rechtsgeschehen in einem Land nicht für ein Schicksal zu halten, das vom Himmel über einen fällt, sondern sich als Teilnehmer an diesem Rechtsgeschehen, als Subjekt und nicht nur als Objekt zu verstehen. Es wäre aber verlogen, wenn ich Ihnen sagen wollte, ich hatte diese didaktische Absicht.'

11. 'Ich sage DDR, weil ich davon überzeugt bin: das, was man mit diesen drei Buchstaben assoziiert, wird es noch lange geben.'

12. 'Ich mache diese Arbeit nicht mit der linken Hand. Besser als ich hier Dialoge oder Szenen schreibe, kann ich es nicht. Bei keiner anderen Geschichte, für keine andere Bezahlung.'

13. The film was highly topical, mirroring the radically changing times of the final GDR years in the fortunes of the various members of a single, representative family.

14. 'Es wird einiges gesagt und gezeigt, was mir im Hinblick auf unsere deutsche Situation angemessen vorkommt. [. . .] Daß so viele Westdeutsche überzeugt davon sind, die DDR wäre mit ihnen nicht zu machen gewesen. Daß sie charakterlich so gefestigt und rückgratmäßig

so beschaffen sind, daß man sie nie so hätte verbiegen können wie die Leute in der DDR. Oder ich möchte den Blick dafür öffnen, daß die unterschiedlichen Ansichten und Verhaltensweisen der Ost- und Westdeutschen so lange existieren werden, so lange die Lebensbedingungen so unterschiedlich sind.'

15. 'Von den vielen Stoffen [. . .] interessierten uns weniger die Bewältigung und die Aufarbeitung der DDR-Vergangenheit, uns bewegte vor allem die Frage, wie die Deutschen nach 40jähriger Trennung und staatlicher Spaltung wieder zueinander finden könnten. [. . .] Uns beschäftigte die Frage: Wie kann man auf amüsante, unterhaltsame Weise der Mehrheit von 60 Millionen Westdeutschen einen Begriff vom Alltagsleben der ehemaligen DDR-Bürger vermitteln?'

16. 'Der Titel will andeuten, daß der Autor für mehr Nüchternheit plädiert: Das Hochgefühl der Vereinigungsfeierlichkeiten ist vorbei, will er sagen. Kommt auf den Teppich zurück, dort ist der beste Platz!'

17. Cf. The excellent analysis of this area in Mcgowan 1998: 36–47.

18. 'unseren Beitrag, das gegenseitige Verständnis der Menschen im Osten und Westen zu fördern.'

19. 'Machen wir uns doch nichts vor: Die Fremdheit ist es, die uns trennt, und ehe wir die nicht überwunden haben, wird der Akt der wahren Vereinigung sich nicht vollziehen lassen . . . [. . .] Das klingt ja wie eine Ferkelei.'

20. 'Es ist nicht ganz unproblematisch, über etwas zu schreiben, wovon man keine Ahnung hat.'

21. 'Ich bräuchte eine typische Familie im Osten, bei der ich sozusagen für eine Weile im Mauseloch leben darf. Die mich einweiht in die Geheimnisse des Ostens, ohne sich durch mich gestört zu fühlen.'

22. 'Mit einem Wort – so eine Familie gibt es überhaupt nicht.'

23. 'Ich gelte als unbelastet, was immer das bedeutet.'

24. 'Ich habe den Verdacht, daß wir bei dieser Fernsehsache irgendwie die Rolle von Insekten spielen sollen, die sich einer unter die Lupe ansehen will, und sehr wohl ist mir nicht dabei. Aber wenn's gut bezahlt wird . . .'

25. 'Diese Lumpen erschlägt man nur noch mit dem ästhetischen Knüppel und im Bündnis mit den Musen.'

26. 'Nach meiner Meinung solltest Du einen großen Roman über dieses Thema schreiben. Das wäre der einzig mögliche *Befreiungsschlag*. [. . .] Dein Fiasko mit diesem Dahnke ist so banal und gemütlich wie ein vollgefurzter Bauernstuhl, der erst aufregend wird, wenn Van Gogh ihn malt. [. . .] Schreib es in haltbarer Sprache auf. Und schreib ihn nieder, den Hund.'

27. 'Später merkt er, daß das nicht stimmt. Der Unterschied ergibt sich schon daraus, daß die Grimms zum Beitrittsgebiet gehören, nicht zum Stammgebiet. Sie müssen sich in einer vollkommen neuen Situation zurechtfinden. Da, wo sie seit jeher wohnen, ist plötzlich Westen.'

28. 'Mit ihren Sorgen, mit ihren Freuden, mit ihren Träumen, mit ihren Fürzen und nicht zuletzt mit ihren Rülpsern.'

29. 'In Deutschland leiden Autoren häufiger als anderswo unter dem Zwang, daß ihre Bücher den letzten ungeheuerlichsten Geheimnissen des Lebens nachspüren sollten. Man will zu selten ein Buch schreiben und zu oft das Buch der Bücher. Es fehlt, so scheint mir, der Mut, alltäglicher zu sein.'

30. 'Es geht mir nicht um die DDR, sondern um Geschichten, die ich erzählen will.'

31. 'Ganz zweifellos habe ich mich, seit ich hier im Westen lebe, privatisiert. In dem Maße, wie ich mich vorher für ein gesellschaftliches Wesen gehalten habe, halte ich mich mehr und mehr für ein einzelnes Wesen, sicher mit gesellschaftlichen Interessen und Aspekten, keine Frage.'

32. 'Wie nebenher erfährt der Leser immer mehr über den Alltag in der DDR.'

33. 'Gerade die Beiläufigkeit, mit der er zahlreiche Facetten der DDR-Historie plaziert, macht seine Schilderung glaubwürdig und eindrucksvoll.'

Conclusion

When he heard of Jurek Becker's death in March 1997, the dissident poet and songwriter Wolf Biermann was not alone in describing him as one of 'the very best the GDR managed to produce'[1] and in ranking *Jakob der Lügner* as 'Weltliteratur' (world literature – *Bote von Untermain* 16.3.1997). In his affectionate tribute to his close friend Jurek Becker, the writer Peter Schneider predicted that he would be one of only five or six authors of his generation in Germany to be remembered in twenty or even a hundred years' time (Riordan 1998: 5); for with his death, German literature had lost a solo-artist: a writer who restored to modern German literature something that had been missing for some fifty years, since the expulsion and murder of the Jews, namely, that 'lightness, melancholy wit, intellectual sharpness and wonderfully effortless sentimentality'[2] so characteristic of Jewish-German writers of the past. And ironically, it was precisely these so 'un-German' qualities, together with his casual yet finely detailed realism, unfashionable with many of his German critics, and his ability as raconteur, another Jewish trait, which made him so popular with his German reading public. Also unique in post-war Germany was the way in which this Polish survivor of the Holocaust mastered the language of his would-be immolators: it became the tool with which he equipped his brilliant imagination in the recreation of the world of his childhood and the search for that part of his identity which he had lost along with his memories of the years in the ghetto and concentration camps.

In all his works, he portrayed his characters as active subjects, not as objects. Just as he showed East Berliners in his television series *Liebling Kreuzberg* becoming participants in legal events, so too he did he avoid the stereotypical portrayal of Jews as passive victims, one of his great contributions to Holocaust literature. Even tormented individuals such as Aron Blank in *Der Boxer* consciously resist the easy-way-out role of victim: like the narrator in *Jakob der Lügner*, Aron detests the pity which he detects in the eyes of others, such as the official in Berlin who gives him his identity papers: 'this *penetrating* pity in his eyes, the sort of sympathy which Aron loathed from the very outset' (B 22).[3]

Becker was also without precedent in East or West German literature in giving an analysis and portrayal of delicate general Jewish issues unclouded by sentimentality or prejudice. And although his works do have autobiographical dimensions, as we have seen, he was also moved to ask the wider, sensitive questions which others in Germany felt unable to ask. In *Bronsteins Kinder*, for instance, as he explained in an interview in 1986, he was posing the hitherto neglected question as to why there were so few recorded individual cases of 'Selbstjustiz' (self-administered justice):

> In terms of statistics, what the novel portrays is not typical, that is true. But the fact that such a case did not occur in reality is, though, the strangest thing of all. In all probability, such a story ought to have taken place a thousand times. I was preoccupied with the question as to why the survivors' anger is so minimal. One subject which has often been discussed is the way in which the victims went to their deaths so obediently. (Hage 1986: 338)[4]

Becker's novels demonstrate, too, that the sheer scale of the Holocaust still made it impossible for an 'unverkrampftes Verhältnis' (relaxed relationship – Riordan 1998: 17) to exist between 'older Jews and older Germans'. Although Becker believed this to be the case on a general level, in his own private life, he had himself come close to such a relationship, as he explained: 'I know of cases where one can observe a very relaxed relationship between Jews and Germans. I would maintain that the relationship between me and my wife is a model example of the possibility of a relaxed relationship' (Riordan 1998: 5).[5] What his novels do suggest, as Becker claimed (Hage 1986: 336–8), is that many Jews had become too dependent on the Shoah for their sense of identity, for being a victim brought with it its own deformities, as the author explained when outlining his motives for writing *Bronsteins Kinder*: he was concerned with awkward, hitherto infrequently raised questions, such as 'in what ways the deformities of the victims manifest themselves. But being a victim also means: being deformed. Can this not also make victims ugly? In films, I am used to seeing nice victims' (Hage 1986: 337).[6] The 'Selbstjustiz' of Arno Bronstein and his fellow camp-survivors, as they turn the tables on their former guard, is an example of such 'ugliness'. Hans eventually realises that the only way to release his father from himself is to free Heppner, but his father dies before Hans's strategy can take effect: his heart attack is a direct result of the stress caused by his violent attempt to settle his scores with the past. The outcome of the novel endorses Becker's view that attitudes and emotions rooted in the past are deformities which prevent survivors from living life to the full in the present and ultimately destroy them.

At the time, Becker also saw evidence of such 'ugliness' in the wider political context in the actions of a Jewish state, Israel: 'There the Jews are taking liberties with justice which cannot be derived from their past. In this book [*Bronsteins Kinder*], I described a similar phenomenon on a personal level.'[7] He claimed, then, that his novel demonstrated that 'being a [Jewish] victim did not give one licence to take the law into one's own hands, or any claim to freedom from criticism'.[8] Becker had written his earlier novel *Der Boxer* in the GDR, where Israel was synonymous with capitalist imperialism, and several critics saw the aggressive personality of one of the central characters reflecting the new Israeli form of Jewishness. The title of the novel refers to an incident when Aron's son Mark is beaten at school and Aron arranges for him to have boxing lessons so that he can defend himself against possible anti-Semitic attacks, warning his son: 'I don't want to make you into a thug, but into someone who can defend himself against thugs' (B 238).[9] But to Aron's dismay, Mark uses his new skill to bully his schoolmates, leading critics such as Chaim Shoham to conclude: 'It can be assumed that Jurek Becker created in Mark the character of the new Israeli Jew: he simply begins to box because he has mastered the art of boxing, as opposed to saving this ability just for purposes of defence' (Shohaim 1986: 234).[10]

Yet this controversial standpoint, shaped by Becker's GDR experiences, only represented one side of the coin, and a temporary one at that. His opinions remained open regarding other aspects of the complex Israeli-Jewish issue. He was only prepared to be persuaded by intellectual argument, though, not by emotion and prejudice, which he abhorred. And by the 1990s, his views on Israeli politics, just as controversial as his earlier ones, had in some ways turned about face. Influenced by personal visits to Israel and by Philip Roth's book *Counterlife*, he found the arguments of the Palestinians for their own state on Israeli territory unconvincing, not only in view of what had happened during the last twenty years, but looking a little further back in history, though 'not back as far as the Old Testament. [. . .] The Jewish need for an impregnable fortress, for a secure refuge, seems to me to be overwhelmingly plausible' (Riordan 1998: 16).[11]

Even in his GDR times, he had been prepared to speak out when his views were controversial, for though his most famous character was a liar, Jurek Becker himelf was a firm believer in truth as the only way to overcome the terrible legacy of the past:

You must not lie to yourself about the past. Otherwise it will not cease to torment you. You must not lie to yourself about what happened, and by telling the truth, you will be able, at some time or other, to cease discussing it. I want people to be enlightened about Auschwitz, because so many untruths are in circulation. And when these untruths have been eliminated, you can gradually cease fighting for the truth. (Riordan 1998: 16)[12]

Notes

1. 'zum Allerbesten, was die DDR überhaupt zustande gebracht hat'.

2. 'die Leichtigkeit, den melancholischen Witz, die intellektuelle Schärfe und jene wunderbar schwebende Sentimentalität'.

3. 'dieses *penetrante* Mitleid in den Augen, eine Art von Anteilnahme, die Aron schon von allem Anfang an zuwider war.'

4. 'Im Sinne der Statistik ist das im Roman Geschilderte nicht typisch, das ist wohl wahr. Aber das sich ein solcher Fall nicht in der Wirklichkeit zugetragen hat, ist dennoch seltsamer als alles andere. Aller Wahrscheinlichkeit nach hätte eine solche Geschichte tausendmal geschehen müssen. Es hat mich beschäftigt, warum der Zorn der Überlebenden so gering ist. Oft ist ja darüber diskutiert worden, wie folgsam die Opfer in den Tod gegangen sind.'

5. 'Ich kenne Fälle, wo ein sehr unverkrampftes Verhältnis zwischen Juden und Deutschen zu beobachten ist. Ich behaupte, daß das Verhältnis zwischen mir und meiner Frau ein Musterbeispiel dafür ist, daß ein unverkrampftes Verhältnis möglich ist.'

6. 'worin die Deformationen der Opfer sich äußern. Opfer sein heißt aber auch: deformiert sein. Kann es nicht auch häßlich machen? Ich bin aus Filmen gewöhnt, schöne Opfer zu sehen.'

7. 'Man nimmt sich dort Rechte heraus, die auch aus der Vergangenheit der Juden nicht abzuleiten sind. Etwas Ähnliches beschrieb ich auf persönlicher Ebene in diesem Buch.'

8. 'daß es keinen Freibrief für Selbstjustiz geben sollte, wenn einer Opfer gewesen ist, und keinen Anspruch auf Kritiklosigkeit.'

9. 'Ich will keinen Schläger aus dir machen, sondern einen, der sich gegen Schläger wehren kann.'

10. 'Es ist anzunehmen, daß Jurek Becker in Mark den Charakter des neuen israelischen Juden schuf, der nur zu boxen beginnt, weil er

die Kunst des Boxens beherrscht, im Gegensatz zur Aufsparung dieses Könnens für Verteidigungszwecke allein.'

11. 'nicht bis zum alten Testament. [. . .] Das jüdische Bedürfnis nach einer uneinnehmbaren Festung, nach einem sicheren Fluchtpunkt, scheint mir überwältigend einleuchtend zu sein.'

12. 'Man darf sich über die Vergangenheit nicht belügen. Sonst hört sie nicht auf, einen zu quälen. Man darf sich nicht belügen, über das, was geschehen ist, und indem man die Wahrheit sagt, kann man irgendwann mal aufhören, darüber zu reden. Ich will, daß über Auschwitz aufgeklärt wird, weil so viel Unwahrheit in Umlauf ist. Und wenn die Unwahrheit eliminiert ist, kann man allmählich aufhören, für die Wahrheit zu kämpfen.'

Bibliography

Primary Sources

Book Editions

Jakob der Lügner, Berlin and Weimar, Aufbau Verlag, 1969. – Further editions: Neuwied and Berlin, Luchterhand, 1970; Frankfurt am Main, Suhrkamp, 1976; Rostock, Hinstorff, 1976; Frankfurt am Main, suhrkamp taschenbuch 774, 1982; Leipzig, Reclam, 1988; Stuttgart, Deutscher Bücherbund, 1991.

Irreführung der Behörden, Rostock, Hinstorff, 1973; Frankfurt am Main, Suhrkamp, 1973; Frankfurt am Main, suhrkamp taschenbuch 271, 1975; Berlin (East), Volk und Welt, 1989.

Der Boxer, Rostock, Hinstorff, 1976; Frankfurt am Main, Suhrkamp, 1976; Berlin (East), Volk und Welt, 1978; Frankfurt am Main, suhrkamp taschenbuch 526, 1979.

Schlaflose Tage, Frankfurt am Main, Suhrkamp, 1978; Frankfurt am Main, suhrkamp taschenbuch 626, 1980.

Nach der ersten Zukunft, Frankfurt am Main, Suhrkamp, 1980; Frankfurt am Main, suhrkamp taschenbuch 941, 1985.

Aller Welt Freund, Frankfurt am Main, Suhrkamp, 1982; Rostock, Hinstorff, 1983; Frankfurt am Main, suhrkamp taschenbuch 1151, 1985.

Bronsteins Kinder, Frankfurt am Main, Suhrkamp, 1986; Rostock, Hinstorff, 1987; Frankfurt am Main, suhrkamp taschenbuch 1517; Leipzig, Reclam, 1990.

Erzählungen, Rostock, Hinstorff, 1986.

Warnung vor dem Schriftsteller. Drei Vorlesungen in Frankfurt, Frankfurt am Main, Suhrkamp, 1990.

Die beliebteste Familiengeschichte und andere Erzählungen, Frankfurt am Main, Insel, 1992.

Amanda herzlos. Roman, Frankfurt am Main, Suhrkamp, 1992.

Wir sind auch nur ein Volk 1–9, Frankfurt am Main, Suhrkamp, 1994–5.

Ende des Größenwahns, Frankfurt am Main, Suhrkamp, 1996.

Liebling Kreuzberg. Lieblings neues Glück, Frankfurt am Main, Suhrkamp, 1997.

Liebling Kreuzberg. Der Verbieter, Frankfurt am Main, Suhrkamp, 1997.

Special Editions

Das Märchen von der kranken Prinzessin. Von Jakob erzählt, with 32 illustrations by Annegret Fuchshuber, Mödling and Vienna, St. Gabriel, 1993.

Jurek Becker. Five Stories, ed. David Rock, Manchester, Manchester University Press, 1993.

Essays in Anthologies, Journals and Newspapers

(Entries are ordered by date)

[Untitled], in *56 Autoren Photos Karikaturen Faksimiles*, Berlin and Weimar, Aufbau, 1970, 22–3.

'Nichtigkeiten. Über Heinz Kahlau', in Annie Voigtländer (ed.), *Liebes- und andere Erklärungen. Schriftsteller über Schriftsteller*, Berlin and Weimar, Aufbau, 1972, 161–6.

'Über verschiedene Resonanzen auf unsere Literatur' (Diskussionsbeitrag auf dem 7. Schriftstellerkongreß der DDR), *Neue Deutsche Literatur*, vol. 22, 1974, no. 2, 55–60.

'Endstation', *Dimension*, Special Issue 1973 on the GDR, 161–6.

'Heilsame Überforderung. Ein Bekenntnis zu Thomas Mann', *Stuttgarter Zeitung*, no. 122, 31.5.1975, 51.

'Das ist ja der Poeten Amt' (review of Hans Joachim Schädlich's *Versuchte Nähe*), *Der Spiegel*, no. 43, 17.10 1977, 254–7.

'Die Zähne. Eine heitere und nachdenkliche Geschichte aus dem Kultur- leben der DDR', *Frankfurter Allgemeine Zeitung*, no. 294, 19.12.1977, 19.

'Mein Judentum', in Hans J. Schulz (ed.), *Mein Judentum*, Stuttgart, Kreuz Verlag, 1978, 8–18.

'Wäre ich hinterher klüger? Mein Judentum', in *Frankfurter Allgemeine Zeitung*, no. 98, 13.5.1978.

'Ohio bei Nacht', in *ZEITmagazin*, no. 50, 8.12.1978, 58–60.

'Brief an Hermann Kant' (1979), in Heinz Ludwig Arnold (ed.), *Jurek Becker, text + kritik*, 116 (1992), 51–9.

'Strauß', in *L'80. Politische und literarische Beiträge: Demokratie und Sozialismus*, no. 13 (1980), 80–4.

'Zum Thema: Literatur und Kritik', in Walter Jens (ed.), *Literatur und Kritik*, Stuttgart, Deutsche Verlags-Anstalt, 1980, 144–50.

'Denk ich an Deutschland in der Nacht', *Frankfurter Allgemeine Zeitung*, 18.10.1980.

'Betroffen sein aus Liebe. Max Frisch zu seinem 70. Geburtstag', *Der Tagesspiegel*, Berlin, 15.5.1981, 4.

'Der Ewige Jude gibt keine Ruhe' (review of Stefan Heym's *Ahasver*), *Der Spiegel*, no. 45, 2.11.1981, 240–6.

[Untitled], *Diskussion Deutsch*, 14, no.72 (1983), 455.

'Ansprache vor dem Kongreß der unbedingt Zukunftsfrohen', in Michael Krüger and Klaus Wagenbach (eds), *Tintenfisch 20. Jahrbuch für Literatur*, Berlin, Wagenbach, 1981, 72–7.

'Ein System von Alarmglocken. Rede vor dem niederländischen PEN-Club', in Ingrid Krüger (ed.), *Mut zur Angst. Schriftsteller für den Frieden*, Darmstadt and Neuwied, Luchterhand, 1982, 96–106.

'Über den Kulturverfall in unserer Zeit', *Die Zeit*, no. 20, 13.5.1983.

'Resistance in *Jakob der Lügner*', *Seminar*, vol. 19, 1983, no. 4, 269–73 and 288–92.

'Bücherverbrennung' (1983), in Jurek Becker, *Ende des Größenwahns*, Frankfurt am Main, Suhrkamp, 1996, 47–9.

'Über den Wert der bürgerlichen Rechte' (1983), in Irene Heidelberger-Leonard (ed.), *Jurek Becker*, Frankfurt am Main, Suhrkamp, 1992, 43–51.

'Antrittsrede', *Jahrbuch der Deutschen Akademie für Sprache und Dichtung, Darmstadt*, 1983/II, Heidelberg, Lambert Schneider, 1984, 115–16.

'Die Ernüchterung', *die tageszeitung*, 19.2.1987.

'Auf- und Abrüstung', *die tageszeitung*, 24.4.1987.

'Er kommt. Vorschau auf einen Staatsbesuch im September', *Die Zeit*, 24.7.1987.

'Nachmittags mit leisem Bemüh'n', (on Pablo Picasso), *ZEITmagazin*, no. 46, 6.11.1987, 9.

'Eine Art von Selbstverstümmelung. Über das Autoritätsgehabe der SED-Führung', *Der Spiegel*, no. 6, 8.2.1988.

'Gedächtnis verloren – Verstand verloren. Antwort an Martin Walser', *Die Zeit*, no. 47, 18.11.1988.

'Das olympische Elend' (1988), in Jurek Becker, *Ende des Größenwahns*, Frankfurt am Main, Suhrkamp, 1996, 63–77.

'Das Bleiberecht der Bücher' (1989), in Jurek Becker, *Ende des Größenwahns*, Frankfurt am Main, Suhrkamp, 1996, 85–107.

'Lebenslänglich Manfred Krug', in Bernd Schultz (ed.), *Manfred Krug.*

Porträt des Sängers und Schauspielers, Bergisch Gladbach, Lübbe 1989, 7–9.

'Die Suppe ist eingebrockt', *Die Zeit*, 6.10.1989.

'Die unsichtbare Stadt', in Hanno Loewy and Gerhard Schoenberner (eds), *'Unser einziger Weg ist Arbeit'. Das Getto in Lodz 1940–1044* (Exhibition, Jüdisches Museum, Frankfurt am Main), Vienna, Löcker, 1990, 10–12.

'Die Wiedervereinigung der deutschen Literatur', *The German Quarterly*, vol. 63, 1990, nos. 3/4, 359–66.

'Über die letzten Tage. Ein kleiner Einspruch gegen die große deutsche Euphorie', *Neue Rundschau*, vol. 101 no.1, 1990, 90.

'Zum Bespitzeln gehören zwei. Über den Umgang mit der DDR-Vergangenheit', *Die Zeit*, no. 32, 3.8.1990.

'Mit den Ohren sehen' (1990), in Robert Kuhn and Bernd Kreutz (eds), *Das Buch vom Hören*, Freiburg i. Br., Herder, 1991, 111.

'Vom Handwerkszeug des Schriftstellers' (1990), in Jurek Becker, *Ende des Größenwahns*, Frankfurt am Main, Suhrkamp, 1996, 147–55.

'Die wünschenswerte Schule' (1991), in Jurek Becker, *Ende des Größenwahns*, Frankfurt am Main, Suhrkamp, 1996, 156–7.

'Eine alte Geschichte' (1992), in Reinhard Appel (ed.), *Wehret den Anfängen. Prominente gegen Rechtsextremismus und Fremdenhaß*, Bergisch Gladbach, Lingen, 1993, 17–19.

'Der Defekt ist der Normalfall. Der Schriftsteller Jurek Becker über Arroganz und Opportunismus in West- und Ostdeutschland', *Der Spiegel*, 47 no. 36, 1993, 86–8.

'Die Stunde der Halbwahrheit', *Börsenblatt für den Deutschen Buchhandel*, 15.1.93.

'Eine Art Einheit', *Freibeuter*, no. 57, 1993, 39–41.

'Für ein Schriftsteller-Treffen in Dublin' (1993), in Jurek Becker, *Ende des Größenwahns*, Frankfurt am Main, Suhrkamp, 1996, 167–76.

'Mein Vater, die Deutschen und ich', *Die Zeit*, 20.5.1994.

'Die Worte verschwinden. Über den Niedergang des öffentlich-rechtlichen Rundfunks' (1994), *Der Spiegel*, 49, no. 2, 1995, 156–61.

'Leserbrief', *Der Spiegel*, 49, no. 4, 1995, 7–10.

'Leserbrief', *Der Spiegel*, 49, no. 36, 1995, 7.

'The Centipede', *World Literature Today*, 69 (1995), 477–81 [Translation of 'Der Tausendfüßler', from *Ende des Größenwahns*, Frankfurt am Main, Suhrkamp, 1996, 216–30].

Interviews

(Entries are ordered by date)

Eberlein, Sybille, 'Ein Filmmann, der Romane schreibt', *Wochenpost*, no. 18, 27.4.1973.

Benckelmann, Jürgen, 'Ich nehme einen ausländischen Literaturpreis an', *Frankfurter Rundschau*, no. 21, 25.1.1974.

Corino, Karl, 'Deprimieren ist für mich kein Schreibmotiv', *Deutsche Zeitung*, no. 11, 15.3.1974.

Wambutt, Marianne and Novotny, Ehrentraud, '"Ich habe die Absicht . . .", Werkstattgespräch mit dem Schriftsteller Jurek Becker', *Berliner Zeitung*, no. 76, 17.3.1974.

Lübbe, Peter, 'Literatur contra Opportunismus', *Deutschland Archiv*, 1974, no. 5, 520–627.

'Über die Historie hinaus. BZ-Gespräch mit Jurek Becker zum Fernseh- und Kinofilm *Jakob der Lügner*', *Berliner Zeitung*, no. 351, 20.12. 1974.

Voigt, Jutta, 'Lust auf Leben. *Jakob der Lügner* eröffnet den Monat des antiimperialistischen Films', *Sonntag*, no. 16, 20.4.1975.

Stapel, Eduard, 'Schreiben als Abenteuer', *Freie Erde* (Neubrandenburg), no. 109, 7.5.1976.

Schlumberger, Hella, '"Die Linken sind leiser geworden." Gespräch mit dem DDR-Autor Jurek Becker über seine bundesdeutschen Eindrücke', *Frankfurter Rundschau*, no. 264, 23.11.1976.

Rumler, Fritz and Schwarz, Ulrich '"Ich glaube, ich war ein guter Genosse." Schriftsteller Jurek Becker über die Nach-Biermann Ära in der DDR', *Der Spiegel*, no. 30, 18.7.1977, 128–33.

Schütte, Wolfram, 'Die Bevölkerung muß endlich so behalten werden wie die Künstler. *FR*-Gespräch mit Schriftsteller Jurek Becker', *Frankfurter Rundschau*, no. 206, 6.9.1977.

Schwarz, Wilhelm, 'Jurek Becker (Interview 17.8.1977)', in Wilhelm Schwarz, *Protokolle. Gespräche mit Schriftstellern*, Frankfurt am Main and Bern, Peter Lang, 1990, 113–30.

Isani, Claudio, 'Übereinstimmung ums Verrecken?', *Der Abend* (Berlin), no. 37, 13.2.1978.

Zipser, Richard A., 'Interview with Jurek Becker (Oberlin, May 1978)', *Dimension*, vol. 11, 1978, no. 3, 407–16.

Hübsch, Reinhard, '"Politisches Verhalten gehört zu meinem Stoff- wechsel." Ein Gespräch mit dem DDR-Schriftsteller Jurek Becker', *Stuttgarter Nachrichten*, no. 12, 15.1.1980.

Schwarz, Ulrich and Becker, Rolf, '"Ja, wenn Stalin ein großer Mann war . . ." Schriftsteller Jurek Becker über seine Existenz zwischen Ost und West', *Der Spiegel*, no. 10, 3.3.1980, 205–12.

Schiffner, Andrea, 'Politisches Verhalten ist optimistisches Verhalten', *Deutsche Post*, no.6, 20.3.1983.

Kalb, Peter E. and Geisler, Wolfgang, 'Ich will Ihnen dazu eine kleine Geschichte erzählen', in Peter E. Kalb (ed.), *Einmischung. Schriftsteller über Schule, Gesellschaft, Literatur*, Weinheim, Beltz, 1983, 56–66.

'Answering Questions about *Jakob der Lügner*', Heinz Wetzel, *Seminar*, 19, 1983, 288–92.

Pfeiffer, Helmut, 'Jurek Becker und Günter Kunert werden in Gespräch und Lesung vorgestellt', in Helmut Pfeiffer (ed.), *Deutsche Autoren heute 6*, Bonn, Inter Nationes, 1984, 4–36.

Hage, Volker, 'Interview mit Jurek Becker', *Die Zeit*, 3.10.1986.

'Interview mit Jurek Becker', *Videotext für alle,* ARD/ZDF, Vormittags-programm, 16.7.87.

Hage, Volker, 'Hinter dem Rücken des Vaters', in Volker Hage (ed.), *Deutsche Literatur 1986, Jahresüberblick*, Stuttgart, Reclam, 1987, 331–42.

Stöhr, Ingo Roland, '"Die wahre Aufregung . . ." Ein Gespräch mit Jurek Becker', *Dimension*, vol. 17, no.1, 1988, 8–29.

Birnbaum, Marianne, 'Das Vorstellbare gefällt mir immer besser als das Bekannte' (1988), in Irene Heidelberger-Leonard (ed.), *Jurek Becker*, Frankfurt am Main, Suhrkamp, 1992, 89–107.

Bodenheimer, Alfred, 'Es können gar nicht genug Einflüsse von aussen nach Deutschland kommen', *Jüdische Rundschau*, 15.6.1989.

Bodenheimer, Alfred, '"Die Republikaner sind ja nicht vom Himmel gefallen". Gespräch mit dem Schriftsteller Jurek Becker über politische Tendenzen in Deutschland', *Allgemeine Jüdische Wochenzeitung*, no.44, 15.9.1989.

Mehr, Max Thomas, '"Eine nicht ganz vollzogene Scheidung." Gespräch mit dem Schriftsteller Jurek Becker über die DDR, die Partei der Flucht und die Schwierigkeiten der Opposition', *die tageszeitung,* no.2919, 25.9.1989.

'Werkstattgespräch mit Jurek Becker', in Karin Graf and Ulrich Konietzny (eds), *Jurek Becker*, Munich, iudicium, 1991, 56–74.

Arnold, Heinz Ludwig, 'Gespräch mit Jurek Becker' (1990), in Heinz Ludwig Arnold (ed.), *Jurek Becker, text + kritik*, 116, 1992, 4–14.

'Interview mit Jurek Becker', in Dieter Arnsdorf and Hans-Georg Knapp (eds), *Literarische Porträts: Jurek Becker*, Munich, iudicium, 1992, 1–10 [Begleitheft zur Videokassette; Eine Reihe des Goethe-Instituts München].

Meyer-Gosau, Frauke, 'Fortschritt kann auch in Ernüchterung bestehen', in Irene Heidelberger-Leonard (ed.), *Jurek Becker*, Frankfurt am Main, Suhrkamp, 1992, 108–22.

Steinert, Hajo, Arnold, Heinz and Isenschmidt, Andreas, '"Ich will kein Scharfmacher sein." Gespräch mit dem Autor Jurek Becker', *Süddeutsche Zeitung*, 30.7.1992.

Traub, Rainer and Becker, Rolf, 'Wunsch nach etwas Obsessivem', *Spiegel Spezial. Bücher '92*, 104–11.

Kamman, Petra, 'Geschichte über Geschichten', *Buch Journal*, no. 3, 1992, 20–4.

Wilke, Klaus, 'Es geht nicht an . . .', *Lausitzer Rundschau*, 22.10.1992.

Höbel, Wolfgang, '"Ich will mir nichts vorschreiben lassen." Jurek Becker über die Aufforderung zum politischen Engagement', *Süddeutsche Zeitung*, 27.10.1992.

'Jurek Becker. Nicht ganz so herzlos', *Stuttgarter Zeitung*, 7.11.1992.

Gaus, Günter, 'Ein Mann, der sich nicht in Schablonen packen läßt' (1993), in Günter Gaus, *Zur Person*, Berlin, edition ost, 1998, 9–26.

Kaindlstorfer, Günter, 'Ich kann meine Bücher gar nicht leiden!', *Die Weltwoche*, 14.1.1993.

Mischke, Roland, 'Herr Becker, ist "Amanda" ein typisch deutsches Schicksal?', *Diners Club Magazin*, no. 4, 1993, 34–7.

Doerry, Martin and Hage, Volker, '"Zurück auf den Teppich!" Der Schriftsteller Jurek Becker über seine neue Fernsehserie, über deutsche Dichter und die Nation', *Der Spiegel*, 48, no. 50, 1994, 195–200.

Köhler, Joachim and Michaelson, Sven, '"Das Fernsehen ist außer Kontrolle!" Über Müll auf der Mattscheibe, Schnüffeleien der Stasi und Manfred Krug', *Stern*, 15.12.1994.

Mehr, Max Thomas, '"Kein Dauergeschwätz." Jurek Becker und Wolfgang Thierse über Macht und das politische Engagement von Künstlern und Intellektuellen', *Wochenpost*, 9.6.1994.

'Überblick verloren!', *Der Spiegel*, vol. 48, no. 15, 1994, 207.

Schütte, Wolfram and Vornbäumen, Axel, '"Ist es Resignation, wenn man aufhört, größenwahnsinnig zu sein?" Der Schriftsteller Jurek Becker über Idole, Bosnien und das Schweigen der Intellektuellen', *Frankfurter Rundschau*, 28.8.1995.

O'Doherty, Paul and Riordan, Colin, '"Ich bezweifle, ob ich je DDR-Schriftsteller gewesen bin." Gespräch mit Jurek Becker' (1995), in Colin Riordan (ed.), *Jurek Becker*, Cardiff, University of Wales Press, 1998, 12–23.

Koelbl, Herlinde, 'Das ist wie ein Gewitter', *Der Spiegel*, 51, no. 13, 1997, 210–16.

Bibliography

English Translations of Becker's Works

Jakob The Liar, translated by Melvin Kornfeld, New York and London, Harcourt Brace Jovanovich, 1975.

'A Week in New York', translated by A. Leslie Wilson, *Dimension,* vol. 11, no. 3 (1978), 386–401.

'My Way of Being a Jew', translated by Claudia Johnson and Richard A. Zipser, *Dimension,* vol. 11, no. 3 (1978), 417–423.

Sleepless Days, translated by Leila Vennewitz, New York, Harcourt Brace Jovanovich, 1979 [and London, Secker & Warburg, 1979] [also London, Paladin, 1989].

'The Wall', translated by Leila Vennewitz, in *Granta,* no. 6, 'A Literature of Politics', Granta Publications, Cambridge, 1983.

Bronstein's Children, translated by Leila Vennewitz, San Diego, Harcourt Brace Jovanovich, 1988.

'Sleepless Days' (Excerpt), in *Bananas. The Literary Magazine*, December 1989, 20–1.

Untitled essay, translated by Michael Hofmann, *Granta 30*, Winter 1990, 133.

Jakob the Liar, translated by Leila Vennewitz, London, Picador, 1990 [Also New York, Arcade, 1996].

Films and Radio Plays

Mit der NATO durch die Wand (short film script for 'Stacheltier', directed by Peter Ulbrich), GDR, 1961.

Wenn ein Marquis schon Pläne macht (TV film script, directed by Peter Hagen), GDR, 1962.

Komm mit nach Montivideo (TV film script with Kurt Belicke, directed by Fred Mahr), GDR, 1962.

Gäste im Haus (TV film script directed by Fred Mahr), GDR, 1963.

Zu viele Kreuze (TV film script directed by Ralph J. Boettner), GDR, 1964.

Ohne Paß in fremden Betten (TV film script with Kurt Belicke, directed by Vladimir Brebera), GDR, 1964/5.

Immer um den März herum (TV film script with Klaus Poche, directed by Fred Mahr), GDR, 1967.

Mit 70 hat man noch Träume (TV film script with Klaus Poche, directed by Fred Mahr), GDR, 1967.

Urlaub (TV film script with Klaus Poche, directed by Manfred Mosblech), GDR, 1967.

Jungfer, sie gefällt mir (film script with Günter Reisch, after Kleist's *Der zerbrochene Krug*, directed by Günter Reisch), GDR, 1968.

Meine Stunde Null (film script with Karl Krug, directed by Joachim Hasler), GDR, 1970.

Jakob der Lügner (film script directed by Frank Beyer), GDR, 1974.

Das Versteck (film script directed by Frank Beyer), GDR, 1976/7.

David (co-operation on film script of Peter Lilienthal, directed by Peter Lilienthal), West Germany, 1979.

Der Boxer (TV film, directed by Karl Fruchtmann), ZDF, 1979/80.

Schlaflose Tage (TV film, directed by Diethard Klante), ARD, 1982.

Rede und Gegenrede (radio play), Westdeutscher Rundfunk, 10.7.1983.

Liebling Kreuzberg (TV series, 6 episodes, directed by Hans Schirk), ARD, 1985/6.

Der Passagier – Welcome in Germany (co-operation on film script by Thomas Brasch, directed by Thomas Brasch), West Germany, 1988.

Liebling Kreuzberg (TV series, 6 episodes, directed by Werner Masten), ARD, 1987/8.

Bronsteins Kinder (film script with Jerzy Kawalerowicz, directed by Jerzy Kawalerowicz), Germany, 1990.

Liebling Kreuzberg (TV series, 7 episodes, directed by Werner Masten), ARD, 1990.

Neuner (film script, directed by Werner Masten), Germany, 1990.

Wenn alle Deutschen schlafen (film script from Becker's short story 'Die Mauer', directed by Frank Beyer), Germany, 1994.

Wir sind auch nur ein Volk (TV series, 9 episodes, directed by Werner Masten), ARD, 1994–5.

Select Bibliography of Secondary Literature on Becker

(For a more complete list see: Paul O'Doherty in Colin Riordan (ed.), *Jurek Becker*, Cardiff, University of Wales Press, 1998: 118–52)

Arnold, Heinz Ludwig (ed.), *Kritisches Lexikon zur deutschsprachigen Gegenwartsliteratur*, vol. 1, Munich, edition text + kritik, 1978,.

——, *Jurek Becker, text + kritik*, 116 (1992).

——, 'Deckname "Lügner". Aus den Stasi-Akten über Jurek Becker', in Heinz Ludwig Arnold (ed.), *Feinderklärung. Literatur und Staatssicherheitsdienst, text + kritik*, 120 (1993), 15–25.

Baum, Gregory, '*Jakob der Lügner* in Christian Perspective', *Seminar*, 19 (1983), vol. 4, 285–88.

Beisbart, Ortwin, and Abraham, Ulf (eds), *Einige werden bleiben. Und mit ihnen das Vermächtnis*, Bamberg, Bayerische Verlags-Anstalt, 1992.

Berger, Karl Heinz, '*Jakob der Lügner*', in Wolfgang Spiewok (ed.), *Romanführer Band II/1*, Berlin, Volk und Wissen, 1987, 6th edition, 52–4.

Brand, Matthias, 'Stacheldrahtleben. Literatur und Konzentrationslager', in Uwe Naumann (ed.), *Sammlung 4*, Frankfurt am Main, Röderberg, 1981, 133–42.

Brecheisen, Claudia, 'Literatur des Holocaust: Identität und Judentum bei Jakov Lind, Edgar Hilsenrath und Jurek Becker', doctoral thesis, University of Augsburg, 1993.

Bremer, Thomas, 'Roman eines Störenfrieds. Über Jurek Beckers *Schlaflose Tage*', *Neue Rundschau*, 89 (1978), 470–6.

Brown, Russell E., 'Radios and Trees: A Note to Jurek Becker's Ghetto Fiction', *Germanic Notes*, vol. 19 no.1 (1988), 22–4.

——, 'Jurek Becker's Holocaust Fiction: a Father and Son Survive', *Critique 30* (1989), 193–209.

——, 'What is Your Father's Name? The Fiction of Jurek Becker', in Russell E. Brown, *Names in Modern German Literature,* Stuttgart, Heinz, 1991, 48–56.

Butler, Michael, 'Fractured Identity' [*Aller Welt Freund*], *Times Literary Supplement*, 7.10.1983.

Cafferty, Helen L., 'Survival under Fascism: Deception in Apitz' *Nackt unter Wölfen*, Becker's *Jakob der Lügner* and Kohlhaase's *Erfindung einer Sprache*', *West Virginia University Philology Papers*, 30 (1984), 90–6.

Chiarloni, Anna, 'Von der Schuld, noch am Leben zu sein. Einige Bemerkungen zum Roman *Der Boxer* von Jurek Becker', *Zeitschrift für Germanistik*, 11 (1990), 686–90.

de Bruyn, Günter, 'Intimes aus der DDR' [*Amanda herzlos*], *Der Spiegel*, vol. 46 no. 32 (1992), 155–9.

Demetz, Peter, 'In der Rolle des Feindes', [*Nach der ersten Zukunft*], *Frankfurter Allgemeine Zeitung*, 4.10.1980.

——, 'Über Auschwitz und das Schreiben in deutscher Sprache: Jurek Becker', in *Fette Jahre, magere Jahre. Deutschsprachige Literatur von 1965 bis 1985*, Munich, Zürich (Piper), 1988, 58–63.

Dobrick, Barbara, 'Eine unsichtbare Frau', *Deutsches Allgemeines Sonntagsblatt*, no. 35, 28.8.1992.

Dorman, Michael, 'Deceit and Self-Deception. An Introduction to the Works of Jurek Becker', *Modern Languages*, 1 (1980), 28–37.

Durzak, Manfred, 'Erfolge im anderen Medium. Jurek Becker als Fernseh-

Autor. Überlegungen zur Fernsehserie *Liebling Kreuzberg'*, in Heidelberger-Leonard (ed.), *Jurek Becker*, Frankfurt am Main, Suhrkamp, 1992, 312–31.

Egyptien, Jürgen, 'Die Riten des Erzählens und das Stigma der Identität. Anmerkungen zum Verhältnis von Poetologie und Judentum in Erzählungen Jurek Beckers', in Heidelberger-Leonard (ed.), *Jurek Becker,* Frankfurt am Main, Suhrkamp, 1992, 279–87.

Figge, Susan G., and Ward, Jenifer K., '"(Sich) Ein genaues Bild machen": Jurek Becker's *Bronsteins Kinder* as Novel and Film', *Germanic Review*, 70 no. 3 (1995), 90–8.

Fink, Adolf, 'Scheherezades jüngerer Brüder. Ein Versuch, den neuen Stadtschreiber von Bergen-Enkheim, Jurek Becker, zu porträtieren', in *Frankfurter Allgemeine Zeitung*, Stadt-Ausgabe, no. 202, 2.9.1982, 27.

Frei, Hannah Liron, 'Das Selbstbild des Juden, entwickelt am Beispiel von Stefan Heym und Jurek Becker', doctoral thesis, University of Zürich, 1992.

Gilman, Sander L., *Inscribing the Other*, Lincoln and London, University of Nebraska Press, 1991.

——, 'Jüdische Literaten und deutsche Literatur. Antisemitismus und die verborgene Sprache der Juden am Beispiel von Jurek Becker und Edgar Hilsenrath', *Zeitschrift für deutsche Philologie*, 107 (1988), 269–94.

Gölz, Sabine, 'Where did the wife go? Reading Jurek Becker's "Parkverbot"', *Germanic Review*, 62 (1987), 10–19.

Graf, Karin, and Konietzny, Ulrich (eds), *Jurek Becker*, Munich, iudicium, 1991.

Graves, Peter, 'Breaking out. Jurek Becker, *Schlaflose Tage'*, in: *Times Literary Supplement*, 20.10.1978, 1236.

Grubbe, Peter, 'Bekenntnisse eines gelernten Deutschen', *Stern*, no.45, 29.10.1976, 167–8 and 172.

Gutschke, Irmtraud, and Drechsler, Sonja, 'Bronsteins Rache – ein legitimes Recht?', *Neues Deutschland*, 3.11.1989.

Hage, Volker, 'Fragebogen. Jurek Becker, Schriftsteller', *Frankfurter Allgemeine Zeitung*, 8.10.1982.

——, 'Wie ich ein Deutscher wurde. Eine Begegnung mit Jurek Becker und Anmerkungen zu seinem Roman', in *Alles erfunden. Porträts deutscher und amerikanischer Autoren*, Reinbek, Rowohlt, 1988, 36–54.

——, 'Die Wahrheit über Jakob Heym. Über Meinungen, Lügen und das schwierige Geschäft des Erzählens – eine Lobrede auf den Schriftsteller Jurek Becker', in *Die Zeit*, no. 12, 15.3.1991, 73.

Hähnel, Klaus-Dieter, 'Jurek Becker, *Irreführung der Behörden'*, *Weimarer Beiträge*, 20 no.1 (1974), 149–53.

Halverson, Rachel J., 'Jurek Becker's *Jakob der Lügner*: narrative strategies of a witness's witness', *Monatshefte*, 85 (1993), 453–63.

Hanenberg, Peter, 'Erinnern und Erzählen. Jurek Beckers "Beliebteste Familiengeschichte"', in Ortwin Beisbart and Ulf Abraham (eds), *Einige werden bleiben. Und mit ihnen das Vermächtnis*, Bamberg, Bayerische Verlags-Anstalt, 1992, 142–7.

——, '"Und sich mühen, aufrichtig zu sein". DDR-Geschichten', in Heinz Ludwig Arnold (ed.), *Jurek Becker*, *text+kritik*, 116 (1992), 60–9.

Heidelberger-Leonard, Irene (ed.), *Jurek Becker*, Frankfurt am Main, Suhrkamp, 1992.

——, 'Schreiben im Schatten der Shoah, Überlegungen zu Jurek Beckers *Jakob der Lügner*, *Der Boxer* und *Bronsteins Kinder*', in Heinz Ludwig Arnold (ed.), *Jurek Becker*, *text+kritik*, 116 (1992), 19–29.

Johnson, Susan M., *The Works of Jurek Becker: A Thematic Analysis*, New York, Peter Lang, 1988.

Joho, Wolfgang, 'Lüge aus Barmherzigkeit' [*Jakob der Lügner*], *Neue Deutsche Literatur*, vol. 17, no. 12 (1969), 151–3.

Kahlau, Heinz, 'Verteidigung eines Vaters. Über Jurek Becker', in Annie Voigtländer (ed.), *Liebes- und andere Erklärungen. Schriftsteller über Schriftsteller*, Berlin and Weimar, Aufbau Verlag, 1972, 17–22.

Kane, Martin, 'Tales and the telling: the novels of Jurek Becker', in Martin Kane (ed.), *Socialism and the Literary Imagination. Essays on East German Writers*, Providence and Oxford, Berg, 1991, 163–78.

Karnick, Manfred, 'Die Geschichten von Jakob und Jakobs Geschichten', in Irene Heidelberger-Leonard (ed.), *Jurek Becker*, Frankfurt am Main, Suhrkamp, 1992, 207–21.

Kasper, Elke, 'Vorstoß zur inneren Grenze. Zu Jurek Beckers Roman *Schlaflose Tage*', in Irene Heidelberger-Leonard (ed.), *Jurek Becker*, Frankfurt am Main, Suhrkamp, 1992, 267–78.

Kaunzner, Hartwig, 'Jurek Beckers Roman *Schlaflose Tage* – ein zeitkritisches Dokument', *Deutsche Ostkunde*, vol. 25, no. 3 (1979), 56–60.

Köhler-Hausmann, Reinhild, 'Aus dem Verlags- und Verwertungsbereich Film. Das Verhältnis von Schriftsteller und "Verteilerinstanz", dargestellt an Jurek Beckers *Irreführung der Behörden*', in Reinhild Köhler-Hausmann, *Literaturbetrieb in der DDR. Schriftsteller und Literaturinstanzen*, Stuttgart, Metzler, 1984, 47–63.

Köpf, Gerhard, 'Einer stellt sich selbst ein Bein' [*Amanda herzlos*], *Die Welt*, no. 190, 15.8.1992.

Krauss, Hannes, 'Jurek Becker. Ein jüdischer Autor?', in Jost Hermand

and Gert Mattenklott (eds), *Jüdische Intelligenz in Deutschland*, Hamburg, Argument-Verlag, 1988, 139–46.

——, 'Sprachspiele – bitterernst', in Heinz Ludwig Arnold (ed.), *Jurek Becker*, *text+kritik*, 116 (1992), 39–43.

——, 'Vor der zweiten Zukunft? Über *Aller Welt Freund*', in Irene Heidelberger-Leonard (ed.), *Jurek Becker*, Frankfurt am Main, Suhrkamp, 1992, 288–300.

Krüger, Brigitte, *Zum Zusammenhang von künstlerisch-ästhetischer Wertung und ethisch-moralischen Wirkungspotenzen im literarischen Kunstwerk als Rezeptionsvorgabe, untersucht an Jurek Beckers 'Jakob der Lügner'*, doctoral thesis, Potsdam, Pädagogische Hochschule "Karl Liebknecht", 1977.

Krumbholz, Martin, 'Standorte, Standpunkte. Erzählerpositionen in den Romanen Jurek Beckers', in Heinz Ludwig Arnold (ed.), *Jurek Becker*, *text+kritik*, 116 (1992), 44–50.

Lauckner, Nancy A., '*Bronsteins Kinder*: Jurek Becker's third novelistic response to the Holocaust', in Karl-Heinz J. Schoeps and Christopher J. Wickham (eds), '*Was in den alten Büchern steht . . .': neue Interpretationen von der Aufklärung zur Moderne. Festschrift für Reinhold Grimm*, Frankfurt am Main, Peter Lang, 1991, 185–99.

Lesley, Arthur M., 'Jacob as Liar in Jurek Becker's *Jakob der Lügner*', *Seminar*, 19 (1983), 273–9.

Lüdke, Martin W., 'Ein Staat, drei Männer und Amanda. Jurek Beckers Prosa-Abschied von der DDR' [*Amand herzlos*], *Frankfurter Rundschau*, 26.9.1992.

Lüdke-Haertel, Sigrid, and Lüdke, Martin W., 'Jurek Becker', in Heinz Ludwig Arnold (ed.), *Kritisches Lexikon zur deutschsprachigen Gegenwartsliteratur*, Munich, edition text + kritik, 1988, 29th supplement, 1–12.

Lukens, Nancy, 'Schelm im Ghetto. Jurek Beckers Roman *Jakob der Lügner*', *Amsterdamer Beiträge zur neueren Germanistik*, 1985/86, vol. 20, 199–218.

McGowan, Moray, 'Zoo story? Jurek Becker's television script *Wir sind auch nur ein Volk*', in Colin Riordan (ed.), *Jurek Becker*, Cardiff, University of Wales Press, 1998, 94–105.

Manger, Philip, 'Jurek Becker's *Irreführung der Behörden*', *Seminar*, vol. 17, no.2 (1981), 147–63.

Matuschek-Labitzke, Birgit, 'Nach dem Roman ein Drehbuch zur Erfrischung. Der Erfolg von "Liebling Kreuzberg" wird fortgesetzt: der Autor Jurek Becker und das Fernsehen', *Süddeutsche Zeitung*, no. 146, 30.6.1987.

Meidinger-Geise, Inge, 'Trauma mit Lächeln' [*Nach der ersten Zukunft*], *Zeitwende*, 52 (1981), 121–2.

Meissner, Otto, "Programm extra" zum Pressedienst Erstes Deutsches Fernsehen/ARD50/94, IV/3.

Möhrchen, Helmut, 'Zur Darstellung zweier Lehrerschicksale in Romanen aus der DDR: Jurek Becker *Schlaflose Tage* und Günter Görlich *Eine Anzeige in der Zeitung*', *Diskussion Deutsch*, 83 (1985), 264–74.

Mohr, Heinrich, 'Erfundene Erinnerung: Zu Jurek Beckers Romanen *Jakob der Lügner*, *Der Boxer* und *Bronsteins Kinder*', in Jens Stüben (ed.), *'Wir tragen den Zettelkasten mit den Steckbriefen unserer Freunde': Acta-Band zum Symposium 'Beiträge jüdischer Autoren zur deutschen Literatur seit 1945'*, Darmstadt, Haisser, 1994, 205–12.

Mugnolo, Domenico, 'Die unbewältigte Geschichte Jakobs. Zu Jurek Beckers *Jakob der Lügner*', *Connaissance de la RDA*, 22 (1986), 91–108.

Müller, Heidy M., 'Wertsetzung als Implikation der Erzählhaltung. Bemerkung zur Judendarstellung in Jurek Beckers Romanen', *Philosophica*, vol. 38, no.2 (1986), 61–75.

———, 'Traumatisierte Überlebende in einem unbeteiligten Staat. Zu Jurek Beckers Romanen *Der Boxer* und *Bronsteins Kinder*', *Judaica*, 48 (1992), 226–36.

Nabbe, Hildegard, '"Wie ich ein Deutscher wurde": Das Problem der Identität in Jurek Beckers *Bronsteins Kinder*', in Friedrich Gaede, Patrick O'Neill and Ulrich Scheck (eds), *Hinter dem schwarzen Vorhang: Die Katastrophe und die epische Tradition*, Tübingen, Francke, 1994, 256–67.

Nägele, Rainer, 'Discourse about Absent Trees, Fiction, Lie and Reality in Jurek Becker's *Jakob der Lügner*', *Seminar*, 19 (1983), 280–84.

Naschitz, Fritz, 'Jurek Becker, der jüdische Geschichtenschreiber', *Literarische Essays. Bekenntnisse und Rezensionen,* Gerlingen, Bleicher, 1989, 266–8.

Neubert, Werner, 'Wahrheitserpichter Lügner' [*Jakob der Lügner*], *Neues Deutschland*, 14.5.1969.

Noll, Wulf, 'Jurek Becker als Gastprofessor in Essen', *Litfaß,* vol. 4, no.13 (1979/80), 104–7.

O'Doherty, Paul, 'Becker's *Bronsteins Kinder* and the Question of Post-Shoah Jewish Assimilation in Germany', in Colin Riordan (ed.), *Jurek Becker*, Cardiff, University of Wales Press, 1998, 45–56.

———, 'Jurek Becker: *Amanda herzlos*', *The Times Literary Supplement*, 9.10.1992, 24.

Ortheil, Hanns-Josef, 'Die Furcht des Geschichten-Erzählers', in Volker

Hage (ed.), *Deutsche Literatur 1997. Ein Jahresüberblick*, Stuttgart, Reclam, 1998, 53–7.

Pasche, Wolfgang, *Jurek Becker: Bronsteins Kinder*, Stuttgart, Dresden, Klett, 1994.

Paschek, Carl (ed.), *Jurek Becker – Begleitheft zur Ausstellung der Stadt- und Universitätsbibliothek Frankfurt am Main*, Frankfurt am Main, Stadt- und Universitätsbibliothek, 1989.

Pegorara, Anna, 'Jurek Becker, *Irreführung der Behörden*', in *Annali. Studi Tedeschi*, Naples, 2 (1975), 133–7.

Pfeiffer, Helmut, *Deutsche Autoren heute 6*, Bonn, Inter Nationes, 1984.

Poche, Klaus, 'Begegnung mit Jurek Becker', *Sonntag. Kulturpolitische Wochenzeitung*, no. 20, 16.5.1971.

Prévost, Claude, 'Die Wahrheit der Lüge und die Lüge der Wahrheit', in Gudrun Klatt (ed.), *Passagen. DDR-Literatur aus französischer Sicht*, Halle and Leipzig, mdv, 1989, 102–8.

Pulver, Elsbeth, 'Kein Trank aus Lethes Fluten' [*Jakob der Lügner*], *Schweizer Monatshefte*, 51 (1971), 201–14.

Raddatz, Fritz J., *Traditionen und Tendenzen*, Frankfurt am Main, Suhrkamp, 1976, 372–4.

Reich-Ranicki, Marcel, 'Das Prinzip Radio' [*Jakob der Lügner*], *Die Zeit*, 20.11.1970.

——, 'Liebe zum Mittelmaß' [*Irreführung der Behörden*], *Die Zeit*, 25.5.1973.

——, 'Plädoyer für Jurek Becker. Aus Anlaß eines mißlungenen Romans' [*Der Boxer*], *Frankfurter Allgemeine Zeitung*, 19.2.1977.

——, 'Abschied von den Träumen einer Jugend', *Frankfurter Allgemeine Zeitung*, 19.12.1977.

——, 'Drei Idioten' [*Amanda herzlos*], *Frankfurter Allgemeine Zeitung*, 19.9.1992.

Reitze, Paul F., 'Jakobs Lüge und der Drang nach Wahrheit' [*Nach der ersten Zukunft*], *Rheinischer Merkur/Christ und Welt*, 10.10.1980.

Ribbat, Ernst, 'Subjektivität als Instrument. Zu Jurek Becker und Nicolas Born', in *Lyrik – von allen Seiten. Gedichte und Aufsätze des ersten Lyriktreffens in Münster*, Lothar Jordan et al. (eds.), Frankfurt am Main, Fischer, 1981, 485–501.

Riordan, Colin, (ed.), *Jurek Becker*, Cardiff, University of Wales Press, 1998.

Rock, David, 'Jurek Becker', in Tracy Chevalier (ed.), *Contemporary World Writers*, New York, St. James Press, 1993, 50–1.

——, '"The reunification of German literature?" Questions of political stance and artistic integrity in Jurek Becker's writing', in Osman

Durrani, Colin Good and Kevin Hilliard (eds), *The New Germany. Literature and Society after Unification*, Sheffield, Sheffield Academic Press, 1995, 395–411.

——, 'Aesthetics and storytelling: some aspects of Jurek Becker's *Erzählungen*', in Arthur Williams, Stuart Parkes and Julian Preece (eds), *Contemporary German Writers. Their Aesthetics and their Language*, Bern, Peter Lang, 1996, 55–69.

——, 'Christoph Hein und Jurek Becker. Zwei kritische Autoren aus der DDR über die Wende und zum vereinten Deutschland', *German Life and Letters*, 50 (1997), 182–200.

——, '"Totalitäre Systeme sind in der Innerlichkeit ihrer Subjekte befestigt, oder sie lösen sich auf." Some thoughts on Jurek Becker's writing and his break with the GDR', in Robert Atkins and Martin Kane (eds.), *Retrospect and Review. Aspects of the Literature of the GDR 1976–1990*, Amsterdam and Atlanta, Rodopi, 1997, 261–77.

——, '"Wie ich ein Deutscher wurde." Sprachlosigkeit, Sprache und Identität bei Jurek Becker', in Colin Riordan (ed.), *Jurek Becker*, Cardiff, University of Wales Press, 1998, 24–44.

Röll, Walter and Bayerdörfer, Hans-Peter (eds), *Auseinandersetzungen um jiddische Sprache und Literatur. Jüdische Komponenten in der deutschen Literatur – die Assimilationskontroverse*, Tübingen, Niemeyer, 1986.

Rosenkranz, Stefanie, 'Westreise ohne Kopfschmerzen (Über einen Besuch bei Jurek Becker und die Fernseh-Serie *Liebling Kreuzberg*)', *Stern tv-magazin,* no. 19, 5.5.1988, 4–9.

Rossade, Werner, 'Zwischen Anpassung und Widerstand. Irreführung der Behörden?', in Werner Rossade, *Literatur im Systemwandel. Zur ideologiekritischen Analyse künstlerischer Literatur aus der DDR*, Frankfurt am Main and Bern, Peter Lang, 1982, 477–523.

Rothmann, Kurt, 'Jurek Becker', in Kurt Rothmann, *Deutschsprachige Schriftsteller seit 1945 in Einzeldarstellungen*, Stuttgart, Reclam, 1985, 36–9.

Rothschild, 'Opfer als Täter als Opfer: Jurek Beckers neuer Roman *Bronsteins Kinder*', *Die Neue Gesellschaft, Frankfurter Hefte*, vol. 34, no.1 (1987), 4–5.

Schlosser, Horst Dieter, 'Der irre "Mittelpunkt der Welt"', *Wirkendes Wort*, 39 (1989), 261–9.

——, '"Wie ich ein Deutscher wurde". Zu Jurek Beckers persönlicher und literarische Geographie', in Carl Paschek (ed.), *Jurek Becker – Begleitheft zur Ausstellung der Stadt- und Universitätsbibliothek*

Frankfurt am Main, Frankfurt am Main, Stadt- und Universitätsbibliothek, 1989, 20–4.

Schmied, Helmut, 'Das unterhaltsame Ghetto. Die Dimension des Raumes
in Jurek Beckers *Jakob der Lügner*', in Heinz Ludwig Arnold (ed.),
Jurek Becker, text + kritik, 116, Munich, 1992, 30–8.

Schmitt, Uwe, 'Vom Schreiben wie man's spricht. Der ungeahnte Erfolg
des Fernsehautors Jurek Becker' [*Liebling Kreuzberg*], *Frankfurter
Allgemeine Zeitung*, no. 80, 4.4.1987, 'Bilder und Zeiten' p. IV.

Schneider, Peter, 'Jurek im Café', in Colin Riordan (ed.), *Jurek Becker*,
Cardiff, University of Wales Press, 1998, 1–6.

Schönfeld, Gerd-Marie, 'Der Liebling von Kreuzberg', *Brigitte*, no. 9,
20.4.1988, 118–24.

Schütz, Erhard, 'Ein Brocken unter den Mittelgebirgen. Jurek Beckers
Roman über altneudeutsche Zeiten' [*Amanda herzlos*], *Der Tagesspiegel*, 26.7.1992.

Schwarzenau, Dieter, 'Heimisch bin ich nur am Schreibtisch. Besuch bei
Jurek Becker, dem amtierenden Stadtschreiber von Bergen-Enkheim',
Rheinischer Merkur/Christ und Welt, no. 13, 1.4.1983.

Shoham, Chaim, 'Jurek Becker ringt mit seinem Judentum', in Walter
Röll and Hans-Peter Bayerdörfer (eds), *Auseinandersetzungen um
jiddische Sprache und Literatur. Jüdische Komponenten in der deutschen
Literatur – die Assimilationskontroverse*, Tübingen, Niemeyer, 1986,
225–36.

Sill, Oliver, '"Lieber Sprechen als hören, lieber gehen als stehen." Jurek
Becker als politischer Kommentator', in Heinz Ludwig Arnold (ed.),
Jurek Becker, text + kritik, 116, Munich, 1992, 70–6.

Simpson, Particia Anne, 'The production of meaning in Jurek Becker's
Schlaflose Tage', *Seminar*, 27 (1991), 153–68.

Staadt, Jochen, 'Zur Situation der Schriftsteller in der DDR. Anpassen
und angepaßtwerden in Jurek Beckers Roman *Irreführung der
Behörden*', in Jochen Staadt, *Konfliktbewußtsein und sozialistischer
Anspruch in der DDR-Literatur. Widersprüche in Romanen nach
dem VIII. Parteitag der SED 1971*, Berlin, Volker Spieß, 1977,
291–7.

Steffens, Günter, 'Der Nachteil eines Vorteils' [*Nach der ersten Zukunft*],
Merkur, 34 (1980), 1157–62.

Steinert, Hajo, 'Hinab in die Niederungen der Literatur' [*Amanda herzlos*],
Die Weltwoche, 13.8.1992.

Stoll, Andrea, 'Das Lebensthema Jurek Beckers im Wechsel der Perspekt-
iven. Zu den literarischen Verfilmungen der Romane *Jakob der
Lügner*, *Der Boxer* und *Bronsteins Kinder*', in Irene Heidelberger-

Leonard, (ed.), *Jurek Becker*, Frankfurt am Main, Suhrkamp, 1992, 332–46.

Tabah, Mireille, 'Ästhetischer Anspruch und ästhetische Praxis in der DDR der 60er und 70er Jahre. Zu *Irreführung der Behörden*', in Irene Heidelberger-Leonard (ed.), *Jurek Becker*, Frankfurt am Main, Suhr-kamp, 1992, 251–66.

Tofi, Leonardo, 'Der Kampf gegen die Müdigkeit: Jurek Beckers Romane von *Irreführung der Behörden* bis *Aller Welt Freund*', in Anna Chiarloni *et al.* (eds), *Die Literatur der DDR 1976–1986*, Pisa, Giardini, 1988, 151–7.

Wallmann, Jürgen P., 'Lügner aus Menschlichkeit' [*Jakob der Lügner*], *Der Tagesspiegel*, 7.3.1971.

Waniek, Erdmann, '"Aber warum verbieten sie uns die Bäume?": Frage und Antwort in Jurek Beckers *Jakob der Lügner*', *Seminar*, 29 (1993), 279–93.

Wehdeking, Volker, '*Der Boxer* und die übermächtige Vergangenheit. Distanzierungsversuche vom eigenen biographischen Trauma', in Irene Heidelberger-Leonard (ed.), *Jurek Becker*, Frankfurt am Main, Suhr-kamp, 1992, 222–35.

Wende-Hohenberger, Waltraud, 'Die verschmähte "Gnade der späten Geburt". Versuche der literarischen Vergangenheitsbewältigung bei Jurek Becker, Gert Heidenreich und Peter Schneider', *Das Argument*, 161 (1987), 44–9.

Werner, Hans-Georg, '*Bronsteins Kinder* im Blickfeld eines ostberliner Lesers von 1987', in Irene Heidelberger-Leonard, (ed.), *Jurek Becker*, Frankfurt am Main, Suhrkamp, 1992, 236–50.

——, 'Zur ideellen Perspektivierung der Gesellschaftsdarstellung in der DDR-Literatur', *Berliner LeseZeichen*, 4 no. 3/4 (1996), 27–37.

Werth, Wolfgang, 'Das Pinguin-Syndrom' [*Nach der ersten Zukunft*], *Süddeutsche Zeitung*, 4.11.1980.

Wetzel, Heinz, 'Four Questions about Jurek Becker's *Jakob der Lügner*: an introduction', *Seminar*, 19 (1983), 265–9.

——, '"Unvergleichlich gelungener" – aber "einfach zu schön"? Zur ethischen und ästhetischen Motivation des Erzählers in Jurek Beckers Roman *Jakob der Lügner*', *Kontroversen, alte und neue*, 8 (1986), 107–14.

——, 'Fiktive und authentische Nachrichten in Jurek Beckers Romanen *Jakob der Lügner* und *Aller Welt Freund*', in Roland Jost and Hans-Georg Schmidt-Bergmann (eds), *Im Dialog mit der Moderne. Zur deutschsprachigen Literatur von der Gründerzeit bis zur Gegenwart*, Frankfurt am Main, Athenäum, 1986, 439–51.

——, 'Holocaust und Literatur. Die Perspektive Jurek Beckers', *Colloquia Germanica*, 21 (1988), 70–6.

——, 'Schreiben, um nicht zu versinken: Jurek Becker, *Warnung vor dem Schriftsteller*', in Paul Michael Lützeler (ed.), *Poetik der Autoren. Beiträge zur deutschsprachigen Gegenwartsliteratur*, Frankfurt am Main, Fischer, 1994, 208–34.

White, I.A. and J.J., 'Wahrheit und Lüge in Jurek Beckers Roman *Jakob der Lügner*', in Gerd Labroisse (ed.), *Zur Literatur und Literaturwissenschaft der DDR*, Amsterdam, Rodopi, 1978, 207–31.

Wieczorek, John P., '"Irreführung durch Erzählprespektive?" The East German novels of Jurek Becker', *Modern Languages Review*, 85 (1990), 640–52.

Wittstock, Uwe, 'Der Jude Hans im Unglück' [*Bronsteins Kinder*], in Volker Hage (ed.), *Deutsche Literatur 1986. Ein Jahresüberblick*, Stuttgart, Reclam, 1987, 141–6.

Zierlinger, Ursula, *Jurek Becker. Jakob der Lügner*, Munich, Mentor, 1995.

Zimmermann, Werner, 'Jurek Becker: *Jakob der Lügner*', in Werner Zimmermann, *Deutsche Prosadichtungen des 20. Jahrhunderts*, vol. 3, Düsseldorf, Schwann, 1988, 10–39.

Zipser, Richard A., 'Jurek Becker. A Writer with a Cause', *Dimension*, 11 (1978), 402–6.

——, 'Jurek Becker', in Richard A. Zipser, *DDR-Literatur im Tauwetter. Wandel, Wunsch, Wirklichkeit*, vol. 1, New York, Bern and Frankfurt am Main, Peter Lang, 1985, 57–9.

General Works on the GDR and its Literature

Arnold, Heinz-Ludwig (ed.), *Feinderklärung. Literatur und Staatssicherheitsdienst, text + kritik*, 120 (1993).

Arnold, Heinz Ludwig, and Meyer-Gosau, Frauke (eds), *Literatur in der DDR. Rückblicke, text + kritik*, Sonderband (1991).

Bullivant, Keith, *The Future of German Literature*, Oxford, Berg, 1994.

Chiarloni, Anna, and Pankoke, Helga (eds), *Grenzfallgedichte. Eine deutsche Anthologie*, Berlin, Aufbau, 1991.

DDR Handbuch, Cologne, Verlag Wissenschaft und Politik, 1979.

Emmerich, Wolfgang, *Kleine Literaturgeschichte der DDR: erweiterte Neuausgabe*, Leipzig, Gustav Kiepenheuer Verlag, 1997.

Hein, Christoph, *Als Kind habe ich Stalin gesehen. Essais und Reden*, Berlin and Weimar, Aufbau, 1990.

Krug, Manfred, *Abgehauen*, Düsseldorf, Econ, 1996.

Loest, Erich, *Nikolaikirche*, Leipzig, Linden-Verlag, 1995.

Müller, Heiner, 'Fernsehen 3: Selbstkritik', in Anna Chiarloni and Helga Pankoke (eds), *Grenzfallgedichte, Eine deutsche Anthologie*, Berlin, Aufbau, 1991, 55.

O'Doherty, Paul, 'German-Jewish writers and themes in GDR fiction', *German Life and Letters*, 49 (1996), 271–81.

——, *The Portrayal of Jews in GDR Fiction*, Amsterdam, Rodopi, 1997.

Rinke, Andrea, 'From Motzki to Trotzki: Representations of East and West German Cultural Identities on German Television after Unification', in: Durrani, Osman, Good, Colin and Hilliard, Kevin, *The New Germany: Literature and Society after Unification*, Sheffield, Sheffield Academic Press, 1995, 231–51.

Soldat, Hans-Georg, 'Die Wende in Deutschland im Spiegel der zeitgenössischen deutschen Literatur', *German Life and Letters*, vol. L, no. 2, April 1997, 133–54.

Wallace, Ian, 'Writers and the *Stasi*', *German Monitor*, 33 (1994), 126–7.

——, 'East German Writers Look Back at the GDR: Two Recent Examples', *Institute of Germanic Studies: Friends Newsletter* (1996–1997), 3–9

Werner, Hans-Georg, 'Zur individuellen Perspektivierung der Gesellschaftsdarstellung in der DDR-Literatur', *Berliner Lesezeichen*, nos. 3/4 (1996), 30–3.

The Polish and Holocaust Background

Adelson, Alan, and Lapides, Robert, *Lodz Ghetto: Inside a Community under Siege*, New York, Viking, 1989.

Bloom, Solomon F., 'Dictator of the Lodz Ghetto: The Strange Case of Mordechai Chaim Rumkowski', in Michael R. Marrus, (ed.), *The Nazi Holocaust*, volume 1: *The Victims of the Holocaust*, Westport CT, Meckler, 1989, 295–306.

Dobroszycki, Lucjan, *The Chronicle of the Lodz Ghetto 1941–1944* (translated by Lourie, Neugroschel *et al.*), New Haven and London, Yale University Press, 1984.

Herschkovitch, Bendet, 'The Ghetto in Litzmannstadt (Lodz)', in Michael R. Marrus, (ed.), *The Nazi Holocaust*, volume 1: *The Victims of the Holocaust*, Westport CT, Meckler, 1989, 340–77.

Hilberg, Raul, *The Destruction of the European Jews* (volumes I and II), New York and London, Holmes and Meier, 1985.

Hilsenrath, Edgar, *Nacht*, Munich, Piper, 1990.

Huppert, Schmuel, 'King of the Ghetto: Mordechai Haim Rumkowski, Elder of the Lodz Ghetto', in Michael R. Marrus, (ed.), *The Nazi*

Holocaust, volume 1: *The Victims of the Holocaust*, Westport CT, Meckler, 1989, 307–39.

Langer, Lawrence L., *The Holocaust and the Literary Imagination*, New Haven, Yale University Press, 1975.

Loewy, Hanno, and Schoenberner, Gerhard (eds), *'Unser einziger Weg ist die Arbeit.' Das Ghetto in Lodz*, Vienna, Löcker, 1990.

Marrus, Michael R., (ed.), *The Nazi Holocaust*, volume 1: *The Victims of the Holocaust*, Westport CT, Meckler, 1989.

Wesie, Ruth R., 'Poland's Jewish Ghosts', *Commentary 83* (1987), 1, 25–33.

Index

Index